D1605848

VIETNAM, WE'VE ALL BEEN THERE

VIETNAM, WE'VE ALL BEEN THERE

Interviews with American Writers

Eric James Schroeder

PRAEGER

Westport, Connecticut
London

Copyright Acknowledgments

The author and publisher are grateful for permission to use the following material:

Eric James Schroeder, "Two Interviews: Talks with Tim O'Brien and Robert Stone," *Modern Fiction Studies*, Vol. 30, No. 1, Spring 1984. Copyright 1984 by Purdue Research Foundation, West Lafayette, Indiana, 47907. Reprinted with permission.

Excerpts from the book *Song of Napalm* copyright © 1988 by Bruce Weigl. Used by permission of Atlantic Monthly Press.

Library of Congress Cataloging-in-Publication Data

Vietnam, we've all been there : interviews with American writers /
  Eric James Schroeder.
       p.   cm.
  Includes bibliographical references and index.
  ISBN 0-275-93561-2 (alk. paper)
  1. Vietnamese Conflict, 1961-1975—Literature and the conflict.
2. War stories, American—History and criticism. 3. War poetry,
American—History and criticism. 4. Authors, American—20th
century—Interviews. 5. War stories—Authorship. 6. War poetry
—Authorship.   I. Schroeder, Eric James.
PS228.V5V47   1992
813'.5409358—dc20   92-16557

British Library Cataloguing in Publication Data is available.

Library of Congress Catalog Card Number: 92-16557
ISBN: 0-275-93561-2

First published in 1992

Praeger Publishers, 88 Post Road West, Westport, CT 06881
An imprint of Greenwood Publishing Group, Inc.

Printed in the United States of America

The paper used in this book complies with the
Permanent Paper Standard issued by the National
Information Standards Organization (Z39.48-1984).

10 9 8 7 6 5 4 3 2 1

Contents

Acknowledgments

This book has taken almost a decade to assemble, and in that time I've gotten advice and help from many people. Rob Pettler watered the initial seed. A number of friends and colleagues told me whom to talk to and what to ask. These people include Raymund Paredes, DeWitt Allen, Lee Zimmerman, and Romey Keyes. Greg Ross deserves a special thanks for all his help and encouragement early on during this project. Mark Tran accompanied me on the ill-fated trip to Arizona. Sam Maio played a big role in the Bruce Weigl interview. Heidi Preschler helped type early draft of interviews. David Reinheimer deserves a special thanks for his work transcribing tapes, and thanks, too, to Jane King for her work on the manuscript. William Searle gave me some very timely (and savvy) advice on publishers. My wife, Susan Palo, displayed lots of patience and gave much-needed encouragement and advice, and toward the end her help was invaluable. My editor Dan Eades at Praeger believed in this project—thank you, Dan, for your confidence. And thanks, too, to John Roberts and Lauren Pera at Praeger for all their help with the manuscript.

Two of these interviews, with Tim O'Brien and Robert Stone, appeared in slightly different versions in *Modern Fiction Studies*. I am grateful for permission to reprint them. Another two, with Michael Herr and Larry Heinemann, are almost identical to the versions published in *Writing on the Edge*. Again, I'm grateful for permission to reprint them. I am also grateful to the University of California at Los Angeles for a travel research grant I received when I first began this project.

Finally, I own a very special thanks to my colleague and friend John Boe. John, without you this book probably never would have got done. Thanks for being there.

VIETNAM, WE'VE ALL BEEN THERE

Introduction

The title of this book comes from the last lines of Michael Herr's *Dispatches*: "And no moves left for me at all but to write down some few last words and make the dispersion, Vietnam Vietnam Vietnam, we've all been there." These lines have haunted me, but only over time did their fundamental truth become clear. Vietnam affected everyone who lived through it. It refused to remain a foreign conflict in a strange country far away; it came home in ways that we're still trying to work out. Those who served in Vietnam were touched most deeply by the war. Statistics continue to testify to the war's devastating, prolonged effects: homelessness among veterans, joblessness among veterans, incarceration rates of veterans—all of these continue to be a legacy of the war.

But the war had cultural effects as well. Numerous articles and books have been written on the media's coverage of the war, for instance. Many commentators agree that both print media and television had difficulty in covering the war. Several of the journalists I talked to claimed that they were motivated to go to Vietnam because they didn't feel that the media was telling the truth about Vietnam. They wanted to tell the truth. In *Dispatches* Michael Herr says, "Conventional journalism could no more cover the war than conventional firepower could win it. All it could do was take the most profound event of the American decade and turn it into a communications pudding." The same might also be said about the way that other forms of media have treated the war, film in particular; the recipes for *The Green Berets* (1968) and *Rambo: First Blood: Part II* (1985) are almost identical— the flavor has been changed slightly but the consistency is the same. And while it's true that there have been plenty of mediocre books written about the Vietnam war, nonetheless literature has succeeded in ways that film can't and won't. Literature, from Graham Greene's *The Quiet American* in 1955 to Tim O'Brien's *The Things They Carried* in 1990, allows form and time enough to shape meaning. And all the writers in this collection have worked with the meaning of Vietnam.

The idea for this book came when I was a graduate student at UCLA writing about the literature that had come out of the Vietnam war. I was interested in the various forms that writers used to write about the war and thought that the more successful writers were those who had stretched the boundaries of particular forms. The best narratives about the war seemed to be those that broke rules. One day a friend who was a bookseller mentioned to me that John Sack, one of the authors I was writing about, was a regular customer of his and lived nearby. If I was really interested, he'd give me Sack's address and phone number, and I could get in touch with him. I wrote Sack a letter (thinking that to phone him would be presumptuous) and was somewhat unnerved when he called me at work two days later saying he was willing to meet with me as soon as I liked. I couldn't believe my good fortune. When I began my research, Sack was one of the writers I first read. His book *M*, one of the earliest full-length Vietnam narratives to be published, remains one of the finest. I can remember being overwhelmed the first time I read it. Sack was one of the first journalists to write negatively about the war. The book is colored by black humor, and as such, it's the first book to use humor successfully in its treatment of Vietnam. But despite *M*'s humor, it's also a very serious book, one of the first harbingers of the war's randomness and incomprehensibility. In the interview, Sack talks about World War II writers like Marion Hargrove, whose book *See Here, Private Hargrove* is a comic account of Army life. Sack makes the point that you couldn't do that with Vietnam because there was nothing noble about Vietnam and certainly very little to laugh about. Yet I think that *M* succeeds as black humor—it's one of few Vietnam narratives to do this. In that sense it transcends books like *See Here, Private Hargrove* and is more akin to Joseph Heller's *Catch-22* (to my mind the best novel written about World War II). In addition to *M*, Sack has written two other books about Vietnam: *Lieutenant Calley: His Own Story* (he spent three months with Calley, taping dozens of conversations) and *The Man-Eating Machine*, a follow-up to *M*, a section of which also concerns Calley.

The best book written about Vietnam is Michael Herr's *Dispatches*. When I first read *Dispatches*, it confirmed my feeling that some of the best work being done about the war was being written by the so-called New

Journalists, writers who argued that objectivity in journalism was an illusion and therefore wrote personal, dramatic narratives that nonetheless were true to the facts of the events they described. But "New Journalist" is a label that Michael Herr would never apply to himself. He had been an editor for *Holiday* magazine and a feature writer for *Holiday* and several other publications in 1967, when he convinced Harold Hayes of *Esquire* to send him to Vietnam where he would write a monthly column. That didn't work, and, as they say, the rest is history. *Dispatches* took six years to complete, but when it finally came out, it lived up to the promise of the "dispatches" Herr had published in *Esquire* and elsewhere.

Dispatches is a narrative that breaks all the rules. Ostensibly it is first-person journalism providing us with a window on the war. We are never allowed to forget that what he describes is real. But *Dispatches* goes way beyond the confines of journalism. Journalism demands facts; Herr insists on much more—on describing psychological states, assessing personal losses, and personifying the war. A scene from the book's first chapter, "Breathing In," is typical of Herr's narrative style; in this vignette, Herr describes his meeting with "Ocean Eyes," a member of an elite reconnaissance team serving his third tour of duty in Vietnam:

> [W]hat a story he told me, as one-pointed and resonant as any war story I ever heard, it took me a year to understand it:
> "Patrol went up the mountain. One man came back. He died before he could tell us what happened."
> I waited for the rest, but it seemed not to be that kind of story; when I asked him what had happened he just looked like he felt sorry for me, fucked if he'd waste time telling stories to anyone dumb as I was.

This scene is typical of Herr's art; like Herr himself, we wait for the punchline, but it doesn't come. Meaning comes to us slowly as we piece together the fragments of Herr's experience.

Herr himself considers *Dispatches* a novel. In many ways it is very novel-like: his rendering of characters, the weaving together of plot and theme throughout the narrative, and his very self-conscious use of language. He also admits to having made up some of the dialogue. Herr recognizes the importance of facts but also their limitations. In the opening pages of *M*, Sack enjoins us, "All this really happened—Do believe." Sack wants us to be convinced of the "truth" of his narrative. It's a testimonial to Herr's narrative that we don't need to be told, "Do believe." Our belief is total.

Studs Terkel, whom Wallace Terry calls "the master of the oral history," legitimized the oral history and gave it shape. The Vietnam war popularized the genre. A number of fine collections have come out of the war, including Al Santoli's *Everything We Had*, Mark Baker's *Nam*, and Gloria Emerson's *Winners & Losers*. One of the most memorable and significant is Wallace Terry's *Bloods: An Oral History of the Vietnam War by Black Veterans*. Terry originally went to Vietnam in 1967 on special assignment from *Time* magazine. He had covered the civil rights movement for both the *Washington Post* and *Time*, and, partly as a result, *Time* asked him to do a story on black soldiers in Vietnam. The story made the cover of *Time* and Terry was asked to go back. He became the deputy bureau chief in Saigon, covered the Tet Offensive, and ended up spending the equivalent of two tours of duty in Vietnam. Like Sack and Herr before him, Terry also went with the idea of eventually writing a book about the war. While he was in Vietnam, he began interviewing black soldiers for the book he intended to write. But it took Terry seventeen years to find a publisher for his book, and in that time the project changed completely.

Bloods is based on interviews that Terry began collecting while in Vietnam but didn't finish collecting until many years later. During that time he added new characters and followed up on some he had met earlier. In its final form *Bloods* is a very polished collection; Terry has referred to the form as "oral novella." And unlike most other oral histories, Terry intended his collection to have an organic unity; he characterizes *Bloods* as "a series of short stories placed in a progression that would give the impact and effect of reading a novel." Terry's shaping is particularly evident in the stories themselves. For instance, Stephen Howard's chapter opens with Howard describing his innocence when he was inducted: "I was going on nineteen when I got drafted. I had graduated from high school the year before, and I was working as an engineering assistant in this drafting firm. My mother went to the bus station with me to see me off to Fort Bragg for basic training, and she said, 'You'll be back a man.'" At the end of his narrative he recounts a story of how a helicopter crew took a water buffalo from some local farmers and dropped it in a minefield from a height of three hundred feet as a lesson to the peasants. He concludes:

> I know the Vietnamese saw it. They watched everything we did.
> I think we were the last generation to believe, you know, in the honor of war. There is no honor in war.
> My mama still thinks that I did my part for my country, 'cause she's

a very patriotic person.
I don't.

C. D. B. Bryan began his career as a novelist. In 1965 he published his first novel, *P. S. Wilkinson*, which won the Harper Prize for fiction. He began writing magazine pieces while finishing his second novel, *The Great Dethriffe*, published in 1970. But while his second novel went mostly unnoticed, his reputation as a nonfiction writer grew. *Friendly Fire* began as a magazine piece for the *New Yorker*. Originally conceived as a six-thousand word piece, the project quickly assumed book proportions. After five years and several fresh starts, the book was published in 1976. Three years later, ABC-TV aired its made-for-television adaptation of *Friendly Fire* in its Sunday night movie-of-the-week slot. It attracted sixty-four million viewers.

Friendly Fire is the story of Peg and Gene Mullen and their quest to learn the truth about their son Michael's death in Vietnam. Michael was the victim of "friendly fire," a U.S. artillery shell that fell short of its intended target. The Mullens, unable to accept the Army's version of the events surrounding Michael's death, begin their own investigation. Bryan himself becomes a player in the story, as does Colonel H. Norman Schwarzkopf, Michael's commanding officer. Finally, though, the facts concerning Michael's death become peripheral to the narrative; the focus comes to rest on Peg and Gene Mullen and their inability to accept the government's explanation of what happened to their son. It is an arresting picture of the war's effects on ordinary Americans.

Norman Mailer's career as a writer has been shaped by war. His first success came with the publication of *The Naked and the Dead*, a novel he wrote after returning from the Pacific theater of World War II and published when he was only twenty-five. *The Naked and the Dead* has come to define the World War II novel; "epic" begins to describe the sweep of its action and the cast of its characters. But it's also a novel concerned as much about ideas as it is about people. And while the politics of the novel are radical, its form is conservative.

In the mid-1960s as Mailer's politics became more pragmatic, his art became increasingly experimental. At the height of the Vietnam war Mailer wrote two books about Vietnam. These books—*The Armies of the Night* and *Why Are We in Vietnam?*—are among his most unconventional. *The Armies of the Night*, subtitled *History as a Novel, The Novel as History*, is Mailer's account of the antiwar demonstrations that took place in Washington, D.C.

over four days in October 1967. One of Mailer's most successful books, it won the National Book Award, the Pulitzer Prize, and the George Polk Award. Within the book's scope Mailer plays many roles: actor, novelist, historian, social critic, philosopher. By structuring the book in two parts, Mailer also makes the *form* of his book part of his subject. He uses the two halves to examine the event subjectively as a participant and objectively as an observer.

Mailer calls *Why Are We in Vietnam?* a "kind of comedy." The novel operates on a number of levels: as parody, as satire, and, most importantly, as allegory, a narrative told on the eve of the narrator's departure for Vietnam. Many early critics, however, were so put off by the book's scatological excursions that they ignored its thematic concerns. Thus while the book chronicles a bear hunt in Alaska undertaken by D.J., the book's narrator, his friend Tex, and his father, Rusty, its theme is a favorite of Mailer's: America as the unstable sum of its various, often antithetical, parts. Toward the end of the novel as the two boys lie huddled, watching the northern lights, the voice of God speaks to them: "Go out and kill—fulfill my will, go and kill." This is the book's final irony—not that they hear the voice, but that they mistake it for God. Mailer knows better; it's America talking. It's this experience that D.J. recalls the night before he leaves for Vietnam.

Although he had been in Vietnam as a correspondent during the latter stage of U.S. involvement, Robert Stone is best known as a writer of fiction. In 1975 his second novel, *Dog Soldiers*, won the National Book Award for fiction. The novel opens in Vietnam but quickly moves to California. We soon perceive, though, that Vietnam and California have a lot in common. Stone structures *Dog Soldiers* as a thriller; characters chase each other in pursuit of three kilos of heroin. But Stone uses this plot to reveal the way that Vietnam was in us. The heroin becomes the embodiment of the war itself. When the characters leave Vietnam, the drug ensures that the war won't leave them. Like the war, the drug causes chaos and leaves the characters wandering in an amoral wilderness. Evil becomes clear enough; it is represented most clearly in Antheil, the crooked federal narcotics agent. The closest we get to goodness is Hicks, who operates according to his own moral code. But the code of Hicks—conceived from Nietzsche, forged in the Marine Corps, and shaped by Vietnam—bears little resemblance to that of a Hemingway hero—Frederick Henry, for instance, also the product/victim of war. Even Hicks's friend calls him a "psychopath," an assessment that often seems to fit. The end of the novel is apocalyptic: the counterculture vision of the 1960s is dead; the war's legacy is omnipresent. Ultimately Stone's allegory doesn't offer us any solutions for America's malaise. His mirror reveals the disease; we must look into ourselves for its cure.

Tim O'Brien keeps returning to Vietnam as he discovers that the subject isn't through with him yet. His first book, *If I Die in a Combat Zone* (1973), was a memoir about his experience of the war. The book was well received, though many reviews and critics referred to it as a novel. After writing his first novel, *Northern Lights*, O'Brien again turned to Vietnam as the subject of his second novel, *Going After Cacciato* (1978). Like *Dog Soldiers* before it, *Going After Cacciato* won the National Book Award for fiction. Moreover, it has been called by many the best novel written about the war. Much of the novel's success derives from O'Brien's ability to yoke realism and magical realism in his parallel narratives. The novel's central story line, Cacciato's trek to Paris, is juxtaposed with scenes of death and boredom that Paul Berlin recalls as he sits in his observation post, trying to make sense out of the war. The questions that plagued O'Brien in *If I Die* and remained unanswered at the end of that narrative—What *is* bravery? What lessons do we learn from war?—find resolution in *Cacciato*. One of the few novels that rival *Cacciato* is O'Brien's own most recent offering, *The Things They Carried* (1990). Unfortunately, my interview with O'Brien was conducted long before *The Things They Carried* was published. But I saw O'Brien shortly after the book came out. He was on a promotion tour for the book and had just read "The Lives of the Dead," the last chapter of *The Things They Carried*, a piece that seems particularly autobiographical. After the reading, the audience sat in stunned silence until the mood was finally broken by the moderator's chipper call, "Any questions?" O'Brien returned somewhat reluctantly to the podium, and before anyone got a question in, said, "I'm not really sure what there is to say about a work of fiction." In a sense O'Brien was right; the questions and discussion that followed seemed like a shadow compared to the substance of the fiction he had read.

Larry Heinemann spent three years in junior college trying to avoid the draft, but when he did graduate he was drafted immediately. When he returned home, however, he was changed; formerly a poor student he was now highly motivated. He began work on a novel. He taught writing at Columbia College in Chicago. And in 1977 his first book, *Close Quarters*, was published. *Close Quarters* is notable for its attention to detail and for Heinemann's ability to capture the language of the war. Like Michael Herr, he is absorbed with getting the voices right. His narrator Dosier could have stepped right out of *Dispatches*, along with the companions he describes:

There were the bad-ass Hell's Angels and Texans and truck drivers, the fuck-up law school dropouts and Mo-Town and Harlem brothers— walking that walk—the John Waynes and Boone County Courthouse loafers and one-eyed Khe Sanh Marines—who had read the JOIN posters and believed them—the Chicanos and clerks and dumb-ass lifers, the village idiots and backwoods farmers, the housecats and walking wounded, and young buck sergeants like me. The winners, the losers, the also-rans, and every notch between.

Heinemann's concern with language becomes even more apparent in his second novel, *Paco's Story*. The novel opens with the narrator's declaration: "Let's begin with the first clean fact, James: This ain't no war story. War stories are out—one, two, three, and a heave-ho, into the lake you go with all the other alewife scuz and foamy harbor scum." But of course the novel is a war story, one told from an unexpected perspective. We learn that the narrator is a ghost from Alpha Company, all of whom have been incinerated by friendly fire, all, that is, except Paco. But Paco himself becomes a ghost of sorts as he drifts into the town of Boone, Texas, looking for work. *Paco's Story* won the National Book Award in 1988.

With many of the writers I chose to interview I was motivated by their willingness to either bend or break the rules of the genres they worked in. Bobbie Ann Mason doesn't do this in her novel *In Country*. The novel is a narrative told from the point of view of Samantha Hughes, a recent high school graduate, whose father was killed seventeen years earlier in Vietnam and who now lives with her uncle, Emmett, another Vietnam veteran. Mason breaks a different sort of rule. Lacking the perspective of an insider, she nonetheless writes about Vietnam and the subsequent effect it has on Sam Hughes. Mason acknowledges that Vietnam was a difficult subject for her but credits her editor with pushing her toward it: "He encouraged me to come face to face with the subject of Vietnam; he said I was avoiding it, which I was. I was scared of the topic. What did I know? I was a girl, I had never been to Vietnam. I felt intimidated writing about the subject. And questioning a little bit whether I had the right to get into that. I guess I knew I did, but still it's not easy to make that leap." I interviewed Bobbie Ann Mason in Tom's River, New Jersey, where she briefly addressed an audience composed mostly of Vietnam veterans who had come to watch a benefit showing of the film *In Country*. When she was introduced, she received a very warm, enthusiastic greeting from the crowd; she had clearly made the leap.

A number of critics, most notably Paul Fussell, have commented on the dearth of poetry that came out of the war. For while it's true that poets like Robert Bly and Denise Levertov wrote poems that were widely read, these were largely voices from the literati, voices from the left, voices from mainstream culture. What was missing were poems written by soldiers. And yet for those who go looking, there is a surprising amount of poetry written by Vietnam veterans. Unlike the poet/warriors of World War I, though, the poet/warriors of Vietnam were, for the most part, much younger and much less educated than their World War I counterparts. For many of these veterans, poetry was catharsis, not art. While that fact accounts for the graphic nature of much of the Vietnam poetry, it also accounts for its roughness.

Bruce Weigl's poetry has been compared to the work of Wilfred Owen, Randall Jarrell, and Robert Graves. And while these claims establish his credentials as the most accomplished poet to emerge from the Vietnam war, I would go further and claim that Weigl is among the most talented poets working in America today. The opening of a poem like "Elegy" recalls those earlier poets—"Into the sunlight they marched,/into dog day, into no saints day,/and were cut down." But many of his poems manage to capture the Vietnam war's uniqueness, its Americanness. The title of the poem "The Last Lie" invokes the tradition of war poetry, but one of the central images in the poem recalls America's favorite pastime:

Some guy in the miserable convoy
raised up in the back of our open truck
and threw a can of C rations at a child
who called into the rumble for food.
He didn't toss the can, he wound up and hung it
on the child's forehead and she was stunned
backwards into the dust of our trucks.

To describe Weigl as simply a war poet is to limit his accomplishments. Weigl is like Tim O'Brien—he and the war still don't seem to be finished with each other.

David Rabe is to theater what Bruce Weigl is to poetry: the war's most talented writer in that genre. Rabe's career, like Weigl's, has clearly been shaped by the war. Six months after he returned from the war, when he had decided he was ready to write about it, he received a Rockefeller Grant for playwriting. Rabe claims it was the good fortune of receiving this grant that turned him to playwriting rather than to fiction, but success did not come overnight. The political and confrontational nature of his work, which was an impediment for many, found an admirer in Joseph Papp. When Papp produced *The Basic Training of Pavlo Hummel* in 1971, Rabe recalled, "Every theater on the East Coast had turned me down." Later that same year Papp went on to produce Rabe's second play, *Sticks and Bones.* Both plays won a number of awards and established Rabe's reputation as one of America's most promising playwrights. And this was at a time when many novelists were having a difficult time finding publishers for their Vietnam narratives. His best-known play, *Streamers,* was produced in 1976 and was eventually made into a film. These plays, together with *The Orphan,* make up what Rabe considers a sequence of four plays, all of which focus on various aspects of the war.

Vietnam is a hard subject to deal with. It doesn't go away. Michael Herr and Wallace Terry—both journalists, neither soldiers—suffered from post traumatic stress disorder and took years to finish their books. The war figures prominently in four of David Rabe's plays. Tim O'Brien and Bruce Weigl keep going back to Vietnam—as a literal place and as a subject. Bobbie Ann Mason has said that the war was something that touched every American who lived through it. I agree with her. And while I would never compare my experience to that of anyone who served in Vietnam, my own experience of the war, limited as it is mostly to my scholarship, is obsessive.

I came of age during the war. In 1971, as American involvement in Vietnam began to wind down, my brother was killed in a U.S. Army helicopter crash in Korea. The next year I was eligible for the draft. By that time, though, no one was being sent to Vietnam. And in 1973 the first of a series of endings to the war came. It wasn't until long after the last helicopters were pushed into the South China Sea that my academic interest in the war was kindled. By that time, the war's legacy pervaded the culture, and most of the stereotypes were still negative. When I was finishing my doctoral dissertation, I dreamed about the war every night. And in the nine years that I have been gathering these interviews, it's been a constant presence in my life.

Following the allied forces' one-hundred-hour land campaign in Kuwait and Iraq, President Bush declared that we'd "kicked the Vietnam syndrome." But as Norman Mailer remarks in the following pages, history is long. I doubt whether the Persian Gulf War—a very brief conflict by most standards—will exorcise Vietnam. Robert Stone thinks that it could take as long as fifty years before we can gauge the full impact of the Vietnam war on our culture. For many Americans, it will take a lifetime to come to terms with the war's effects on their lives. Implied in Michael Herr's dispersion "Vietnam Vietnam Vietnam, we've all been there" is his belief in the need to move forward with our lives. It's important to remember where we've been, though. The work of these writers helps us to remember where we've been and brings us closer to the wisdom we need to move forward in our own lives and our country's future.

John Sack:
"Playing a Diabolical Trick on the Reader"

Schroeder: Vietnam wasn't your first experience covering a war, was it? Didn't your career as a journalist actually begin when you were a soldier in the Korean war?

Sack: I was on the *Crimson* at Harvard, and after college I wasn't drafted— I volunteered for the Army to avoid being drafted, and I volunteered for Korea because I had a specialty as a public information writer. I got onto *Stars and Stripes*, and I was in a safe position to volunteer for the front. I say safe. In fact the death rate for war correspondents, both in Korea and Vietnam, was higher than the death rate for soldiers. But I covered the western front in Korea for *Stars and Stripes* for about half a year. What I liked about writing was being out in the field, being out in the cold, driving a jeep, going back and forth on the road from Seoul to the front, jumping into shellholes and foxholes and bunkers, and 10 percent of the time sitting down at the typewriter and knocking off the story.

Schroeder: Were you conscious of this as a traditional American role? In other words, the tradition of Hemingway, the war reporter?

Sack: I never thought of Hemingway as a war correspondent or a foreign correspondent. I do remember that Hitchcock movie *Foreign Correspondent* that featured that foreign correspondent in his trench coat. Perhaps such associations made it seem like an exciting job. But I'm not sure that if there weren't a war, I would have chosen to be a foreign correspondent. I don't know.

But as long as I was going to be in the Army, God knows I couldn't imagine anything else in the Army that could be any fun. I you're going to be in the Army for two years, being a war correspondent offered a wonderful chance to be able to see a war and to leave it whenever you want. It wasn't so much the glamor of it because there wasn't anybody whom I could impress with the glamor. I couldn't go visit my girlfriend in Seoul. There weren't too many people that I was writing to back in the States. There was just really something exciting about the job, about waking up at odd hours and driving the jeep north to Panmunjom, getting the stories, getting the scoops. I was twenty-two or twenty-three years old and really liked being outdoors, the adventure, the camaraderie with the other guys on *Stars and Stripes.*

And of course when I got back to the U.S. everyone said, "You're a writer; you're supposed to sit home all day at a typewriter, writing." That's what writing turned out to be most of the time, and it's not what I wanted. The part that was always fun for me was being in the field and then, only second, organizing the experience and making some sense out of it.

Schroeder: Was writing that difficult, then, back in the States after an experience like that?

Sack: Oh, it's terrible for me to have to create something out of my own head. In the late fifties, I was writing humor for the *New Yorker*; it all came out of my head. I would be home all day long just trying to think of funny things to say. I'd much rather have an experience and feel that it had to be expressed, had to be explained, and then sit down and organize it.

I can't remember what we would be laughing about in Korea; I just remember that it was a wonderful, wonderful time. Mike Herr makes a similar point in *Dispatches* about Vietnam—how much fun it is to be a war correspondent, that war can be fun. It's really true. Understand that I was against the war in Vietnam. In the end, I spoke against it at eighty colleges from Seattle to Florida, from UCLA to Maine. I spoke for the Mobilization, Moratorium, and Resistance. I testified to Congress. But that doesn't mean that being a war correspondent in Vietnam wasn't fun.

In Korea it was wonderful fun on *Stars and Stripes.* I just remember the nights of sitting there and laughing and laughing all night long with the other correspondents. One night we were sitting there, all typing our stories, and an air raid alarm sounded. We were used to Bedcheck Charlie (one Chinese plane used to come over Seoul and drop a few bombs), but this was the first time we'd ever heard an air raid siren. We all looked at each other. No one had told us what to do during an air raid. What were we supposed to do? Was there an air raid shelter around? We remembered something out back that looked like an air raid shelter, or maybe it was a potato bin. We didn't know. So we just sat there laughing. The Army hadn't told us what to do. We tacked some blankets over the windows and sat there laughing at the absurdity of the whole thing.

Schroeder: As an Army correspondent was your experience that different than that of the infantrymen? For instance, wouldn't the rest of the infantrymen have known what to do in case of an air attack?

Sack: Oh, I doubt it. I went through the same training as they had. I went through sixteen weeks of basic training. The first time I was at the front in Korea, Second Division, a guy from the PIO Office took me up to the top of a hill, and he pointed out the Chinese lines and a tank that was abandoned in no-man's-land. All of a sudden I heard this whistle, and we both dived under another tank. As mortars started falling around, I began laughing, because I had just had sixteen weeks of basic training and no one had ever mentioned that if you hear a whistling sound, that's incoming artillery and you should dive into a hole or under a tank. The reason I knew this was from seeing movies. Finally, we went running down the hill while things fell all around us. We got into a bunker and the guy who's with me asks this other guy what's happening. "Oh, the Chinese always mortar us at three o'clock every afternoon." "Well, why didn't you tell us when you saw us going up the hill?" "Yeah, I wondered what you were doing."

No, the infantry didn't know any more than we did. I was in a funny position: I was a PFC, but because I was a correspondent, I had the acting rank of full colonel. So I could bump captains off planes; I could eat, if I wanted to, at the field officers' mess; I could even sleep in the VIP billet. (And, of course, what I chose to do was to sleep in the VIP billet and eat at the enlisted men's mess because it was free.) I think I felt closer to the enlisted men than to the officers. Certainly when I was out in the evening I wanted to be with the enlisted men. My friends were mostly the people on *Stars and Stripes* and the other reporters.

Schroeder: How did you get the idea to do *M*?

Sack: I was with CBS News, and my first awareness that something was happening in Vietnam was when I was in Spain as bureau chief in Madrid. I began thinking that it might be interesting to go there. When I came back to the U.S. in September 1965, there really wasn't much to do at CBS. I was just drifting around there, doing dumb little projects and reading about the war. And then there was a very specific moment: I was reading *Time* magazine at CBS on West Fifty-seventh Street in New York, and *Time* was gung-ho about the war; it wrote of some soldiers jumping out of a helicopter and described them as "lean, mean, and looking for a fight." At that point I rebelled immediately. I'd been in Korea and I'd never seen a soldier who was lean, mean, and looking for a fight. Scared shitless was more like it. But all the reportage about the war in Vietnam was written in that same gung-ho World War II style, and I knew that that's not the way the Army was. No one was writing about it the way it really was. The first images that came to me were the eggshells in the scrambled eggs, shit on a shingle, KP, and people grousing, goldbricking, getting the wrong bullets in the rifles, shooting each other—everybody screwing up: all the stuff that was in *See Here, Private Hargrove.* In World War II you could write books like *See Here, Private Hargrove* and *C/O Postmaster.* Because our cause was so noble, you could have civilian soldiers with two left feet going into battle. But in Vietnam our cause was ignominious, and the press couldn't have dunderheads going into an ignominious war; it had to play up how gung-ho the men were.

I remember—this must have been a few days later—waking up at four in the morning and thinking it seemed obvious that the way to write about this would be to follow a basic training company to Vietnam. Everybody told me later that was a brilliant idea. At the time it seemed utterly, utterly obvious to me; to write about an event you must start with the people before they're in the event: establish their characters, carry them into the event, and then see what happens to them as the event affects them. You don't pick them up in the middle of the war: then they're already soldiers, and if they die, it's because they're supposed to. But if you pick them up as civilians back home, then they're people being swept up into something unknown. Any important book about war starts in the United States—*The Naked and the Dead, Catch-22.* You've got to establish character at the outset. It's just obvious.

Anyway, the next thing I did was call the Pentagon to find out if it would be possible to go to basic training for a month or two. Tom Wolfe makes it sound as if I wangled the Pentagon into letting me do it. Not at all. Anybody could have done it. Obviously a newspaper reporter who wants to write about basic training can call the Pentagon and then Fort Dix and at both places the answer will be, "Yeah, come on." He'll then spend two hours there, interviewing people and taking notes. All I was asking was to spend a month there instead of two hours. And to the Army there's no difference: that's my right as a reporter. I wasn't joining the company or re-enlisting— I was still a civilian—but I was spending so much time with the company that a few little changes had to be made. They gave me some fatigues and something on my arm to identify me as a correspondent (they made me a black armband with a "C" on it that the soldiers thought meant complaints or chaplain, so they came to me with all their stories). But the Pentagon had said, "Sure," and when I asked, "What about going to Vietnam?" the answer was the same, "No problem." To be a correspondent in Vietnam was incredibly simple.

Schroeder: Robert Stone has said much the same thing, and in fact writes about a similar situation in *Dog Soldiers.*

Sack: Oh, you don't even have to tell anyone that you're coming! You just get on a plane and go. When you arrive you go to JUSPAO [Joint United States Public Affairs Office], show them a letter from your bureau or editor, and you're accredited. That's all there is to it. The only thing that the military said I couldn't do, of course, was to fly on the same plane with them across the Pacific. Other than that, it was all open.

So I wrote Harold Hayes at *Esquire* that they're not "lean, mean, and looking for a fight," but that the Army is a place where eggshells get in the scrambled eggs. I said that I wanted to write a humorous article about soldiers going to Vietnam. In some ways it would be just like the World War II books, like *See Here, Private Hargrove*, but because of the nature of the war it wouldn't be simply straight humor but would become black humor. Well, Harold bought it, and I took a leave of absence from CBS.

I wanted to go to a camp that I thought would represent a cross-section of the Army population; I thought that I would have to go to a camp in the South. But the Pentagon said, "They're all cross-sections, and Fort Dix is as much of a cross section as any." I even went down to the Pentagon to assure myself of this. And, in fact, in order to maintain this feeling of generality, I never mention Fort Dix in the book, nor do I mention the name of the division or the battalion or where they are in Vietnam.

When I arrived they put me up in the guest house—I didn't sleep in the barracks—and I had breakfast every day at the officers' mess. I would get over to the barracks around six or seven in the morning. And then I would stay with the soldiers all day. But I wasn't going through training. Some reporters did actually do this—they would be going through the training and doing the pushups and everything. But I didn't need to do that; the soldiers' job was to do the pushups and my job was to take notes.

I had a rented car and checked out various things around the camp when what they were doing wasn't of any interest to me. Once I even said that I was going to be at Headquarters checking on something, and instead I drove to Newark Airport and flew down to Washington. I went to the Pentagon to see the process by which the members of the company were chosen to go or not to go to Vietnam. I came back that evening knowing who was going to go to Vietnam and who wasn't, but never told them, of course, that I knew it.

Schroeder: During your time at Fort Dix did you feel conspicuous?

Sack: I felt very awkward. I felt like a little boy and was hoping desperately that I wouldn't be the absolute last one chosen for the baseball team.

Schroeder: Did the fact you'd been through it yourself as a soldier help?

Sack: Oh, it helped tremendously in terms of intuiting what was going on in their minds. I identified with them. I absolutely saw everything as they would. That helped me tremendously all the way through because what I was feeling, I was almost sure, was what they were feeling. Of course I couldn't come out and say, "This is what they were feeling" merely because I was feeling it, but I could go to them and ask and they would usually confirm, "Yeah, that's how I felt." An example of this is when the colonel at battalion headquarters in Vietnam is briefing them and saying something like, "You're not going to help your buddy if you get V.D." Immediately my first thought was "You can get V.D. here? Where can you get V.D.?" And immediately I turned to look at Sullivan, who's the big cocksman there. I could see his eyes looking around. I went over to him afterwards and asked, "When the colonel said that, what were you thinking?" And he said, "Where do you get V.D.?"

   While I was with them at Fort Dix they were just so happy to have me there. Nobody cared about them. The sergeants didn't care about them; the civilians didn't care about them; Washington didn't care about them. They were just pushed around and hassled. All of a sudden here comes this man of his own free will and volition who's going to sit there and listen to their problems. They took me into their confidence. And so because of that I was able to identify with them probably more than I was able to identify with the soldiers in Korea.

Schroeder: The differences between soldiers in Vietnam and in previous wars were significant; were the correspondents in Vietnam different than the correspondents in previous wars?

Sack: Well there was nobody in Vietnam like Ernie Pyle from World War II or Jim Lukas from Korea. I can't imagine anybody in his forties or fifties doing the type of journalism that I was doing or that Mike Herr was doing. Michael did a brilliant thing that occurred to no other person. Perhaps it should have occurred to me, but my defense mechanism—self-protection— stopped it from occurring to me until I had read Michael's book and realized what he had done (and that's why I think that his book is by far the best Vietnam book of the ones I've read). As a journalist I was trying to feel what the soldiers were feeling by going through basic training with them, being on the operation with them, and imagining what was going on in their minds. But there comes a point when you've been out with them in the field for a week, and you realize that it's beginning to affect your own performance. And you think that because you're a writer and must stay relatively clear-headed, you'd better get out of the war zone for a few days and get some rest. It never occurs to you that this experience of going nutty, of being exhausted, of losing track of things, is the very experience of being in Vietnam that you should be writing about. Now Michael realized this and allowed himself to live it. I once read in a review of *Fear and Loathing in Las Vegas* how noble it was for Hunter Thompson to donate his sanity to the cause of journalism. But of course Hunter exaggerates a lot. Michael was really the one who donated his sanity to the cause of reportage; he had a hard time for several years afterwards. *Dispatches* came out years after it was supposed to. And that was because he lived that experience and survived enough to be able to write the book. But the rest of us, certainly, when we felt that this thing was getting to us, when we felt shaky, scared, and confused, we went back to Saigon to clean out the tubes. We did what the soldiers couldn't do.

But getting back to your question, anybody in his forties or fifties would have been interpreting things so much from the point of view of his recollections of World War II that he would not have been able to grasp what was going on over there. An example of this can be seen in Bill Styron's review of *Lieutenant Calley* in the *New York Times Book Review*, where Styron could not assimilate the fact that American soldiers were going around Vietnam killing civilians. Styron was a Marine captain in World War II. And in spite of all the evidence in the book, he kept insisting that when Calley said something good about himself he was lying and that when Calley said something bad about himself Sack was trying to undercut Calley.

So basically, I guess I could write as well as other people who were thirty-six, but as far as my feelings went, I was twenty-two and a soldier again. I completely identified.

Schroeder: How would you then describe the point of view in *M*? It certainly doesn't seem to be that of a twenty-two year-old soldier.

Sack: I'm playing a diabolical trick on the reader of *M*. In my first three books the "I" was evident throughout. It was always my point of view. In *M* there is no "I." I never say "I." There's never any suggestion that I'm even there. You can never tell which scenes I witnessed and which were reported to me second-hand. And I don't have my photograph on the book for the same reason: because I want the reader to feel that he or she is being handed raw information, raw facts. "This is the way it is," as the *Los Angeles Times*, I think, said. That objective facts have just been plunked in front of the reader and haven't passed through anybody else's consciousness. I did not want the reader to see a picture of me on the back of the book and think, "Oh, this is the guy who has arranged and interpreted the facts for me."

This is a shuck. Obviously everything has passed through my consciousness, and I'm just taking advantage of this whole American belief in objectivity. I myself don't believe in objectivity—no New Journalist does. Other reporters feel that they have to restrict themselves to objective facts, although there's really no such thing. So I was going along with this whole newspaper ethic (I don't know how consciously at first) where I report who, what, when, where, and how. A reporter writes, "President Reagan said today in the East Room of the White House that 'Blah, blah, blah.'" He doesn't write, "He looked old and tired" or "He looked shifty-eyed" or "Look, between you and me it's a crock of shit." And like that reporter, I never say "I" in *M*, but I'm imposing my point of view, my consciousness, by choosing what facts I'm going to report. I'm not being sneaky about this. I'm not thinking, "Oh I won't say this because this is against my thesis; I'll just cut it out." No, I'm merely recounting the incidents that are important to me, and recounting them the way I happened to see them. Somebody else, anybody else, could go through the same experience and see it quite differently.

At the same time, when I was with M and going to Vietnam, I was so wrapped up in the soldier's point of view that I was not yet against the war; in fact, I was probably for the war, grudgingly for the war. I recall feeling that "it's a big messy war, but we have to do it, there's no choice." I knew that when M screwed up on its first operation and killed that girl it was a good story, but I did not believe that it was in any way typical of what was going on in Vietnam. After that operation was over and we were back at brigade, I was talking to the chief of staff of the brigade, Lt. Col. Sam Walker, and I apologized to him. I said, "Look, I'm really sorry about this; my plan was to join this company in training, follow it to Vietnam, accompany it on its first operation, and then the book would end. And they went on this operation and it was a terrible mess. All they did was kill one girl. That's my story and I'm stuck with it. I'm sorry, I know it isn't typical." And Col. Walker said, "It's typical." He said it, but I didn't believe it. It wasn't until half a year later reading a story in the *New York Times Magazine* by Tom Buckley where I read that the same thing was happening in the Delta that I began thinking, "Maybe it was typical." It took months before I was against the war.

Schroeder: Did you single out Demirgian as your main character for any particular reason?

Sack: No, I didn't single him out. It was not until well along—maybe even during the operation—that I realized Demirgian would be the central character of the book. When I started, I was taking notes on almost everybody—there were two hundred soldiers in the company—and I was taking heavy notes on the ones who I felt had interesting characters, who were different from the mass.

Schroeder: You were conscious of that?

Sack: Well, yes. In the beginning Prochaska was to me the most interesting person. And then perhaps Yoshioka and McCarthy. I don't think I even knew who Demirgian was for about a week and a half. But I must have had my eye on him during their last week before they left to Vietnam because he was the one that I chose to see saying good-bye in Boston. Then again, he was the obvious choice because I didn't want to spend the money to follow Morton back to Texas, and Prochaska and Yoshioka weren't going any-where, they were just sitting around the base.

Demirgian emerged very slowly as the main character. It wasn't at all (as some have felt) because his name was Armenian and sounded like Yossarian that I chose him. In fact, I thought that that was a disadvantage, that it would seem derivative. But when the soldiers went home on leave, I didn't want to follow Prochaska because he wasn't going to Vietnam; Yoshioka was going to Vietnam, but he wasn't going home to California, he was just going to stay on the base; Bigalow was going up to New York City and wander around—he didn't know what he was going to do, stay at the Y, I think. But meanwhile I had two characters who were friends who were going some-place close that I could fly to—Boston—so it was clear that I should go with them. Not because I had decided that they were going to be the main characters of the book, but because convenience sent me there, and the rest of the people I would just have to pick up later. And somewhere along the way it became clear that Demirgian would be the main character.

Schroeder: In a sense, then, your choice of main character seems to have been out of your own control. As a writer don't you find that alarming: the fact that you're so locked into your characters' actions?

Sack: Oh no, that's the fun part. Every time I've tried to write fiction I've really been unable to do it, starting at Harvard where I got a "C" in fiction. I once tried to write a "movie of the week" for television, and I just couldn't manage to get the characters under control. I just lost all sense of form. I don't know how writers of fiction do it. Finally I began wondering what I was doing, inventing all these characters in order to make a story that fits together.

No, for me it's much more exciting to see real people and watch them behaving in utterly inscrutable ways. "Why is this man behaving in a way that is totally inconsistent with anything that I know about human nature?" Smith's behavior, for example. To try and understand what was going on in his mind when he was charging up the hill and doing the best job he could when he was against all war—to try to figure out what's happening there is fascinating. To get a character, a real person, and start investigating him and to see what makes him work opens up all sorts of boxes. It's an exciting pursuit. But to invent a character is frustrating for me. I can't handle it.

Schroeder: Why don't you think that anybody wrote this type of nonfiction about World War II? All of the major books about that war are novels: *From Here to Eternity, The Naked and the Dead, Catch-22.*

Sack: That's an interesting question. I guess the closest thing in World War II would be Ernie Pyle's writing, but it's really not the same, is it? Do you know what I think the reason is? In the fifties to be a writer meant to be a novelist. If you thought of writing, you thought of writing a novel. Even now people introduce me as a novelist because to write a book is to write a novel. That's the only reason that I can think of.

Oh, also, I suppose, if you're not writing a novel, you've got to take reams of notes or else have a fantastic memory—or perhaps both, like Truman Capote. I guess that in World War II, the writers weren't taking notes.

Schroeder: Do you see the Demirgian of *The Man-Eating Machine* as being the logical extension, the natural progression, of the Demirgian of *M*?

Sack: I do now. I didn't then. I returned from Vietnam in May of '66. Then the book was sold to NAL [New American Library] and I worked all summer to complete it by the October 10 deadline. At that point the guys were still in Vietnam and I felt terrible being in the United States. I felt like a deserter. And I just had to go back, so I arranged with Harold Hayes to do a story on their last month in Vietnam. And at the time I returned, nothing seemed logical to me. Perhaps everything would have made better sense if I'd originally had unlimited resources and had just stayed with M for the year and written at great length while watching the changes come over them. When I went back I was noticing, quite obviously, that the soldiers didn't like the Vietnamese. It got to be overwhelming, how much they hated the Vietnamese. I couldn't figure out why they hated them to such an extent that they were already committing atrocities: for instance, Sgt. Condron shooting those two Vietnamese laundry boys. But now I understand it.

Schroeder: Earlier you mentioned that you identified with many of their experiences. Why, then, was this so difficult to comprehend?

Sack: Because I hadn't been with them during that whole time.

Schroeder: If you had, do you think that your reaction would have been the same?

Sack: If I had been with them for a year, I'm sure that I would have started hating the Vietnamese too. In a sense I did hate the Vietnamese. Even in Saigon I really disliked them—I wouldn't say hated them—but in my own experiences with them I really disliked them. When I got to Vietnam I was planning to spend half my time writing the book and half my time doing good things for the Vietnamese. To my knowledge, I was the only member of the American Center of the International Pen Club in Vietnam. I called the Vietnamese Pen Center and said that I'd like to meet them and even offered to help them. And they said, "Ah, so, so, so," and never returned my call. Having also been a producer at CBS I called the Vietnamese television station and offered my services, free. They never did anything. It was impossible to meet any Vietnamese. The only Vietnamese you could meet were prostitutes. You were never invited into Vietnamese homes. Like the

American soldiers, I really started disliking them. But of course the soldiers were going to dislike them even more because they were being killed by faceless people who they assumed were the Vietnamese whose faces they saw during the daytime. If I'd gone through that, I'm sure I would have hated them.

After their first operation I went down to Saigon to write, and M was left wandering around in the field for weeks and weeks, getting killed like Morton or wounded like Yoshioka. So when Demirgian came into Saigon one night and said, "I'd like to burn this whole country down and start again with Americans," I could vaguely understand it, but couldn't really appreciate the depths of it or why he would feel that way. But then when I came back at the end of the year and saw them really full of hatred—Demirgian wanting to kill a VC because he was a Vietnamese, Condron shooting those two laundry boys—then I was really puzzled by it, and in my second *Esquire* article I ascribed it to racism. When I came back home in 1967, I remember being on a radio program at CBS at which the host asked me, "How do the soldiers feel about the Vietnamese?" To which I replied, "They hate them." He was tongue-tied. "What? What? Are you saying that our soldiers hate the Vietnamese?" I answered, "Yes, they do." He continued sputtering, "What do you mean? I, I, I thought they, they were there to defend them!" The switchboard lights up. There are calls pouring in and I'm fielding angry questions: "How dare you say that? I was in World War II and we passed out candy to the children. We loved the children. How can you say that Americans hate the Vietnamese?"

Schroeder: Do you think that this feeling was unique to Vietnam?

Sack: To the Vietnam war? Well, it was much stronger in Vietnam. We didn't particularly like the Koreans in the Korean war. We called them the "indignant personnel" instead of the "indigenous personnel." Apparently there was some annoyance with our South Korean allies. But nothing to the point of purposely going out and trying to shoot them. These feelings were certainly much stronger in Vietnam. I started thinking about it, and finally I began reading books on racism. I finally decided that it was not because of racism. In fact, I make this point explicit in *The Man-Eating Machine*. This is an idea that I had a tremendously difficult time getting across. I finally realized that we hated the Vietnamese not because they were yellow people, but because they were people, period, and in an efficient society people stand in the way. We would kill the Vietnamese simply because they were people and prevented our war machine from going forward. But this is still so difficult for people to accept. *Mother Jones* bought a section of *The Man-Eating Machine.* Then they changed the sentence "It wasn't racism" to "It wasn't *just* racism." And I insisted, "No. It wasn't racism. This is exactly what I'm trying to say." They got very upset by this. Just before going to press they had a meeting and didn't invite me; the result was that they cancelled the whole article.

Schroeder: Your technique in *M* is at times self-consciously literary. For instance, in several places you foreshadow things to come. Yet we are kept guessing throughout the book who is a marked man and who isn't.

Sack: That was, of course, the plot of the book, in so far as there is a plot. The first sentence implies that some of them are going to die—at least one of them is going to die. And then every major character who is introduced is introduced with a little hint that it might be him. Prochaska is introduced and just when everybody thinks, "Oh boy, is he being set up to be killed," I say, "He's the sort of person who in a mediocre war novel would die in the next chapter to last," leaving the question open: Is he going to die or not?

Schroeder: Or perhaps your comment undercuts the initial foreshadowing and makes us certain that it's not going to be him.

Sack: I was hoping that it would be ambiguous, that everyone would wonder. And Morton, of course, telling his mother about the coffin. And Demirgian with the sergeant telling him, "You're the one that's going to die." The question is left open so as to give the book a plot.

Schroeder: Yet the tone is, as you characterize it, black humor. And because in many places the tone is so light, when people actually do get killed, the reader's sensibilities are offended; he thinks, "This person can't really be dead." There's an analogous situation in *The Naked and the Dead.* Hearns's death comes so unexpectedly and seems to pass almost unnoticed—except by the reader, of course, who says, "Wait a minute. This hasn't really happened—he couldn't be dead, he's the main character!" We simply don't want to accept the fact of his death. The same sort of thing, I think, happens in *M.*

Sack: Well, that's the way it is in war. And I suppose that that's the best way to write about it—not to suggest anything in advance. But of course I was never there when any of the people in the company died or were hit.

Even if I had spent a year with M, it would still have been very unlikely that I would have witnessed anything of that sort. In Demirgian's company nobody was killed after the first operation. That would have been the company that I would have been with, most likely. And even if I were there, all of a sudden something explodes and somebody is dead—[*slowly*] I don't know how you could embroider on that.

Schroeder: In *M*, though, after someone is killed life seems to go on. There's not a great sense of tragedy about it. It's forgotten because it's something that does happen. But then—

Sack: [*interrupting*] That's my fault. There was a great sense of tragedy accompanying Morton's death. The book would have been better if I had really been able to elaborate on that.

Schroeder: I think the book's last section, the summing up of what has happened to all of the principal players in the last six months, is very effective: "So and so was killed, so and so was wounded, so and so never made it to Vietnam, and good old Demirgian, still in Vietnam, only now a sergeant." The ending conveys a strong sense of these young innocents who went into Vietnam thinking that it was going to be a turkey shoot or an extended vacation or various other illusions; they lost these illusions and some of them also lost their lives in the process. The compactness of the last page brings all of this home so quickly.

Sack: It's good if that happens. If that actually happens, great! I'm afraid the real reason for that is that I just wasn't there when Yoshioka and Morton were hit. I was supposed to be there with Yoshioka; I'd gone up to talk to him about something, and when I got there, they said that he was a casualty. They'd assumed that I was coming up to see Yoshioka, that I'd known about what happened. I didn't. As soon as I did, I went rushing down to the hospital and then was there with him in the hospital. So the scene at the hospital is much more detailed than the one on the road where he got hit. The reason that the scene on the road transpires so quickly is because I wasn't there to get all the notes that I needed.

But Morton, I found out about Morton a week or two later. When I went up to his company the captain was unhappy and disturbed about it. I explained I'd been following Morton since basic training and I'd like to find out what had happened. The captain said, "Rather than going to see the men, I think it would be better if we bring a guy up here because the men are feeling pretty disturbed." And the sergeant from Morton's squad came up, and he was very angry. I mean, he was homicidal. He approached me holding an M-16—the guy wanted to kill me. They'd been on this operation and people had died, and he was scared with the rest, and, finally, here's this reporter coming in to ask them about how this guy died. I could only talk to him for a few minutes and then the humane as well as sensible thing to do was to let him go back to his bunker. I did talk to one or two others who were there. I got much more information later on when *M* was optioned by CBS as a mini-series (it was never made). I had to write some more material for them, and it was then that I found out more about Morton's death.

But as I think about it, I couldn't have used that in the book; at that point the book was clearly drawing to a close, and things had to be summed up.

Schroeder: Were there any specific influences which caused you to forsake traditional journalism in favor of *M*'s new journalistic technique?

Sack: One thing comes to mind immediately. I read Michael Herr's story on Fort Dix in *Holiday* magazine; I had no detailed description in *M*, and he had such wonderful description in his article that I realized my piece needed something similar, so I inserted sentences such as this one on page nine of the paperback [*reading*]: "The air was thick with the smell of floor wax and rifle oil." And I went through the whole book putting in such descriptions. You see, before I went to Vietnam I hadn't read any New Journalism—I had read very little Tom Wolfe and had just glanced at Truman Capote.

Schroeder: Were you familiar with the term "New Journalism" at that point?

Sack: No; the first time that I heard the term was in 1968. I read a review of Mailer's *The Armies of the Night* in *Look* magazine—the review was called "The New Journalism"—and I said, "If there's such a thing I should learn about it." I started reading the piece, and *Look* offered a list of the four great New Journalists. And I was one of them. That was the first time I heard the term. I wasn't that familiar with Tom Wolfe, so I read a little more of him.

People in 1966 had been talking about Truman Capote, and I was afraid he was doing something I wouldn't be able to do, so I read about thirty pages of *In Cold Blood* just to make sure that he wasn't doing anything I couldn't even imagine how to do. Of course I'm incapable of writing descriptions as beautiful as his. But at least it wasn't something unimaginable.

So the reason that *M* is New Journalism is because having been a producer at CBS News the scene-by-scene construction came naturally to me. You see, I originally wanted to do *M* as a documentary for CBS, and when I couldn't do that, I left CBS to do it for *Esquire*. I saw everything as movie scenes; that's why there's a sort of soundtrack running through it; that's why *M* has no flashbacks; that's why everything is set up scene-by-scene—it's a camera setup. I really had *M* in mind as a movie. Fortunately, that turned out to be the way things were done in New Journalism. And that's also why I had very little description. I hate writing description. Every time I have to think of some metaphor to describe what things look like I just rebel against it. For Christ's sake, give me a camera. On film I can show it in two seconds, instead of having to agonize over finding the right words for it.

Schroeder: One of the most controversial of the New Journalistic techniques is point of view. Tom Wolfe talks about the need for the author to keep out of the narrative and, in fact, does this in most of his work. Others like Mailer and Thompson, though, are often at the center of their narratives.

Sack: That was a specific, conscious choice in the case of *M*. As I mentioned earlier, I wanted readers to think they were getting undigested, raw material.

At one point I violated that in the *Esquire* article in the scene where the operation begins. When I first went out that morning I wasn't really planning to go, and Dan Rather said, "Come on, you'll like it; it's no problem." They were planning on going into the Michelin plantation. At that time as far as we all knew we were going into a terrible firefight. And at the last moment I decided to go along. The VC all knew we were coming. And I knew that the VC would know. There were all these horror stories circulating about what it would be like and what it was like the last time. And when we got onto the helicopters, both the soldiers and I thought that we were going into this incredibly hot landing zone. When this passage was first written for *Esquire* it said: "M wasn't anywhere near the Michelin funland; in keeping with the truly secret order"—this is overwritten—"it was twelve merciful miles to the South. Hooray for the American Army!" And then I had "Author's Note" in parentheses, signifying how *I* was relieved. I meant thank *God* that the Army had some brains. Since everybody knew that we were going to the Michelin plantation, they sent us someplace else. Hooray. But then looking at the *Esquire* piece I realized that no one's aware that I'm there on the helicopter. No one's aware *where* I am. And to say "Author's Note" doesn't really make sense to the reader. So I just took that out; it was the only place where the author appeared.

Eliminating myself was a literary choice. In a way it's the opposite of egocentric, but in another way it's even more egocentric: the art becomes so important that I'm willing to do anything—including keeping my picture off the book—for the sake of the art. When I wrote the story on Lt. Calley I could have very easily said, "Calley and I sat down; he ordered a gin and tonic and as he was sipping it he recollected that"—I hate that stuff. But after I interviewed him I realized that everything I knew about Calley that I wanted to say could be said in Calley's own words, if I just arranged them right. So I started writing it as just Calley's words, but vaguely in the back of my mind I wondered how I'd ever get a byline here. The byline actually became a problem with Viking, but the material dictated that it had to be written in Calley's own voice.

I don't really like this book. I stuck to Calley's words and just cut and cut and cut, and finally the text was cut down to the point where it doesn't read like a human voice.

Schroeder: How did you come to feel about Calley?

Sack: [*pause*] Well, remember that I'd already written that piece in *Esquire* about Sgt. Condron, who did exactly the same thing. He was a lovely guy who went and killed some people and was court-martialed and sent to Leavenworth. It was written very sympathetically from his point of view, not because it's OK to kill Vietnamese, which of course it isn't, but because I wanted to show how logical it seemed to the soldiers to kill Vietnamese. So the Calley book was a repeat of the Condron story, but people knew Calley whereas they didn't know Condron. When I first met Calley it was important for me to establish whether the guy *was* a homicidal maniac (in which case I had no interest in writing a book about him because it doesn't prove anything except that occasionally homicidal maniacs get into the Army) or whether he was an average soldier. I was very lucky and astonished to find out that, better than being an average soldier, he was in the upper 3 percent of the soldiers in Vietnam as far as compassion and consideration and love of the Vietnamese went. In fact, after a few months in the field without any idea that he would be tried for My Lai or any idea that My Lai was anything out of the ordinary—because it wasn't—Calley went to the colonel and asked to be transferred to S-5, where he worked passing out food for the farmers and getting feed for the pigs and setting up sewing courses for the nurses. For six months he worked in this job that no other officer had been able to last in for more than a month. He was and is a very considerate, caring person. I liked him, and I had good times with him.

So did everyone else who knew him, yet he committed mass murder in Vietnam. That tells us something about the war in Vietnam.

Schroeder: Did you find a difference between the mainstream media's reporting of Vietnam and the kind of writing that you were doing and that Michael Herr was doing? Did you get the sense that there were almost two different wars?

Sack: Yeah, of course. Because the media was following those Galilean rules of objectivity. For instance, here's an example from *Lt. Calley*. This is right after My Lai and the Army wants a body count [*reading*]:

> Medina said, "What is the body count?"
> I said to Medina, "I don't know."
> "What is your estimate then?"
> "I don't know. Go to the village yourself. Or go over there to the ditch. And count 'em."
> "Anything off the top of your head—"
> "Oh, hell. Thirty. Forty."
> "Lieutenant Brooks?" Medina had all the platoon leader there, and asked every one. He then called the Colonel, and he reported fifty for the first platoon, fifty for Brooks's platoon, fifty for the third platoon, fifty for the mortar platoon, fifty for the helicopter units, and fifty for the artillery. And maybe some for the headquarters troops: it appeared as one hundred and twenty-eight in the *New York Times*. Front page.

Now where did the *Times* come up with 128? They get it from the official news briefing—the Five O'Clock Follies—in Saigon. Where did *they* get 128? God knows. But the *New York Times* with its objective reporting is forced to print the JUSPAO story even though the *reporters* are laughing about it and criticizing it. But the *New York Times* has to tell it, it has to say, "The Army said we killed 128 people." It can't say, "The Army said that and the Army's full of shit." The *Times* has to put its story on the front page. It's trapped by its own rules.

Homer Bigart, who covered the Calley trial for the *New York Times*—I respect him, he's a two-time Pulitzer Prize winner—he felt he's doing the right thing, but I intensely disagreed with his method of reportage. He felt that his reportage would be biased, would be hurt, if he ever met Calley. He did not allow himself to meet Calley, or to talk to Calley, or to find out anything about Calley as a person because it might bias his coverage of the facts of the trial. So to me, the press coverage, the *Times*'s coverage, of Calley's trial was *insane.* Any time I'm involved with a story and know what's going on and then see the press coverage of it, it is utterly insane how wrong they are, and how wrongly they misinterpret it. Objectivity is just impossible.

Photograph by Dudley Reed

Michael Herr:
"We've All Been There"

Schroeder: Perhaps you might begin by describing your journalistic apprenticeship and subsequent motivation to write about Vietnam?

Herr: I don't know how to answer that at all. In a way it's so boring. I always wanted to write. Even since I was a kid I wanted to write. I began living in New York when I was nineteen or twenty. I worked for magazines, first as an editor, then as a journalist doing pieces, travel features, film criticism. And yet I never had any training as a journalist and have never ever thought of myself as a journalist. This is a touchy subject because I have many friends who are journalists. I'm not putting them on another side of any line, but I've just never thought of myself as a journalist. I don't have a journalist's instincts and have absolutely no training or discipline as a journalist. I had a long personal relationship with Harold Hayes, who was perhaps the last great magazine editor during his tenure as managing editor of *Esquire*. The anthology of collected *Esquire* pieces that he edited, *Smiling Through the Apocalypse*, reads like a time capsule. It's a fabulous record of those times and the evolution of the so-called New Journalism.

I don't know why I was attracted to Vietnam. I couldn't really begin to answer that except to say that I felt that it was *the* story at the time, and I also felt that it wasn't being told in any true way. Lots of journalism, but it wasn't saying what was happening there or at least what I felt, my hunch. I asked Harold to send me there and he agreed. It was really quite simple. I went actually to write a monthly column. I was there about a week when I realized what a horrible idea that was. Because he had taken great expense and risk to send me, I wrote to him explaining the situation. He replied: "Well, you're there. Do what you want to do." It was quite extraordinary.

Schroeder: Had you planned on staying as long as you did?

Herr: I had no plan. I went to write a book. Harold knew that. Whatever arrangement I had with him—whether it was pieces, or a column, or even a regular feature—the idea always was to write a book. Having thought of myself not as a journalist but as a writer, I thought that it was time to write something. I was twenty-seven years old when I went there, and I had spent all the time previous travelling and writing pieces about places, but not writing what I felt I should be writing. So I believed before I ever got there that that was the time and the place and the subject. I was very ambitious for the work and had large expectations for it.

Schroeder: Did you envision the book as having a certain structure, as following a certain form?

Herr: That's hard to know. Vaguely, yes. Consciously, specifically, no. I think that when an idea comes to you for a book, in a way that book is already finished. Somewhere it's inside, waiting to be taken out. Everything but the design and the cover and the ad campaign. It's all in there. Right now I'm going through hell with the book I'm writing, but I know it's all in there somewhere, the whole shape of it is there. My great problem as a writer is organization. I can't see the connections between bits of a book. So in a way, yes, the book was all there and I knew what it was, but in a way I had to find it. And I had no idea what it was going to do to me, what the search for the book was going to do to me. Because I had no idea what the subject was. In one sense, however, that's what the book is about—*Dispatches* is really a book about the writing of a book. If somebody were to ask me what it was about, I would say that the secret subject of *Dispatches* was not Vietnam, but that it was a book about writing a book. I think that all good books are about writing.

Schroeder: Yet *Dispatches* isn't just concerned with writing; it's concerned with a specific *type* of writing. This critical distinction surfaces several times, most notably when you comment, "This war could no more be covered by conventional journalism than it could be won by conventional fire-power." You distinguish between people who were doing what you were doing and people who simply reported the official story.

Herr: Related to this—this is a very delicate area—is the fact that when the book was finished there was some question as to whether it should be published as journalism or as a novel. In my heart of hearts, I've always privately thought of it as a novel. The "I" in the book shouldn't be taken—at any rate, always—as me. As it's a book about a journalist, there is a certain distance implicit, a certain construction.

Schroeder: Nonetheless, the viewpoint in the book remains very immediate and exerts a powerful effect on the reader. It propels the reader right into the heart of the events described.

Herr: Finally, that's not by accident, but that's because it was required by my experience to do it that way.

Schroeder: Can you imagine *Dispatches* being told from a traditional journalist point of view where the "I" disappears?

Herr: No, it would be another book. Writing a book can be a very messy business, filled with all kinds of excessive, hysterical moments, especially for someone who is as afraid, not of writing, but of publishing, as I am. I have absolutely no fear of writing. I write a lot. My concern is in having it read. Finishing it. Letting it go. The blank page gives me no fear whatsoever. It's the full page that frightens me.

Schroeder: Was that your major problem, then, in getting out *Dispatches*?

Herr: I had several problems, not the least of which was the famous post-Vietnam syndrome. I came back from Vietnam having written only a very small part of the book while I was there. I wrote two-thirds of the book in eighteen months after I came back, and at that point there was some kind of massive collapse, a profound paralysis that I can't *directly* attribute to Vietnam, although Vietnam was certainly the catalyst. Vietnam was the last portion of a long journey. To blame my collapse on Vietnam without looking at all of the rest of the factors would be blind indeed. I think that that's the tragic confusion of a lot of veterans. This is hard to talk about. It's also one of the reasons why I've never been more public with my feelings about the veterans. It's a really heavy dilemma. I think about them all the time. But whenever I've been in correspondence with them (which is seldom because I don't do much letter writing), when I tell them what I *really* think, I find that more often than not they never write back again. They think that I'm some kind of brutal-minded, totally unsympathetic asshole, when in fact all that I'm saying to them is "*You* went to Vietnam, *you're* the one who went there. If Vietnam was so bloody terrible, don't be there anymore.

Vietnam was a part of your life. Look at *all* of your life. Don't be bitter and don't blame it on anybody." At the time when I was utterly paralyzed and couldn't write, I wasn't so easy about it. But nor did I necessarily connect what I was going through with what had happened in Vietnam and what happened in the immediate time after my return. In a way, the heaviest of it was after I came back from Vietnam.

Schroeder: Whenever the subject of Vietnam arises the same basic sets of responses are evident: veterans often exhibit one of two extremes—they can be obsessed with the experience, still living it, or completely silent about it. The public's response is generally similar to this latter response—people neither want to hear about Vietnam nor discuss it. *Dispatches* seems to me to mediate between these two poles. It tries to create a perspective which captures the experience, sympathizes with the participants, and yet allows the reader to see the necessity of walking away from it in the end.

Herr: This is just a human perspective.

Schroeder: Very much so. But this has shocked some people.

Herr: I know. I've experienced that. One of the ways that I can tell that I did what I really wanted with that book is the responses I get from extremely political people. People of the left think that I'm some kind of bloody-minded, militaristic monster, and people of the right think that I'm the worst kind of bleeding-heart liberal sob sister, when, in fact, I don't really know what politics is. Politics is language, and as such I find it completely worthless and useless; it describes nothing but attitudes when the situation is changing every second. In writing *Dispatches*, I had no political ax to grind. Where I did, it's quite obvious and I say so in the book: we never should have gone to that place; it was an act of unspeakable arrogance for which we are still paying. But once you're there and you're in the scene then you need another expression—"should have been," "could have been," "would have been"—that's not going to help anybody. It's certainly not going to describe what happened.

Schroeder: You mentioned *Dispatches* as having a human perspective, as being concerned with the human side of the war.

Herr: That's the only side I saw. I didn't see any concepts in Vietnam. I went looking for them, but I never touched one or saw one. All I saw was real life. And it's just a piece of your life. A very heavy piece of your life. I have friends, men and women, who have had very horrible things happen to them in so-called peace time situations in New York City on the street. And many of them are frozen in those moments. It's the same situation, just the same. I say something similar in the book: "Don't let it wipe you out; it's only your life. If your life happened to take you to Vietnam, rather than blaming a corrupt government and a careless government, why don't you blame yourself? You might actually feel better if you can take it on yourself." That's a very hard thing to say to a guy who's in a wheelchair, or has had his young life cracked open for him. But in a way, that's who you've got to say it to.

The other thing is that I don't want to have my head in that subject any more. It's a big world and there are lots of things to write about. It's really important just to get on with it. The Vietnam war ended in 1975. It's over. It really is over. Whether I still think about it or find little tag ends of an old obsession or have dreams about it—that's another story. But in real life on the ground it's over.

Schroeder: But don't you think that America has been very slow in coming to terms with Vietnam?

Herr: America has never come to terms with Vietnam. Vietnam is big in the culture now. It's right up there on the surface. I suppose that *Dispatches* broke it as a story in the culture. But that's still not quite dealing with it. There are these twelve-part PBS series and treatments of it. And I suppose that's useful—it's better than pretending that it never happened. But there is some profound way in which it is not going to be dealt with. We are not a great introspective or retrospective people. It's not in our nature. We're very ignorant of our history. We're great perverters of our tradition.

Schroeder: Do you think that we'll learn anything from Vietnam?

Herr: I don't know. I think that's an individual matter.

Schroeder: Do you think that we've learned anything thus far?

Herr: No. I would say no. I would say no and say that it's too much to ask of us because we would have to call things by their real names, shave off all the rhetoric and defuse a lot of emotionally inflated words. Inflation of a kind got us into Vietnam. Vietnam's legacy has been inflation. Maybe if we had never gone to Vietnam we would be up to our nostrils in El Salvador, rather than being in just up to our knees. I don't know. I have a suspicion that we're not great at telling the truth about certain kinds of national behavior. The war sure twisted us. We haven't felt the same about ourselves since Vietnam. We're haunted by it, but we won't name the shape of the ghost; we won't say what it is.

Schroeder: Do you see *Dispatches* as trying to do something that all the media coverage—TV, newspapers, and magazines—failed to do?

Herr: Always. I always did. Even before I went to Vietnam that's what I wanted to do.

Schroeder: What do you think was the effect of the media coverage?

Herr: I think it prolonged the war. I think it anesthetized the people's minds about the war, about what the war was. I think that the coverage turned the war into something that was happening in the media wonderland that we are all increasingly living in. Unless we keep ourselves extremely alert, we're going to be utterly consumed by that horribly homogenized, not real and not unreal, twilight world of television. Cathode poisoning. Numbness.

Schroeder: In our technological society are novels still able to compete with the media, television in particular?

Herr: Not in the marketplace and not for a wide audience, but in individual consciousnesses, absolutely. I think that television just can't compete with a piece of writing. For all the talk about Vietnam being a television war, I never believed it was television's war; I always believed it was a writer's war. And in my arrogance and ignorance I wanted to be the one to prove it.

Schroeder: You see Vietnam as a writer's war; it was also a young man's war.

Herr: Well, you know, the old men make the war for the young men to go fight in; that's classic, that's eternal. The old men in this case happened to be chronologically young men.

Schroeder: But the median age of a Vietnam combatant was much younger than his World War II counterpart, and it seems to me that the people who were doing the type of reporting that you were doing—

Herr: —were quite young. It's true.

Schroeder: I think in many instances World War II and Korea must have been an inhibiting influence on the older writers, journalists, reporters. And when they did write about the war, their writing often had little impact. For instance, James Jones. He went to Vietnam after the U.S. troop withdrawals and wrote *Viet Journal*, a book-length nonfiction account of his experiences. The book made practically no impact at all. No one's ever heard of it.

Herr: I didn't know that James Jones wrote a book about Vietnam. As a rule I don't read Vietnam books, but that, I think, would be an exception. I have read a few, but that's one I would certainly read; I think Jones is a great writer.

Schroeder: Why don't you read Vietnam books?

Herr: Well, first of all, for the same reason that I have no Vietnam souvenirs anymore. I had them. But I no longer want them in my life. In a strange way, it wouldn't be untrue to say that as a subject I'm no longer interested in Vietnam. Because as a subject I'm not. And because I have to try consciously all the time to keep it out of my life.

For the same reason I don't write about it anymore. I'm not sitting in L.A. now writing Vietnam stories for all the people who ask me to come out and write Vietnam stories for them. I'm through with Vietnam. I mean to be through with Vietnam.

Schroeder: The Vietnam stories are certainly pouring out now.

Herr: I'm told that there's just a flood of Vietnam books, films, et cetera. The only Vietnam book that I've read every word, cover to cover, is *Going After Cacciato*. I think it's a truly great book. It had two strikes against it because of its subject, but again it was not really a book about Vietnam. It had a completely other subject. It's just a great novel. Its companion is *Dog Soldiers*, most of which doesn't take place in Vietnam. But still there's not an issue or matter of the time and of the war that isn't totally and beautifully and skillfully rendered in that book.

Schroeder: Those two books are interesting to juxtapose with *Dispatches* because they're both books which open in Vietnam and immediately take off, leaving the war. How would you compare what O'Brien and Stone are doing with the novel form to what you're doing in *Dispatches*?

Herr: I don't. I can't. Except that we were all trying to find a form and an expression for a very extreme experience that all three of us, one way or another, lived through. We had to find this in order to save our lives. I would say that all three of us understood completely the necessity of exorcizing the experience. You can't carry it around with you because it's just too heavy. It fucks you up for other activities like having a family and writing other books.

Schroeder: John Sack said something very interesting to me about you. We were talking about New Journalism and he mentioned a review that he had read a few years ago about Hunter Thompson. The review dealt with *Fear and Loathing in Las Vegas* and the critic said something like, "Hunter Thompson has done the ultimate; he has given his sanity for the cause of his work." John Sack took issue with the statement, saying, "No, no, it's not true because as everyone knows Hunter Thompson is given to extreme exaggeration." He continued, saying, "The only person who's ever done anything like that is Michael Herr; what he did in Vietnam was to put himself completely into the situation, refusing to take himself out for a moment, and to live that situation for a year." Sack finally concluded that "Michael Herr has outdone us all; he's given his sanity for the cause of reportage."

Herr: [*laughing*] I hope not forever. I've paid too much if it's true. But I was pretty crazy when I came back. For a long time I was, in fact, *very* crazy. Sometimes I was crazy in a very public way, and after I crashed I was crazy in a very private way. Except during the very worst of it, I always knew that it was redeemable. And I felt like I would do whatever I had to do. I also felt that I didn't have a lot of choices. There was a certain point at which I realized that whatever I thought I was doing, I wasn't completely conscious of what I was actually doing. So as long as I didn't know what I was doing, I would do whatever came up. I always believed that there was another door on the other side of me that I could go through and come out of with a book under my arm.

Schroeder: Was the writing helping to relieve the craziness or was it compounding it?

Herr: The writing compounded it before relieving it. Plus I had an utter and complete paralysis of will and was overcome by fear. I was writing, but I was writing like that scene in *The Shining* where all the pages are filled with the same sentence. It wasn't much more developed than that. I was writing the same paragraphs over and over and over.

Schroeder: One of the famous pieces of Michael Herr apocrypha has you writing two or three thousand pages of manuscript and then tossing them all out and beginning over from scratch.

Herr: It would be closer to the truth to say that I wrote a few pages so many times that it came to be thousands of pages. But that isn't really a true account. I've heard so many stories about what I was doing in those years that I don't even bother to answer them because they are all filled with absurdity. All of them are true and at the same time completely false. For example, in spirit I may have been a junkie in the street, but never in body.

Schroeder: What about the problems which you mentioned as having with the book's organization?

Herr: They took care of themselves somehow. I think you finally reach a point of concentration which whatever you're writing that, all of a sudden, you find what it is that you're saying. How you're saying it and the order of it all then come naturally. With *Dispatches* the problem just dissolved.

Schroeder: You have said that you like to think of *Dispatches* as a novel. Yet you don't introduce your main "characters" until towards the end of the book in "Colleagues." In novelistic terms, this late introduction of characters central to the story's action is backwards. How do you describe the book's organization?

Herr: I wrote the book inside out. Chronologically, the first piece I wrote is the second chapter of the book; the next piece I wrote is the Khe Sanh piece, followed by "Illumination Rounds," and then I wrote "Colleagues." So I had the whole central part of the book, but I didn't have a book. I didn't want it to be a collection of pieces, I wanted it to be a book. I didn't have the energy to rewrite very much of all that material. I wanted the first and last chapters to be a kind of—if you'll pardon the military language—perimeter that would somehow miraculously make a book out of these separate pieces. So I spent years, five years, six years, fucking around with that form, trying to write a first chapter and a last chapter that would be a circle to draw around the rest of the pieces and somehow make it a book. Since I haven't been able to read it since I finished writing it, I can't tell for myself how successful I was.

Schroeder: You've never gone back and looked at the book?

Herr: I did once, but it was out of one eye, very shy. You know, I spent so much of my life with my head in that place and in the subject that this is why I don't read Vietnam books—unless they're by friends. I read friends' books. At least I try to.

Schroeder: The chapter "Colleagues" must have been especially difficult for you because these people *weren't* characters in a novel—they were very good friends of yours. Is there a reason, other than the book's chronological composition, for having this chapter at the end of the narrative?

Herr: It was very difficult. But "Colleagues" is not actually at the end. It's the next-to-last chapter of the book. It just seemed somehow to make sense to place it there. It seemed to be the best order for the book. I don't really know why. There is a vague chronological order in the book. Time was the bugger. Time was ostensibly the biggest technical problem that I had. And like all problems in writing, it disappears at a certain point—hopefully. You can't think about the problems. You can't think and write at the same time. When you're thinking you're not really writing and when you're writing you're not thinking. They are mutually exclusive activities.

Schroeder: Yet it's obvious that revision figures very largely in your writing. Your style, in particular, must have taken a long time to develop.

Herr: Sure. I'm sure it's been a long time in the developing. I can't, however, really talk about my style. It's like talking about your looks. That's just the way it is. In a way it's too personal to talk about; it's something that I really have no control over. I just work a sentence or a paragraph over until it clicks for me and when it does I don't think about it anymore. But *why*, I can't really say.

Schroeder: When you write are you conscious of shifting gears, of moving from a subdued, almost classical rhetorical mode to your trademark, super-charged hyperbolic, allusive, run-on style?

Herr: I see it when I'm doing it. To that extent I'm very conscious of it. But just how it happens I don't know.

Schroeder: *Dispatches* moves constantly between the two styles and it moves so effortlessly between them—

Herr: —[*laughing*] So it seems—

Schroeder: —and yet when you break these styles down and analyze them, they are very different; the first is a very balanced, meticulous, clear, concise style, while the second one is much more like speech—it's often frantic, it's constantly filled with slang expressions and references to popular culture, and yet it too is obviously very carefully crafted.

Herr: I'm always looking for permission to do those latter things. I say to myself, "Oh, no, you can't say *that*! It isn't done. You can't move from this to that. So and so never did it. And since he never did it, *you* can't do it." But you reach a point where you realize that of course you can do it. You can do anything. You just have to issue yourself a license to do those things. And then you do them.

Schroeder: Those "licensed" passages in the book seem not only central to your role, to your character as narrator, but they also seem to serve as the common denominator for an easy, open communication with the soldiers.

Herr: That's because I had their voices in my head. They were finally my inspiration. Even though I'm a horribly literary person—I really am, I lead a completely literary life and always have done—they inspired me in spite of myself and my resistance to them. I found, especially after I came home, that they were my real inspiration; they inspired me more than any writer or body of writers ever did. They made it real for me.

Schroeder: In the book it seems that in your relationships with them you had little problem communicating with them. And yet at one point you comment on the difficulty that other "literary" people had in establishing a rapport with the soldiers. How is it, then, that your own interaction with them appears so spontaneous and so open?

Herr: Well because I hope to God that I'm a "real" person before I'm a "literary" person. It's not always easy because writers are very private and deceptive—generally very hidden people. Most of the soldiers, however, were very open. They always found the subject. I didn't pose the subjects of our conversations. They would tell you. They would tell you *very* eloquently and *very* beautifully. I don't think that it's any secret that there is talk in the book that's invented. But it is invented out of that voice that I heard so often and that made such penetration into my head.

Schroeder: Can you give me an example of this type of invention?

Herr: Not off the top of my head. [*pause*] Nor would I if I could. I don't really want to go into that no-man's-land about what really happened and what didn't really happen and where you draw the line. Everything in *Dispatches* happened *for* me, even if it didn't necessarily happen *to* me.

Schroeder: This does bring us back to a point that we were discussing earlier—that sometimes gray line between journalism and fiction. It's becoming increasingly difficult to distinguish at times when something becomes fiction or when it remains journalism.

Herr: Well, that's the anxious little secret of New Journalism—which is why I have never called myself a New Journalist.

Schroeder: What do you think of the tag itself? Do you think that it accurately describes a literary genre?

Herr: I used to think that it was very rhetorical. But now, in fact, I think that it captures a rather fabulous moment in our literary history.

Schroeder: Do you think that moment is over?

Herr: I think that all moments end. There is another moment that's going on now that maybe in its own way is wonderful (although it doesn't seem so to me). New Journalism does have great resonance. It has dominated American writing for twenty years. It dominated the imagination of a lot of writers who weren't novelists.

Schroeder: Tom Wolfe's thesis is that journalism had a bad name as a serious literary pursuit until the sixties, that true writers were novelists, that journalists were inevitably seen as lower life forms in the great artistic chain of being, and that only with the advent of the New Journalism did the form gain respectability and finally achieve a status equal to that of the novel.

Herr: I think that's rather true. I think of people like Tom Wolfe, and—God knows—Norman Mailer (who I really think of as the daddy of New Journalism just on the basis of his bravery and audacity—Mailer has the courage to write out of a mood and forget about formal requirements), and Hunter Thompson—these people absolutely elevated journalism in people's minds and made it culturally acceptable. It *was* new. But was it really journalism?

Schroeder: When you went to Vietnam, did you initially see yourself as doing what these people were doing?

Herr: Yeah, I suppose I did. Mailer certainly was a great inspiration to me in the early sixties: reading Mailer's pieces in the *Village Voice* and in *Esquire* and realizing that you could absolutely think of yourself as a serious writer and adopt that mode; you had that option if you treated it seriously and with respect and did not patronize it and did not in your heart condescend to it as being some lesser form. This was writing too.

But on the other hand, in my own work I was not always bound by the facts. That was a choice, it wasn't an accident. The first piece I ever wrote from Vietnam had in it a fictional character who was so fantastic and so obviously fictional that the only people who ever believed for a moment that he was a real character were people in the legal department at *Esquire* magazine. They were a little nervous. Everybody else completely understood that I was making this general up. He's not in the book because by the time I got around to putting all the stuff together, I realized that I didn't need that kind of fantastic creation anymore, that so-called real life was quite fantastic enough. There are enough excesses and exaggerations in the book as it is.

Schroeder: You didn't have any legal problem with the book, did you?

Herr: No, I never did.

Schroeder: I ask because I recall John Sack's account of how he had to go out and collect releases from his main characters.

Herr: No, I never did. I had a few rather nasty letters, but that's all. And while I never had any problems with individuals, I did, however, make journalistic mistakes. There are errors of fact in the book. I'm not happy about this. When the Khe Sanh piece was published, I had a really beautiful letter from a colonel who had been stationed there; he corrected me on various points of fact. I lost the letter, and it didn't turn up again until after the book was in print. As I have a very good editor whom I trust completely, I never went through my galleys, and so in this instance I couldn't bear to go in and make the revisions myself. I was tapped out. I was exhausted from the project. Including the year in the war, I had spent eight years working on it, and I just couldn't do any more. So unfortunately there are errors of fact of which I'm not proud, but I don't think that in the long run they matter.

Schroeder: Well, your aim was never to write a history.

Herr: Definitely. A secret history maybe.

Schroeder: You use that term several times in *Dispatches.*

Herr: Yes. As many people have called me as a novelist as have called me as a historian. I only call myself a writer. I don't really ascribe to any of those other titles. They don't matter much to me.

Schroeder: That should certainly prevent you from receiving letters which correct your presentation of facts. And yet even novelists, I'm sure, are not immune from this. Did the colonel, however, have any larger purpose than simply correcting errors of fact?

Herr: No, I think that was his main concern. The reason this colonel bothered to write and straighten me out about the facts was because he was moved by the writing of the piece. So that was a great letter and it was a great response—they weren't always that great, believe me.

Schroeder: Do you think that much of the positive response from officers and "straight" journalists was due to an inherent truth which they perceived in your account? An analogous situation which comes to mind is Hunter Thompson's *Fear and Loathing on the Campaign Trail.* He noticed that the other reporters—including the older veteran political correspondents— were wiring their home offices for copies of *Rolling Stone* to see what he had written because they felt that he had much more freedom to write what was actually going on than they did, and that in a sense he was telling the story much better than they ever would or could.

Herr: Sure. Well, that's my little joke in the book. Once there was a little gathering given by the press muscle of Vietnam—JUSPAO it was called— to meet Teddy Kennedy. Hundreds of reporters were present. Barry Zorthian, the press godfather in Vietnam, introduced us as "the gentlemen of the press and Michael Herr." I was terribly flattered. It was a joke me and my chums were always making because I *wasn't* a reporter in that sense; I wasn't a working journalist. I was there doing something else. At the time there was no one else carrying a press card who was doing that. I carried the honorary rank of colonel. I was a bureau chief. I was accorded all the privileges of a bureau chief.

Schroeder: Did you have problems with that from the military? You gained the respect of your colleagues, but did JUSPAO resent what you were doing?

Herr: They didn't know what I was doing. I only published one piece while I was there. *I* didn't know what I was doing.

Schroeder: And there were no problems from that one piece?

Herr: None.

Schroeder: Isn't it odd, then, you were able to achieve the degree of notoriety you did, publishing the little that you did during that time span?

Herr: I guess any notoriety I had there I was unaware of; it must have been purely because of my personal behavior, which was rather circumspect, with the exception of a few blowouts.

I do recall an incident in particular worth mentioning. I was sitting in the press club at Danang having dinner at about the time that the piece called "Hell Sucks" was published. A guy came in with a funny look on his face and said that there were some Marines outside who wanted to talk to me. I went to the door and I saw a bunch of *big* Marines—grunts. I didn't know whether I should go all the way out there or go back inside because I didn't know what they really had in mind. What they really had in mind was that they were guys whom I had seen in Hue, and they had a lighter inscribed which they gave to me.

The stupidity and arrogance of certain commanders aside, there is a strange way in which I was on their side. In the situation, in the moment, not politically, not geopolitically, not ideologically, but humanly I was on their side because they were in a real shitstorm and you'd have to be some kind of monster not to be on their side.

My quarrel with the liberals and my quarrel with the peace people is that they never explored their own violence. I found their attitudes extremely smug and complacent. I saw more human violence at peace demonstrations than in many situations in Vietnam—not all, but many. These people never wished to confront those things. They would like to pretend that they haven't got those capacities, that they are *not* violent people. But in their dreams and in their wishes and in their hearts they were in Vietnam too. Their shadow was in Vietnam. They're part of it too.

Within six months of returning to New York from Vietnam, I utterly alienated all my so-called friends. I found them so blind and so hypocritical and so smug, drawing lines that in real life I didn't believe existed anymore. I'm not a liberal. I don't know what I am politically, but I'm certainly not a liberal. For me that's synonymous with hypocrisy: lying about your own feelings and experience.

All the people I know who got thrown out of SNCC [Student Non-violent Coordinating Committee] in the mid sixties—all the white boys—were outraged. But the blacks at SNCC knew what they were doing; they know more about the racism coiled up in the heart of a white liberal than the white liberal knew, or probably knows today. By saying that it's not there doesn't make it go away. It's the same with Vietnam. The Vietnam war was a national spectacle, an American manifestation that all Americans knew, whatever their position on the war or whatever they said it was.

Schroeder: *Dispatches* confronts the issue of hypocrisy to the extent that at times you are even merciless with yourself as the narrator of the piece.

Herr: It's got to be that way. If you don't do it on a personal level, you don't have the right to do it anywhere. If you're going to lie with yourself and be heavy with everybody else, you can never tell the truth. Even if you're correct in what you say, you're still a liar. It's not what somebody says that makes truth or untruth; it's who he is when he's saying it that determines the value of a statement.

Schroeder: Quite early in the book you confront your own motives. In examining the conditions of personal involvement, you encounter a soldier who says, "We're here to kill gooks. Period." Rather than trying to smooth over this unsettling viewpoint, you immediately say, "Which wasn't at all true of me. I was there to watch." Your moral position may be ambiguous, but your role certainly appears clear to you. Was your role always so clear to you?

Herr: It became clearer. It was not clear at the beginning. I really believed there was a space between myself and what I was watching. That I was on the clean side of a line and not a participant. But after a couple of months— certainly by the time of the Tet Offensive—I saw my position all too clearly.

Schroeder: You allude to the fact that you ended up behind a machine gun during Tet. From your description of the situation, it sounds as if it wasn't a question of choice, but rather a matter of survival.

Herr: It was definitely not a question of choice. But there were other times when there *was* a choice, at which I declined to become a participant. But it was always there to do if you wanted to.

Schroeder: Were you familiar with Robin Moore's *The Green Berets* before you went to Vietnam?

Herr: No, but I did see the film while I was in Vietnam. It was shown at a theater in Danang that was full of Marines and had about a dozen Green Berets sitting in one row—they were really shat upon by the rest of the audience; you would have thought you were watching a comedy from the laughter of the Marines.

Schroeder: I bring up *The Green Berets* because for years it was the final word on Vietnam: it was one of the first books to come out of the American experience in Vietnam, and the American public bought it like candy—it sold several million copies. The same was true of the film.

Herr: Well really, the first and last book about Vietnam is *The Quiet American*. If you want to travel light, you don't need any other books about Vietnam.

Schroeder: Greene's book is visionary.

Herr: Yes, it's really extraordinary. The only thing that it stops short of foreseeing is the horrible karmic wash that Vietnam left behind. "Karma" is not a word that you hear applied to the Vietnam war, and yet it would be difficult to find a more accurate and concrete word for what it really is that left America so dispirited and frightened and violent and divided—to say nothing of Southeast Asia and the suffering that we stirred up there and then walked out of. Or so we thought, because we can't shake it. I do feel that Vietnam—however it's being dealt with in America—is still the single prevailing fact of American life. All of our present anguish comes in the wake of the Vietnam war; it is the accumulations of the Vietnam war.

Photograph by Mario Ruiz
Used by permission of Ballantine Books

Wallace Terry:
"It Became an Absolute Crusade"

Schroeder: What first got you interested in journalism? Had you always wanted to be a journalist?

Terry: As far back as grade school I was editor of something. We had different publications in this all-black school (segregation was still in place in Indianapolis). I was the editor of the *George Washington Carver School-O-Gram*. Shortridge, the high school I went to, was a college-prep school where people like Booth Tarkington, Dan Wakefield, and Kurt Vonnegut had gone. There was a heavy emphasis on writing skills at the school and on working on the school daily, one of three in the country. I liked sports, so I eventually became editor of the Tuesday edition of the *Shortridge Daily Echo*, which was put to bed on Mondays and carried the sports scores. After I broke my wrist playing football, a teacher said it was safer for the school if I wrote about sports instead of trying to play them.

Every summer my parents helped me go to a college somewhere in the Midwest to participate in a journalism institute for high school students. The first year it was at Butler College near home, the next summer it was at Franklin College, and then it was the big time—Indiana University, where the journalism school was named after Ernie Pyle. I was very impressed by that because he was a Hoosier writer who became a great war correspondent. That was one of the influences on me in wanting to be a war correspondent one day. I thought there was no one like Ernie Pyle, except maybe Ernest Hemingway and Stephen Crane. Those writers had the greatest influence on my own writing.

Before my senior year I went to Northwestern, which tried to recruit me for journalism. But I wanted to go to the best small college that I could get into and study the classics. I applied to several and Brown offered me the best scholarship. My family did not have the money to send me to college, which meant I had to go where I could get the best financial aid. Brown too had a daily paper, and full of myself as I was, I was going to show them a thing or two. When I visited the paper's offices during freshman recruiting I announced I was going to be editor one day. Well, they deliberately delayed my induction to the staff. I had to heel longer than anyone in history just to cool me down. Eventually I did become editor, largely, I think, because of some of the innovative things I tried to do, like get an interview with Arkansas Governor Orval Faubus when the desegregation of Little Rock High School was taking place. That incident landed my picture on the front of the *New York Times* and newspapers all around the world. My stepfather said, "You've landed on the front page of the *New York Times*; you're going to spend the rest of your life trying to get there again." He was right. [*laughs*]

My first summer in college I did some freelance writing for my hometown paper, the *Indianapolis News*, and the second summer I worked as a trainee, carrying coffee to Dan Quayle's uncle and writing obituaries. This was the big time. I still have a photocopy of my first check from the *Indianapolis News*. Finally, I went off to the *Washington Post* before my senior year. I was treated like a regular reporter, paid union scale. That was a bit phenomenal because I was only nineteen when they offered me the job. I don't know if that makes me the youngest reporter in the *Post*'s history or not.

After college I went to seminary as a Rockefeller Fellow at the University of Chicago. I was still convinced that I was going to follow a combined career in the ministry and law.

Schroeder: What happened to change your mind?

Terry: I missed journalism so much that I decided I wanted a part-time job. No one around Chicago would hire me because I was black. I didn't want to work for the black press because I saw it as specialized. I believed I should work in the mainstream. While I was interested in stories that related to blacks, I thought those stories also related to whites. They were American stories. Well, one day I was sitting in the offices at the *Chicago Sun-Times* where I had gone to get some advice about finding a job. My aunt had made contact for me with a reporter named Fletcher Martin, who had been the first black to win a Nieman Fellowship at Harvard. I told him I had worked the previous summer for the *Washington Post*. He said, "Son, it took me twenty years to get to where you got to before you even got out of college. You don't need to talk to me. You need to go back to the *Washington Post.*" He picked up the telephone and dialed Al Friendly, the managing editor of the *Post,* and asked if they'd take me back. They said yes. So I moved to Washington as a regular staff member of the *Post.* After a year or so I got deeply involved in covering civil rights. To me it was the biggest story in the country. It was a story that I passionately cared for because it was going to affect me, my family, my children, and generations of black people to come.

In 1963 I left the *Post* and went over to *Time* magazine. At that time there were no black correspondents working for the news magazines. *Time* made it clear to me that I wasn't going to be pigeonholed into black reporting. But having learned that writing black stories could get me off night rewrite for the *Washington Post,* I was damned sure going to get out of being a catch-all junior member of the Washington bureau for *Time.* They doubled my salary and agreed to let me be a Washington correspondent. This was highly unusual: (a) I was very young; (b) the usual procedure was to start you in a domestic bureau—like Chicago or Boston—to get you trained. But because I had covered national stories for the *Post* on loan from the city desk, I was able to pull it off with *Time.* I covered a wide range of things, like housing and labor, back-up on the White House beat.

Schroeder: And you continued to do civil rights stories?

Terry: My main focus was civil rights, a subject that would allow me to work on a lot of cover stories. I had a run from '63 to my Saigon war years, where I was working on perhaps as many cover stories as the White House correspondents were. Invariably, there would be a cover story when there was a major riot like Watts, Harlem, Detroit, Newark. Civil rights leaders like Martin Luther King would frequently appear on the cover of *Time.* Of course there would be covers on Whitney Young and others within the movement. And I had a piece of that action.

Schroeder: How did you first get interested in Vietnam?

Terry: I went off to Vietnam in '67 to write about the Negro soldier, a story that I suggested. I came back home after a few weeks of reporting there. A big deciding factor in my decision to go to *Time* had been *Time's* large staff of overseas correspondents. I think at that time those of us who belonged to the *Time-Life* news service were a match for the national and foreign reporters at the *New York Times* and certainly ahead of everybody else. Anyway, I was asked if I wanted to go back to Vietnam.

Schroeder: *Did* you want to go back?

Terry: The first time I went, when I suggested doing that story, I didn't think they would ask me to do it *myself*. When they asked me to go, that was exciting. On that first trip I could get in and get out. Just be there for a few weeks. But when they proposed I go back, this wasn't anything I sought or expected. I saw how uncomfortable even some of the professionals were who were there. But I came back because it was the biggest story in the world. And also in the back of my mind, I thought that I would write a book.

After that first Vietnam cover story came out, Bill McPherson, who had worked with me at the *Post*, called me up. He was an editor at a publishing house. He said, "Wally, you should write a book for us about the black soldier." And I said, "All I got are these *Time* files; this is stuff we put together in about two or three weeks. I don't have enough material. This is a month of reporting by three or four of us." But when the prospect of going back to Vietnam arose, it was irresistible. It was the biggest story. It was the chance to do a major book. Now I had wanted desperately to write a book. I tried on four or five different occasions and something would always happen; the project would unravel. Either it was not what the publisher wanted, or I didn't want to do what they wanted, or co-writers with whom I was working couldn't get their acts together, or I felt uncomfortable somehow working with them. There were all books somehow related to the civil rights movement, and none of them happened. I always kept giving these small advances back.

Schroeder: One of the most striking things that Michael Herr said about the war was "I went to cover the war and" [*Terry chimes in simultaneously*] "the war covered me." Was that experience typical for most correspondents? Was it inevitable that that would happen? He also talks about slipping over to the wrong side of the story during Tet. He talks about firing a weapon, covering a team trying to get back inside the camp.

Terry: He says he fired a weapon? I don't think he had any business doing that. I don't think reporters should be participants. Unless you find yourself in a very, very desperate situation. I would have fired a weapon to save a friend. Or a fellow American. Or a South Vietnamese. I was in a couple of touchy situations where there was a prospect that we would be overrun, and I was handed weapons by my escorts, and even told that if I didn't want to be taken I should use a grenade on myself. I don't know if I'd ever do something like that. But there were indications that we were really in deep water. I wouldn't, though, be out there firing a weapon with assault forces because they would be doing their job and I wouldn't be doing mine. Mine is to watch what they're doing and try to keep a balanced head and be alert, keep myself alive, and pick up the flavor of what is happening. I don't know how you do this while participating in it. I think it's wrong, a violation of journalism ethics. But then I don't consider Mike a journalist. A journalist is one who covers events and tries to give some background on the events. People who ride around writing impressionistic pieces and are not responsible for informing the public on a daily or weekly or whatever basis are not part of the mainstream journalistic news-gathering operation. I look at Mike as a novelist who was collecting not only material but also experiences. For me *Dispatches* is one of the best novels to come out of the war. But I don't call it journalism.

Schroeder: What *do* you think of the job that the media did in Vietnam? What do you think of Peter Braestrup's contention in *Big Story*, for instance, that the media misreported the significance of the Tet Offensive?

Terry: The main point that Peter makes is that journalists, either because of overanxiety or in their rush to be first, misreported what happened at the American embassy. He accuses some of the news organizations of reporting that the Vietcong got inside the chancery, the main building. As it turns out, the American command made an announcement to the press when the grounds were made secure that no one had been inside. And the press by and large retracted their stories. But the damage of those early reports had been done. Imagine the impact this story made. You've been at war using main forces for three years, since the Marines landed in '65, and here you cannot protect your own embassy grounds and chancery—the VC can get inside in the capital of the country that you came to shore up and defend.

Well, Peter Braestrup was mistaken, and the big story of *Big Story* was that he was mistaken. If he had interviewed me, he would not have made the mistake he did. But I'm not surprised that he didn't interview me because he may be like a lot of my other fellow Americans who do not see me as a mainstream journalist but as some black appendage who is dragged out to interview some black people or to cover civil rights but who cannot be relied upon to cover mainstream issues.

Schroeder: But you were there for the biggest years of the war—

Terry: I was there as a regular correspondent, I was the deputy bureau chief of *Time*'s Saigon bureau. I was responsible for the coverage, for determining who would cover what. That was my job. After the initial battles of Tet blew over, I decided to send at least one member of our bureau to each of the war zones—I Corps, II Corps, III Corps, and the Delta—to do an evaluation of what had happened. We discovered the Vietcong had been annihilated, that Tet was a magnificent battlefield victory. I went to II Corps. I was the first reporter into places like Banmethuot and Quinhon and Pleiku. This was within the first few days after the initial attacks were launched. Once we got things settled in Saigon we really took off. Braestrup gives us high points for this. But he didn't interview me. He interviewed Bill Rademaekers, who was the bureau chief at the time. But Bill wasn't responsible for that reporting.

I'll tell you why I know what happened, why Braestrup was mistaken. When Saigon was attacked, Rademaekers went to MACV [Military Assistance Command—Vietnam] to be briefed. I sent Nguyen Nguyen, a Vietnamese reporter, to the An Quang pagoda. I sent John Cantwell over to cover the embassy grounds. Cantwell told me, "They're inside." I said, "Send the story to New York." We're operating on a different deadline than, say, AP or the networks, who were, to quote Braestrup, "sending erroneous information." Later on that morning after everything had been secured, I was walking with a black officer in the vicinity taking pictures of the VC lying on the embassy grounds. That officer's name was Major Beauregard Brown; he worked at MACV. Brown and I asked a black sergeant on the scene if the VC were inside. He said yes. That was good enough for me until the official denial came. And when the denial came, I had to go along with it because I couldn't find that sergeant again. And everybody else who was involved (as I would learn in later years) had been sworn to secrecy. But I was convinced that we were right, that we had not been mistaken.

In 1972 I was in Europe working for the Air Force. I ran across a black airman named Don Browne. And I said, "Don, what'd you do in Vietnam?" That's the kind of thing you say to guys even today. "It was secret," he said. He was a part of a secret Air Force unit who were involved in embassy matters including the Phoenix Program. He told me then what I wrote about in *Bloods*. Yes, the Vietcong were inside the chancery. Because they operated in secret, his Air Force unit was used to kill them and mop up. They went inside under orders to kill *any* Vietnamese they saw. If they ran into the janitor, he's dead. So I was right, Cantwell was right, the other reporters were right. So we were not being irresponsible.

Schroeder: The story was too politically loaded. The military didn't want it released.

Terry: Of course not. It was devastating. Bunker's bunker has been captured by the Vietcong? Now the VC *couldn't* have held it. If you look back in Don Browne's account, that's clear—there weren't enough of them to hold it. In his book *Vietnam* Stanley Karnow is very clever because he doesn't say what happened inside the building. I think he had his suspicions.

Schroeder: Wasn't it very hard to cover the story when there were so many impediments to keep you from doing so, the main one which was probably the Army itself?

Terry: As an American reporter I did as much as I could to observe the classification of materials. I didn't want to violate the rules. I disliked the thought of violating the rules in covering a war because I didn't want to do anything that might endanger my fellow countrymen. Even if it's a wrong-headed war. Now I don't think Vietnam was an *immoral* war from our standpoint. (On the other hand, if I had been a German reporter covering my German countrymen as they slaughtered millions and conquered defenseless nations—that's immoral behavior.)

I wanted to see us do it right. We weren't doing it right. And I smelled that the first time I got there. For instance, soldiers in the field would tell me "The ARVN aren't pulling their load; they're not going to be able to handle it when we leave. When we go, this place is going to the Communists quicker than you can imagine." I could not believe the war effort was going to work when I saw how corrupt the Saigon officials were. I knew, for instance, that Thieu's relatives were taking a piece of the action any time American supplies came into the city. Those supplies would then show up on the black market. I couldn't think that the war effort was going to work when I saw an enormous population of eighteen-, nineteen-, and twenty-year-olds—we called them "cowboys," the privileged South Vietnamese youths—riding around on Honda motorbikes when they should have been out there taking the places of eighteen- and nineteen-, and twenty-year-old American boys. Or when I saw us go out in the field and chop up a village to save it rather than inserting two or three Lurp [long range reconnaissance patrol] team members to take out the VC who were threatening and controlling the area. We were doing it the wrong way.

And I believe racism and arrogance were contributing factors because if we had better understood the history of Vietnam or at least read the people who were telling us the history of Vietnam, we would have understood their great fear of China and we may have cut our losses a lot earlier and left when the French left. The outcome would have been what it is today except that we would have been spared fifty-eight thousand American dead and untold numbers of Vietnamese dead. The losses got too high. We tried desperately to Vietnamize the war and it didn't work. The ARVN was no match for the aggressiveness and the determination of the North Vietnamese soldier. Those guys were tough. It's very hard for Americans to believe that a foe would commit the lives of an entire nation and not sue for peace at some point; it's very difficult for us to imagine that, after our defeat of the Japanese, there could be an Asian army that could hold us at bay—at considerable loss to themselves and without air power in the South. But the North Vietnamese were special. The Vietnamese army is right now undoubtedly one of the half a dozen best armies in the world, partly as a response to their experience with the French and later with us.

Schroeder: What happened when you came back?

Terry: When I came back from Vietnam I got a Nieman Fellowship and started transcribing my tapes. I took six months off before I went back to the Washington bureau. Finishing that manuscript, I was so committed to getting that book published that it would absolutely change my life. I left *Time* in order to see what would happen to my life. When the book came out, I thought I would have an enormous degree of leverage as a journalist. I thought I would be able to call my own shots. And I thought that having gone through what I went through in the sixties, covering all the major civil rights episodes, all the major urban uprisings, and over two years in Vietnam covering the war, I thought I deserved something like Paris, or Rome, or London.

At the time I had no idea that I was beginning to develop PTSD [post traumatic stress disorder] because my book was not getting published. But I never felt in this early period any loss of hope that it would happen. I still felt really pumped up. When my first publisher decided not to publish the manuscript, I went through a long period of sending the manuscript out. There would be times when my hopes would just soar, when I would get a letter like I did from Toni Morrison who, said, "I read the first half of *Bloods* and if the second half is anything like the first, you have something fantastic." I rushed up to Random House to have lunch with her, and she said that she not only wanted to publish it, but that she would give me a contract for its sequel.

None of this would happen. It was a question of salability. This is what I would hear more frequently than anything else. This was not to say that I couldn't get a university press to publish it. I could have. But I was being advised by my friends—especially since so much time had gone by—why not wait a little longer and see if something turns up? I was being advised not to go with a university press because there would be no promotion budget. A few thousand copies of the book would be published and that would be the end of it.

Something else was happening to me as well. The subject had grown to such proportions within me that it had become a crusade, an absolute crusade, and I wasn't quite aware of this. I began to take on other work that allowed me to control my time. I would not go back to *Time* or to the *Post* or to network television, where I might be sent anywhere overseas. Instead I worked as an account manager for J. Walter Thompson; I could call my own shots. My account: the Marine Corps. This was wonderful because it introduced me to two of the fellows who eventually landed themselves in *Bloods*. I also worked for several months in Europe as a special assistant to the commanding general of United States Air Force, Europe. I was to advise him on human relation matters. I would lecture, conduct a survey, and investigate racial tensions. At the same time, I found more characters for *Bloods*.

Next I began to teach at Howard University as the Gannett Professor of Journalism. I controlled my time. I decided what classes to teach and when to offer them. I taught on Tuesdays and Thursdays; on other days I was still trying to get this book done. And I was still getting rejection letters. Until finally I got a letter from Marc Jaffe of Ballantine Books, who said, "You have the missing pages." This took fifteen years. Jaffe, in turn, introduced me to Erroll McDonald, a black guy at Random House, because we needed a hardcover publisher. Ironically Erroll had been Toni Morrison's protégé.

Schroeder: In the introduction to *Bloods* you tell the story of the sixteen-year-old Marine from Brooklyn, the youngest American killed in Vietnam—

Terry: [*interrupting*] You know what? He was fifteen. I found this out when I went to see his name on the wall. I looked him up in my original notebooks and discovered he was actually fifteen. And then I found out he wasn't on the wall.

Schroeder: Do you think he was left off deliberately? Perhaps because he was so young?

Terry: I don't think so. I just think that there's some people who got left off. I don't know.

Schroeder: When you mention him, you say that it was at the point you learned about him that you knew you wanted to do a book about the blacks who fought in Vietnam.

Terry: I was already committed to doing the story. In the last couple of months I was in Vietnam, *Time* agreed to let me go out in the field and do some legwork on my book project. In return I would write a piece for them. I did a two-page signed piece about black power in Vietnam, how things had changed since the '67 cover story. When I went into the field I wanted to do a couple of things. First, to survey the attitudes of black and white soldiers. I ended up surveying hundreds of soldiers. I asked them social and political questions: how they felt the war was progressing; were we doing it the right way; should we invade the north; what they thought of draft-card burners and the antiwar movement; what they thought of each other and the Vietnamese; were blacks being discriminated against. I carried these surveys around with me, and sometimes I got into trouble.

At the start, I got some help from Winant Sidle, who had been the information boss and spokesman for Westmoreland and now for Abrams. He looked over the questions, which was highly unusual. It was against regulations because outside people and independent agencies cannot and must not survey armed forces personnel. The armed services survey themselves. But, Eric, I wanted to do this because I didn't think that my reporting alone would be sufficient proof of what I suspected was going on: a kind of black soldier revolt, a racial crisis on the battlefield. If I could show that a high percentage of the black soldiers, even black officers, were saying they were being discriminated against, this would add weight to the words of my subjects. I wanted to talk to guys who were heroes, guys who were officers, guys who could tell me about racial conditions.

So what would happen is this. A contact in the unit—and I went all over the country, from the DMZ to the Delta—would set up interviews for me. The word would get out: "A black reporter's coming, man! I hear he's a cool dude." Suddenly I'm not talking to one guy; the room's full of guys. Instead of taking notes, I would have to turn on the tape recorder. The session would become a little piece of theater. I would ask a question and they would start responding and then bouncing off of each other. (Eventually I took some of that material and went into A & R Studio in New York and produced the only documentary record that came right from the battlelines. It's called "Guess Who's Coming Home" and was put out by Motown. But the Motown distributing network was a little bit frightened of it because by that time there was a lot of antiwar stuff going on, and so the record went nowhere. Now it's an incredible collector's item if you can find one.)

So I would show up and these guys would gather and it was like theater. I knew I was onto something really big. The piece I based on those interviews was called something like "Black Power Comes to Vietnam." It was about the rising militancy and the racial conflicts that were leading to riots and killings.

Schroeder: Your original manuscript was quite different from *Bloods*, wasn't it?

Terry: Oh, yeah. It was a different manuscript altogether. *Bloods* has nothing to do with the original manuscript. As a matter of fact, I protected some of the main characters from the original manuscript because when I was writing this book, I didn't want to steal from that first book—that was my heart! That's the material I gathered in the field while I was getting shot at.

When I completed my first manuscript, in order to protect many of these GIs—because some of the things they were saying were very militant, very angry, and they could get into deep trouble if they were still in service or maybe even if they were out—I put the manuscript together as part oral history, part narrative. It was written almost like a series of one-act plays or like a film script. But that first manuscript never went anywhere.

When I came back from Vietnam, I thought, "Hey, I'm going to stop the war. Between me and Sy Hersh, that's going to be the end of Vietnam." After the My Lai massacre, here comes Wally Terry saying the black and white guys are fighting and killing each other. Who would want to support *that* kind of foolishness any longer? With the help of Harvard social scientist Tom Pettigrew I published a two-part story in the *New York Times* based on the surveys I collected. But I didn't get a book out on the story; only now are we turning those survey materials into a book. Again, back in 1971, '72, nobody wanted to publish that survey. It now stands as an important historical document because it was the only survey conducted of American troops in battle, in the war zone.

Schroeder: Why do you think you had such a terrible time getting your manuscript published? By that time all sorts of books about Vietnam were beginning to be published.

Terry: Publishers by and large believe there is only a limited market for black books although blacks make up 11 or 12 percent of the population. That's twenty-eight or thirty million black people, a population that's equal to many European countries. This population has a GNP that equals Canada's or Spain's buying power. But the publishers believe that black people don't buy books. If we were thought of as a book-buying people the way Jewish people are, *Bloods* would have been published immediately. I also think that if *Bloods* had been written by a white person, it would have been published immediately.

Schroeder: One of the things I've noticed is that very few books have been written about the war by black veterans. Off the top of my head I can think of only one, *Coming Home*, a novel that has no relation to the movie of that name.

Terry: Right, it's by George Davis. He sued the filmmakers because he thought they had appropriated his title; his book came out before the movie. David Parks—son of Gordon—wrote a book called *GI Diary* about his year as a helicopter pilot. A guy named Clyde Taylor did an anthology of speeches and articles called something like *Vietnam and Negro America*. That's three so far. There was a novel by a veteran which came out not long ago that had the word "mojo" in the title—*Got My Mojo Working*. And then there is an oral history done by a white professor that's based on interviews he did with two black soldiers; it's called *Brothers* and it's in paperback. That's about it. Out of maybe thirty-five hundred books, we're looking at no more than ten that are by and about blacks.

Schroeder: This seems particularly disturbing to me because, initially at least, blacks were disproportionately represented in Vietnam.

Terry: Exactly. I'm very worried that not enough is being done. This is why I've committed myself to writing more volumes and maybe even a novel one day. But I'm not a novelist, so I'm very leery about embarking on a project like that. I'm not going to presume there's any relationship between a good journalist and a good novelist and that one can necessarily become the other. Writing a novel scares the hell out of me. I look at novelists with great awe because they create in a way that I don't. I'm a good editor, I'm a good producer, and I'm a good speaker; I do all of those things better than I write. As a writer I'm a good reporter, but I'm not a great creative writer.

Schroeder: In some ways, though, *Bloods* is a very innovative oral history. Did you decide that the form was perhaps more flexible than most people think?

Terry: When Erroll McDonald at Random House asked me to write an oral history instead of publishing the narrative I'd been carrying around for eleven years, I wanted to do something a little different. As much as I respect Studs Terkel—and he's the master of the oral history—I didn't want what I was doing to look like his work or like Al Santoli's, or anyone else's, for that matter. I wanted to do something distinctly different and innovative. I remembered a short story writing course I took at Brown. I wanted to incorporate as much of those techniques as I could. So I decided I didn't want to use a question-and-answer format; I did not want to get in the way of the narratives. Essentially, the book would be a series of short stories placed in a progression that would give the impact and effect of reading a novel. I believed that doing it that way would make it more readable, more exciting, would give it a wider appeal, especially for very young people; I wanted children to be able to read it. If you don't read it by the time that you're fourteen or fifteen, your butt may be on its way to the Marines or to the Army. I saw one of my own kids come out of high school and seriously toy with the idea of joining the service—he talked to a recruiting sergeant. The idea is to read this book so you know what really goes on out there if you're ordered into combat.

Schroeder: So truth telling was a primary motive for using that form.

Terry: Oh, absolutely. That was the ultimate motive. You see, for me the book became greater than just telling the story of forgotten black soldiers, or even making a statement about racism in America through the experiences of black soldiers. It was bigger than that in my mind. To me there is no greater subject to write about than war because it's the worst thing that we do to each other. Almost all of the human emotions are involved in war; it's the most desperate time for man.

I've had people tell me that I was an advocate journalist. So what? So I'm reporting things in a way, or selecting material to use to try to convince you of something. What I'm trying to do in this book is convince you of the sacrifice of the men who went to Vietnam—whatever their color—and of the respect they deserve for that sacrifice. And also to convince you that we need to treat each other differently and get racism out of our lives, and finally to convince people not to have wars. To convince people that wars are not like what you see in the movies or in comic books, or anything in between. The book is journalism, but it's also more than that because I make these artistic decisions about how I present the material.

I decided if *Bloods* was going work, I'd have to do it as a series of short stories. Originally, I wanted twenty-one stories because that's the age of adulthood, but I ended up with twenty; I dropped a guy just before press time because I didn't believe him. I knew that if a person was found out to be exaggerating about his life, it would destroy the credibility of the book, the other soldiers, and myself. So I ended up with twenty. I'll know better next time, I'll have a backup. [*chuckles*]

This old college course of mine had taught me how to write a short story. And each piece in the book is a short story—it has a beginning, a middle, and an end. There are flash-forwards, flash-backwards. I wanted each story to have a hook; when you started reading I wanted you to feel like you couldn't put it down once you were inside the first three or four paragraphs. I also believed that on every page you should be moved to laugh or to cry or to feel that you'd gotten some information that you never had before. There had to be something memorable on each page. If that wasn't there, I felt I'd failed.

Former students of mine helped to transcribe this material. But the principle transcriber was my son Wally, who at the time was nineteen, the average age of those who fought the war. He became my sounding board. I would test the material on him. When I thought that I had the story where I wanted it (I made up a word for this form, I called it an "oral novella"), I would take the piece and meet my wife, Janice, at our neighborhood Italian restaurant, where we would have dinner and I would read to her. If we were not in tears at the end of it, we knew that I had failed and I had to get back to the typewriter.

Schroeder: Were the stories primarily based on interviews you had done in Vietnam? I know that you talked with some of the men after they returned to the States.

Terry: I interviewed some of the men in Vietnam and then went back to those old interviews. And then I looked them up later and asked more questions. Next I went and found men whom I had met along the way.

Finally, I used contacts to look for people whom I wanted to include because of something they had done. For instance, I called Bobby Muller—you know that name—and I said to him, "Hey, Bobby, I need a black guy who's been back to the 'Nam since the war." He said, "You need Bob Holcomb; Bob recently went to Hanoi with us." These kind of contacts would provide a whole set of experiences that I needed in the book.

So I went up to New York where Holcomb lives, and I took him out to lunch for a pre-interview. While we were talking to each other, I discovered that he had been married to my godmother's daughter and that I had *seen* him a couple of times—I just hadn't paid any attention to him because I thought these kids were young. Right away we were relating to each other. He'd grown up in Gary and I'd grown up in Indianapolis, and New York had been a part of our lives too. So we just had an immediate liking for each other. He was an artist, a painter. He calls me every once in a while—he lives down in Ft. Lauderdale now—and he says, "This is Chapter 15 reporting in."

Steve Howard was a little bit reluctant to be interviewed, but we had known each other in Vietnam, so he couldn't really turn me down. He suffered; he has suffered from PTSD for many years—he was a combat photographer and door gunner. He said he has never been able to discuss Vietnam with his mother, so he gave the book to his mother, and it changed their lives. He called me up and said, "Hey, man, Moms loves you; we pulled it off."

Schroeder: You mention Steve Howard's reluctance to be interviewed, yet it appears you had little difficulty in establishing a strong rapport with your subjects.

Terry: The secret to good oral history is the questions. You've got to have good questions. If you're dealing with a difficult subject and people are reluctant to talk about it, what allows you to get close to them is your background. Many of the soldiers I interviewed were able to confide in me because of the degree of trust they immediately felt. They knew that I had been to Vietnam. They also knew I'd been there more than a regular tour; I had been there the equivalent of two tours. So their reaction was "Hey, man, you didn't have to go at all; you were there twice as long as the guys that had to be there, twice as long as me." That gave me credibility. I had traveled all over Vietnam. So I knew a lot about their respective units. I would ask, "Who'd you serve with?" They'd say, "The 25th." I'd say, "Oh, you were based at Cu Chi." I'd find out what time they were there and say, "You were in the Iron Triangle" or "You were at Khe Sanh." So I knew the lingo and I also knew the history of their units. This was very important to them.

Finally, I was black. And I don't think that was an overriding factor, but it helped in getting into some very delicate issues. I was aware of certain things that a white interviewer might not be aware of. I'm not saying black soldiers could only talk to a black face, but being black did have some advantages.

Schroeder: What was the editing process like?

Terry: I had anywhere from 60 pages to 150 pages on a given person. I listened to the tapes to make sure the transcriber followed the speech patterns of the subject. I had a brilliant piece of advice from Errol McDonald, who said, "It's very important for you to make sure that each voice sounds different, grammatically; if you don't, it's going to read like articles in the *New York Times*." And he was absolutely right, though some critics didn't understand this and said, "This book needs editing; people are saying 'I wanna' in it." But that's the way we talk. And I wanted these voices to come alive, exactly like they really speak. Of course this reflects upon their education or sometimes just their sloppy speech behavior, like I myself sometimes have. This gave an originality to each voice, since I didn't physically describe these people or describe them in any other way either—they're telling their own stories through me.

After I listened to the tapes and compared them with the transcripts, I made a selection of material. I underlined what I wanted to use: I cut it all out and separated it by subject matter. Then I made a creative decision on what I'd use first and then on the order of the rest of it. Sometimes I was dealing with more than 150 different subjects, as I was with the guys who were POWs. I then arranged whatever that person said about that subject in the order in which I wanted it said, sometimes breaking sentences up and recreating sentences, so that in fact I am writing it for them.

Schroeder: This is *very* different, as you say, from most oral histories which are simply transcriptions, sometimes roughly edited for grammar and coherence.

Terry: This is very, very different. This is taking the techniques of the novelist and applying them to oral history.

Schroeder: I think perhaps it's most apparent in the leads.

Terry: Of course, because people don't start off so clear, so dramatic. They typically start off, "Ahh, umm, lemme think. Man, I can't remember that." [*laughs*] But then again that technique also comes from being a journalist, from knowing what a lead is all about.

Schroeder: I thought Joe Biggers's lead was very strong: "The first one I killed really got to me"; and Gene Woodley is particularly memorable: "I went to Vietnam as a basic naïve young man of eighteen. Before I reached my nineteenth birthday, I was an animal. When I went home three months later, even my mother was scared of me."

Terry: Right. Nobody just opens up and starts off like that. Also, when I decided that I needed a transition, I talked to the subject about it because I think it's dishonest to say that they said something that they didn't say. So I may go back and do another interview while I'm working on the piece.

Schroeder: You seem to be conscious not just of shaping individual pieces but also the whole book's structure. In particular, I'm thinking of two chapters near the end—the chapters about Gene Woodley and Dwyte Brown—their experiences were so extremely different.

Terry: Absolutely. Dwyte was the comic relief, before you come to Fred Cherry. In Fred Cherry you get the senior officer who goes through this incredible hell. He begins his story by saying he wanted to be a pilot like the guys in the Tuskegee Airmen and he ends his story by saying that he's out there looking for the next pilot, the next generation. It's schmaltzy, but I love it. I'm an emotional writer. I think that having been trained in the ministry and been given a social consciousness because of it, I couldn't be otherwise.

Schroeder: You mention your religious training. It seemed to me that an unexpectedly high percentage of your subjects talked about their religious views.

Terry: When I was getting the questions together, Janice noticed that I had none that dealt with God. And she said, [*laughing and mimicking his wife*] "What kind of minister are *you*?" [*still laughing*] Not to mention what kind of writer, who's not going to deal with faith and God in talking to people about war. I started to think about it and realized she was right. So with her help I began to write some questions. And I got some wonderful responses. One guy thought he heard the voice of God on three different occasions. I ended a chapter with Lightbulb Bryant saying, "You know, I've been reading the Bible every year trying to figure out Vietnam and I still can't find anything in the Bible about Vietnam." [*laughing, then very somber*] Fred Cherry, as a POW being tortured, talks about his faith.

I think that a writer without a religious background would have left out those questions. But in my case the religious background was there and I was still about to blow it. Fortunately, I had a wife who is a partner and editor as well. Everybody needs editing, needs a sounding board.

Schroeder: You've become a very sought-after speaker on college campuses. What made you want to talk on college campuses?

Terry: I like to talk. [*again, laughing*]

Schroeder: [*laughing too*] But there's lots of places to talk, why college campuses?

Terry: I want to reach this generation. I got started doing this about the time that the book came out because it was a way to help students with the book. And in time it evolved into more than a lecture, or a reading, or comments from an author, or an evening with an author, or questions and answers with an author. It developed into a program, like a one-man show or a one-man play. I just felt compelled to carry this story because not only do I reach the audience I see that night which may number anywhere from fifty to twelve, thirteen hundred, but stories are written by reporters who cover the event or interview me (I stopped counting at eight hundred interviews over the past five years). This keeps the story alive, it keeps the message moving, it wakes people up not only to the war but to the sacrifice and also to the lessons to be learned, not only about American military and foreign policy but lessons about human relations.

Schroeder: One of your subjects, Stephen Howard, said, "Vietnam taught you to be a liar. To be a thief. To be dishonest. To go against everything you ever learned." Many of your other subjects are equally eloquent about the devastating effects the war had on blacks. Did anything good come out of the war for black Americans?

Terry: Well, black soldiers were killed, were maimed, were scarred in disproportionate numbers. So the answer is no. The movement towards The Great Society was stalled by the monies that had to go to the war effort, by the attention that the White House gave to the war effort, by the loss of the White House by Johnson to Richard Nixon. All of that damaged the black community.

I think because the black community has been slow accepting the Vietnam veteran, we have suffered the loss of potential leadership more than the white community. Many of those men remain outside the mainstream and outside of an opportunity to lead and influence the black community. Now I've seen exceptions. There's a black veteran in the Connecticut legislature who's hell on wheels. But we don't have these people out there like we ought to.

Blacks in disproportionate numbers separated from the service with less than honorable discharges, which cost them their medical and education benefits. Many of them would find themselves unemployed and unemployable because they had no transferable skills except the ability to fire a weapon, which is not a transferable skill. Some of them ended up involved in criminal activities and wound up in our jails. And there are disproportionate numbers of blacks among incarcerated veterans. There is a disproportionate number of blacks among our homeless veterans. There's a disproportionate numbers of blacks among jobless veterans. The biggest problem black veterans have is being unemployable or underemployed. It's scary to realize that black soldiers who fought in the Tet Offensive are middle aged: they are around forty-five years old. When you turn forty-five and you're not working, social scientists will tell you that you've been lost to this society. So if they're not retrained or reclaimed, we've lost them. And I think we're going to lose a lot of them. That's terrible. And it's sinful. So I'm propelled by that fact and by all that I've seen to keep telling this story.

It doesn't get better for me when I see films like *Platoon* and *Born on the Fourth of July* and *Full Metal Jacket*, the most popular of the Vietnam films, all of which dismiss black participation out of hand and diminish our heroism and our leadership. I hope it's not deliberate because if it's deliberate, it's racist. I want to believe that it's oversight, but I have the feeling that if it's not racist, these directors and writers are at least recreating Vietnam in their own white image. We're watching a whitewash in Hollywood, and I've seen evidence of it elsewhere.

I was sitting on the Veterans Administration's Advisory Committee on the Readjustment of Vietnam-Era Veterans when I heard a woman from the Bureau of Labor Statistics say that blacks accounted for only 10 percent of Vietnam casualties. I told her, "It took seventeen years for me to get this story; it's going to take me another seventeen years to undo the damage you've just done to me and to every black man who ever served in Vietnam."

Because people writing term papers, dissertations, books will go to those figures, and those figures are lies. Our government is lying right now.

Speaking at a conference about the war that was held at George Mason University in Virginia, Jim Webb [former secretary of the navy and author of several Vietnam novels] said that there are several myths about the war that need to be disproved and one is the disproportionate service of black men.

Schroeder: James Webb said that?

Terry: Yes. And I think that's dangerous. It destroys truth and it diminishes a service to our nation and denigrates a people. He's wrong. NBC called me up and said, "We don't understand; the Pentagon is saying that only 10 percent of the casualties in Vietnam were blacks and now you're saying that 17 percent of the casualties at the height of the war were black soldiers. Well, we don't understand why you have those figures." I said, "I don't understand the Pentagon; my figures came from the military in Vietnam during the war, from MACV. And at the time the war was going on, the Pentagon concurred. Now why the Pentagon has chosen to reduce black participation and black casualties is beyond me, but I imagine that if I live to the turn of the century, I'll get another phone call from you telling me that the number is down to 5 percent, and eventually I'll get a call telling me that there weren't any black people in Vietnam at all."

If you look at the movies and the TV shows you certainly get that impression. When *Tour of Duty* first came on I watched the first episode and that was the end of it for me. Because initially the only blacks were privates (they made some changes later in the season). The Asian was a medic so he's not supposed to have a gun, he's emasculated. The officers and the senior sergeants are all white. It's just like Oliver Stone's mindset. In *Platoon* the only person who knows what he's doing at the end is the narrator, the Oliver Stone character, the Yalie. The movie has a white elitist viewpoint: "Only people like us knew what we were doing out there." The sergeants were alcoholic no-goods; the blacks were potheads who were stabbing themselves in the feet to keep from going back into battle or were running into trees—they were like Mantan Moreland jumping out of the pantry saying, "Ah thinks ah see a ghost; feets do yo' duty." All he did was update the coons that were first established decades ago in *Birth of a Nation* and were replayed as Prissy in *Gone with the Wind*. I hate *Gone with the Wind*. I love *Glory*! I respect the way *Platoon* treats violence and war, but it slanders a people and their patriotism.

To me Vietnam is like the Civil War; this is a part of our culture now, and it's something we're going to go back to and back to and back to. We'll *never* get away from it—not in the foreseeable future. Certainly not in the generation of children whose fathers served there. The academics will be looking at it a hundred years from now like they still look at the Civil War. McPherson's *Battle Cry of Freedom*, which was published just a couple years ago, is the best single volume book on the Civil War. And tens of thousands of books have been written on the Civil War. The Ken Burns's series on the Civil War may be the greatest documentary film ever made. I think Vietnam is going to be like that too. Granted, Vietnam's not like World War II; it's more difficult. You can't romanticize it. It's too ambiguous. But we'll be writing about it forever. And the best books, the best films, are probably yet to come.

Photograph by Ray Solowinski

C. D. B. Bryan:
"Propaganda in the Purest Sense"

Schroeder: Although you're probably best known as a writer of nonfiction, you began your career writing fiction, didn't you?

Bryan: The first place I published was in the *New Yorker* back in '61— a short story. Then I did a couple more short stories. They were all about the same character, P. S. Wilkinson, who became the protagonist of the first book I wrote. It was published in 1965 and did very well. It won the Harper Prize. I was primarily a fiction writer until after Wilkinson was published; after winning the prize I really got clobbered. Critics either loved the book or hated it, but in any case my winning the prize seemed to really have pissed them off. "Prove it" seemed to be their attitude. I knew I was neither as bad nor as good as they said, and I also knew I still had a great deal to learn about writing. And so I started trying some nonfiction. I did some pieces for the *New York Times Magazine*. And at the same time I started to do an occasional travel piece for *Holiday*, which was a way of getting a vacation.

Schroeder: It sounds a bit like Michael Herr's early career; he worked for a while as an editor and then a writer at *Holiday*.

Bryan: Was he at *Holiday*? I thought he was at *Esquire*.

Schroeder: He started at *Holiday*, did some travel pieces for them, and went to *Esquire* when he did his profile on Fort Dix. But he was initially at *Holiday*.

Bryan: *Holiday* was a wonderful magazine at one point and then it just rapidly went into decline.

I wrote a second book that disappeared without a trace—*The Great Dethriffe*—which I liked, but it didn't sell. That was 1970. I began casting about for something else to do and by that time the Vietnam war was really getting to me. I had served in the Army and been an intelligence officer in Korea after the war in '58. I knew both the good things and the bad things about military life. One of the good things was that—[*pause*] I was a nuclear targeting officer—

Schroeder: This was in *Korea*?

Bryan: Yeah. And in Korea the military people who were euphemistically referred to as "special weapons" people in those days were wonderful people. They were really concerned about nuclear weapons, scared by them, and worried that they might have to use them. This was very encouraging to a smart-ass ROTC kid who came along thinking that all of these people were Dr. Strangeloves. That simply wasn't true, though.

While I was there, Korea's President Syngman Rhee was finally expelled. He was a crook. And as I understood it he left with $28 million in gold aboard a U.S. Air Force flight to Hawaii. That was sort of a loss of political virginity for me. Thirty-three thousand Americans had died in Korea, and I wondered what the hell all of these people had died for.

So *Friendly Fire* was born out of a sense of frustration about the war. I had been attending antiwar rallies. The first ones still had that confusion, that blur—they were still sort of love-ins too. For instance, one of the first pieces that I did for the *Times* was out in L.A. I was covering a love-in [*laughing*] which was really fun. Somebody named Captain Acid parachuted out of a Cessna over Elysian Park. He floated down with a black parachute and handed out acid.

But mostly those times were frustrating. You'd write letters and sign your name to ads and it just seemed so academically futile. By that time I had been teaching at the University of Iowa and loved Iowa. When I left I moved to Connecticut. Just shortly after I moved here a friend wrote and asked if I'd heard about Peg Mullen, the woman who had taken out the ad in the Des Moines *Register* protesting the war. The Mullens paid for it out of the money the Army sent them to bury their son. It sounded like a magazine piece, and the *New Yorker* was interested. But then when I got out there to Iowa I saw the story was something different. It was not so much "why did she take out the ad?" but how she felt about what the Army was doing, why was there some sort of conspiracy to prevent her and her husband from learning how their son died? Seymour Hersh had just done *My Lai 4* and I thought, "Boy, I can really bring the Army to its knees."

Schroeder: You said in a brief interview that you did with *Publisher's Weekly* that "it was already more than anybody wanted to read. Sure it was important to read about Vietnam, but people weren't just writing about it anymore; they were shouting." In the face of that literary and political climate, what motivated you to undertake a major lengthy work?

Bryan: I didn't go there thinking that it was going to be lengthy, Eric. I thought it was going to be a six thousand word piece on "mom's apple pie gone sour." And the more I looked into it, the more I got sucked into it—just like the U.S. got sucked into Vietnam—suddenly we were there for twelve years! I was there for five years on the book. One interesting thing is that I spent about a year on the book and did it wrong and realized that I had to start all over again. And I thought that the voices of these people I had been talking to were so good that it would be possible simply to be an editor and let the interview transcripts tell the story. I had something like nine hundred pages of manuscript and then found that they read flat. *I* would read it and *I* could hear their voices with all their emotions, but it didn't really come across in print.

Schroeder: Your problem sounds a lot like Michael Herr's problem with *Dispatches.* It took him nine years to finish the book. Were the problems that you had primarily problem with form?

Bryan: They weren't really problems of form; they were mostly the problems of tracking down the people to talk to. Writing the book was a very painful event. The book kept extending as I wrote it: more things happened that were going to end up being part of it. Friends began kidding me, "Where the hell are you going to end this book?" One of the great problems occurred when the Mullens went to visit Lt. Colonel H. Norman Schwarzkopf down in Walter Reed Army Hospital, then came to Connecticut to tell me what he'd said. At that time they believed he was responsible for the death of their son. I doubted, from my experience with the Army, the sort of things they were reporting to me, that a colonel wouldn't say anything. And it wasn't that they were lying; it was that they couldn't hear the truth.

I took a break and did a trout-fishing piece in Arkansas for *True* magazine. And while I was down there, I realized that that's what the book was about—

the Mullens, what had happened to the Mullens, not what had happened in Vietnam to Michael, their son. So there was that shift—that was probably in about April of '72 (it's clear in the book when the shift took place). And then there was the problem of the Mullens saying what had happened; going down to see the colonel, and hearing the colonel say what happened, and the two stories didn't jibe. But both were valuable. So what do you do? And that's when I turned to *In Cold Blood.*

Schroeder: I was going to ask you about that because it seems to me that *In Cold Blood* was a specific model for you. There's the obvious affinity of subject matter in the Cutters and the Mullens, but moreover there seem to be stylistic similarities as well. In the opening sections of both books, for instance, you and Capote seem to eulogize the landscape.

Bryan: Do you have any personal knowledge of Iowa, of the Midwest?

Schroeder: I've driven through it.

Bryan: Even having that experience, you have a sense of the land, of the enormous space there. And this is particularly so if you farm there. There was also that need to establish the Mullens's credentials. To show that Michael would have been the fifth generation to farm the same land. This family weren't crackpots, they weren't war protesters, they weren't hippy freaks; they were the earth. I think I said something in the book about when the government loses the trust of a family such as this something very serious is wrong. But the land is very much part of the family and is obviously very much part of the story. It's like that particular, peculiar light of Los Angeles that I've never really understood.

In Cold Blood, as I remember, does open with a scene set in farmland. But Capote had the same sort of problems with sources that I had. He has a scene where the two boys, the murderers, are together in a car. Rather than blend the two accounts, he did one person's recollection in one chapter and then in the following chapter did the other's. And for me as well that was the only way to do it.

Schroeder: *Friendly Fire* shares another structural similarity with *In Cold Blood:* a suspenseful opening. It's soon resolved and yet it's not resolved— we wait for a complete version of what happened to Michael Mullen until the very end. Capote does something similar—we know *what* happened to the Cutters, but we don't get a full picture of it until the end.

Bryan: Another problem that I had with *Friendly Fire* was how to get people to read the story. And my idea was to turn it into a mystery story. By the time that you find out it isn't a mystery story, you're hooked. The other problem that I had was how to get you to read almost forty pages of family history—the book's second and third chapters. So I'm very pleased with the first chapter; I'm proud of the way that it picks up and things begin to move faster and faster and faster, until the last line, "And one year after that his mother was under surveillance by the FBI." And that's the hook. You want to know why. And from there I can go into the wonderful business about the family.

It was hard keeping it to just those two chapters. I had to throw away something like ninety pages on the Indian chief Black Hawk, who just intrigued me. God, he was a marvelous character. Abraham Lincoln was sent out to get him, and Jefferson Davis escorted him back to the Jefferson Barracks. I've always wanted to do a book about him, but there isn't a big market for Indian books. Certainly nowhere near as big of a market as there is for Vietnam books.

I later wrote a piece for *Harper's* on Vietnam literature. I wanted to say something about the literature, about books I like—I've got a bunch of Vietnam books here [*gestures toward his bookshelf*].

Schroeder: Do you find yourself still reading a lot of Vietnam narratives?

Bryan: I still read them. Obviously I get a lot of them sent to me. About half the time I'm asked to review them and I ask them to get somebody else. There's too many of them.

Schroeder: Do you think that the best books are still to come?

Bryan: I think that *Dispatches* was so good and said something so important about the war that I don't think that anybody is going to do anything better than that. I really don't. I thought that *Cacciato* was overrated, frankly. I found it very hard to keep going with that book and I slogged through it because it had won the National Book Award. And because I like O'Brien.

Two other books interest me, but for the wrong reasons. Gloria Emerson's book *Winners and Losers* interested me, not for so much what it said about America, but for what it said about Gloria Emerson, about what had happened to her. In fact I reviewed that book. I liked Robert Mason's *Chickenhawk* right up until the end. I thought that he shouldn't have put that stuff in there about standing trial for smuggling marijuana. The whole book suddenly became something else and that wasn't what I wanted. There's another book I remember liking—I can't remember the name—like *Chickenhawk* it was also about a helicopter pilot; it was a novel but it seems to be tacitly an autobiography.

Schroeder: There's so much cross-over with Vietnam narratives between fiction and nonfiction. O'Brien start off by writing a nonfiction memoir and then wrote Cacciato; even somebody like James Jones—a very successful novelist who went to Vietnam in 1972 and ended up writing a nonfiction account of it.

Bryan: It seems to me that fiction wasn't the way to deal with Vietnam. If *Friendly Fire* had been fiction, it wouldn't have worked. People simply wouldn't have believed it. How could the president write the Mullen family a letter praising the Vietnamese at this stage in the war when the family thought their son had been killed by the Vietnamese? People wouldn't believe that kind of bad taste. And Senator Jack Miller writing that it had been his experience that the families bearing the greatest burden had been the least complaining and that he regretted that Peg Mullen was one of the exceptions. The story just could not have been fiction. It had to have that resonance as you read it that this actually happened.

But to do this, to find out what actually happened—that's very hard. The idea of putting that last chapter, "The Mission," almost as an appendix was a way of making clear that the book was not about what happened. I don't think that the Mullens, Peg and Gene, still believe that's what happened. I've had some correspondence with their daughter and I think that they still think that something's going on.

Schroeder: Have you stayed in touch with anybody else from the book?

Bryan: I just came back from a long trip with now Major General H. Norman Schwarzkopf. When I saw Schwarzkopf I was in California doing research for a magazine piece, a story for the *New Yorker*. I was near the end of my trip out there, at the desert warfare training center out there. They were using live fire with a computerized targeting mechanism—really astonishing equipment. There were some troops on a hill and the artillery was firing over their heads and all of a sudden the soldiers started taking some short rounds.

Schroeder: It sounds exactly like what happens in *Friendly Fire*.

Bryan: I'll play it for you, because its really extraordinary—

Schroeder: —You've got it on tape?

Bryan: I've got it on tape. [*Plays tape of training exercises; the voices on the tape become alarmed as the shells begin falling short. Shouts of "Cease fire! Cease Fire!" are heard. Afterward we both sit in silence for a moment, a bit stunned by what we've heard.*]

Schroeder: Getting back to *Friendly Fire*, I wonder what you think about your own appearance in the book. When you appear as a character, it's startling, to say the least. You've indicated you would have preferred to stay out of the book entirely, but you were unable to do so. Are you satisfied with your presence in the book? Do you think that the decision to put yourself in the book was simply an individual one, based on the requirements of *Friendly Fire's* particular narrative, or do you think that this is an issue raised by the genre, the nonfiction novel, and that as is oftentimes the case with this genre, it's impossible for the author to stay out of the narrative? In this latter category I think of people like Norman Mailer and Hunter Thompson, who have often made themselves the subject of their nonfiction.

Bryan: I think in the case of *Friendly Fire* it happened more the way Joe McGinniss came into *Fatal Vision*. Suddenly you become a character in the story. In my case, the way that the Mullens responded to me is telling. No, I had not wanted to be in the book.

The voice of the Bryan character in the book should not be a surprise because it's the same voice used throughout the book; there's sort of a conversational tone that prepares you for the conversations themselves, so they shouldn't be jarring. By the time of the Bryan character's appearance, I think that the reader wants to know what the hell is going on. The reader is beginning to make some judgments about the Mullens, and the voice of reason and calm (which is the author's voice, one hopes) is actually the reader's voice too. What is going on? Has this woman gone around the bend?

But I had two advantages in doing the book. One, my feelings for Iowa and for the family and the obvious affection that I have for them, and, two, my experience with the military and my sense that Lt. Col. Schwarzkopf was a decent man. One of the problems with the polarization from that period was that it was inconceivable for people to believe that Gene Mullen and Norman Schwarzkopf could both be decent men. And I think that *Friendly*

Fire stands up now better than it did then; people are now more able to respond to it, to its polarities.

Schroeder: Don't you think one of the things that has changed is that people are able to be more understanding of the military—I'm thinking specifically of the soldiers who fought in Vietnam. We're finally able to say, "Yes, you are Americans and you did what your country asked you to do," instead of treating them the way they were treated in 1969 and 1970, when they were shunned after returning from Vietnam.

Bryan: Mark Baker's book *Nam* has some wonderful scenes in it of soldiers still in combat fatigues landing in California—there was a particularly powerful one in San Francisco where a guy in a full-dress uniform has to be rescued from a bar by his friends.

Schroeder: *Friendly Fire* itself also came under attack; it wasn't unanimously well received. Often the criticism seemed overtly political rather than artistic. I'm thinking especially of Diane Johnson, who wrote that "sinister forces crept in and finished the book." She claims to detect not only a note of condescension towards Peg Mullen, but also that "the author betrays his work." She also questions the book's organic integrity. Do you feel that there is this shift in the second half of the book away from sympathy towards the Mullens?

Bryan: No; at least I hope not. There is that process of withdrawal—you have to pull back at some point—and it occurs at the point in the book as it occurred with the Mullens. I finally felt, "This is what happened to Michael; this is how he died." And there's no question about it. Schwarzkopf, who is a career military officer (and so, to the Mullens a right-wing Nazi), and Willard Polk (a draftee ghetto black) who had been court-martialed (I interviewed him in the federal penitentiary at Terre Haute), as well as several others who were with Michael—all of these knew exactly what happened that night, as did the company commander and the medics and various other people who I talked to. I also had the artillery report, so I felt I really knew what had happened. There was no question as to how Michael had died.

So I drove out to Iowa like a white knight thinking that I could set this family at ease now. I could tell them, "This is the truth of how your boy died." I told them, and they didn't believe it. And they don't believe it because (1) I was not an Iowan—I was an Easterner who had gone to Yale; (2) I had been an intelligence officer. Therefore, I was part of the conspiracy.

Peg had said, "There's only one side when you lose your son." And my saying that Schwarzkopf was a decent man, that Schwarzkopf wasn't even on the hill when Michael was killed, and that Schwarzkopf had nothing to do with directing the artillery, and that he was the one who went up and raised hell when he found the beer cans, that even the guns had been aimed correctly, that it was this poor lieutenant back at the fire direction center who had failed to take into account the height of the trees—all of this seemed to have no effect on them. I was very frustrated at their not understanding this and said, "God, I don't know what you want from me." And Gene replied, "What we want from you? We didn't want anything from you. You wanted something from us. You wanted a book." And they were right. I wanted a book.

Schroeder: That sort of realization is something that you encounter elsewhere in the writing that came out of the war. I'm thinking in particular of correspondents in Vietnam. Michael Herr talks about this at some length. Sooner or later you come face to face with the fact that you were there to watch all of this. You had to come to terms with this fact and to live within that knowledge.

Bryan: You have to exploit the grief of others. There's no question about it. That was true of the Mullens. But they were willing to have it exploited because that's how they were going to get their story told. And I think I did the Mullens proud, frankly. I'm not ashamed of that book. And I don't think that I used them any more than they used me. I suspect we're friends still. We may disagree on how Michael died. But I love that family still. They occupy a major part of my life. To this day I think about them all the time.

Schroeder: Actually, I disagreed with Johnson's criticism regarding your relationship with the Mullens. I felt that your feelings came across very clearly in the book—and their feelings for you as well.

Bryan: Well, you have to understand too the politics of the *New York Review of Books*. For them I was a fascist swine while for some of the more conservative papers I was a liberal wimp. You've got to roll with that.

Schroeder: Johnson raises an interesting question that she doesn't pursue. She seems to feel that part of the tension which she experiences is inherent in the genre itself: accounts of the real world often violate the formal quality which we expect from art and from fiction in particular. Novels have their own truth which is somehow distinct from what we do in life. When you try to use the structures and techniques of the novel to describe actual events, there is a tension between these two different types of "truth."

Bryan: Well, the tension, perhaps, is the temptation to shape your material, so that it becomes a piece of literature rather than journalism. That's the problem you have with journalism—it's the problem of the news reporter rushing out to cover the fire and there's this woman screaming that her children are in the room, and you ask, "How do you feel about it?" The children are burning up.

That was a side of me that I had not run into before. It rather surprised me and bothered me a lot. For instance, I'd be talking to the Mullens and Gene would start to cry, and I'd check the tape to make sure I had enough left to catch it. But I don't remember ever consciously twisting a knife to make him cry. He was effusive in his tears. Peg, however, cried very rarely, only when the issue came up of whether she would have wanted Michael to have avoided the draft. And at that point she confronted what she felt was parental guilt: that they had raised their boy in such a way as not to question his responsibility to serve.

Schroeder: It seems to me that you're suggesting that your presence is not in fact disruptive but that their interaction with you was a normal part of their lives, that your presence really serves two functions: that you are a sounding board for their emotions and reactions and also a recorder, and that those two things ultimately aren't separate.

Bryan: And it's a way of telling the story. An important part of the story is their grief, and their anger, and their frustration at what had happened. And Peg's last lines in the book are something like "Michael's death was an obscenity. Am I always going to be angry? I have to be angry." And she is. And that anger is such a pure force in her life. She's a marvelous woman. And Gene's a marvelous man. I was very lucky, I felt, that it had turned out to be that family. I could not believe—this is awful to say—but I could not believe what good material these people were. How wonderfully articulate they were about their emotions.

Because they were so articulate you also get that particular Midwestern quality of the narrative form: "I said and then he said and then I said, and then he said." You get these lines of dialogue shooting down a page, and you check it out and it's virtually what happened. (As I pointed out in a note at the beginning of a book, if I could not confirm a conversation from more than one source, I would not use it.) One of the questions people raised about *Friendly Fire* was since I was not there, how could I record the dialogue? For instance, Peg would go in to see the lawyer in La Porte and the lawyer would say certain things to her, and a year later she would tell me, "This is what happened." I would go to see the lawyer and he would tell me what happened. The two of them would agree. I would assume that was all that was said.

Schroeder: Your method sounds very similar to what Capote did in constructing scenes for *In Cold Blood*. Do you think, then, that in nonfiction there can be such a thing as objectivity?

Bryan: Yes. [*pause*] I think that *Friendly Fire* is objective. Ultimately. Don't you?

Schroeder: I do, but in a limited sort of way. Any time that you've got a writer at work, he or she is going to be filtering information. I think that *Friendly Fire's* objectivity lies in its ability to synthesize various points of view. I like something Gene Mullen says in *Friendly Fire*: "Schwarzkopf has had plenty of time to think of his own self, his story, his 'I.'" In a sense, *Friendly Fire* is about two competing stories, two "I's"—Peg and Schwarzkopf. You become the mediator between Peg and Schwarzkopf. Now obviously in real life you aren't going to be able to make these two people see eye to eye. But in the book you're able to achieve a balance between their points of view. And in that sense I think that the book is objective.

Bryan: Also, the question of objectivity arises when you consider the reason for writing the book, which was subjective: opposition to the war. But this was balanced against my feelings about the military, which were also subjective; my father's side of the family is Southern and has a sense of the military tradition and honor, duty, country. I knew enough about the military that Schwarzkopf trusted me. He opened up. But then again he had no reason not to; he had nothing to lose. Nor had he anything to gain from talking to me. At one point after we met, he sent me a long tape, of his feelings about what had happened, and he said, "Maybe it just helps to talk about this."

I had dinner recently with two friends who had both been in Vietnam. We were talking about the Vietnam monument in Washington, D.C., and I asked one of them who's involved in counseling other Vietnam vets if he'd seen it yet and how he felt about it. He just dissolved into tears. The war is still that much of a presence to him.

Schroeder: Were you satisfied with the TV version of *Friendly Fire*?

Bryan: Yeah, I think I got off easy. They could have made John-Boy Walton gets his in Vietnam and they didn't. I thought they were particularly brave to permit a certain amount of ambivalence at the end of the story. My great pleasure in it was that it was done by my best friend, Brandon Stoddard, who became the president of ABC movies. Brandon was the one who bought it and Brandon was the one who sat on it and watched it as it got done.

Schroeder: Did TV give you the audience that you didn't get in print?

Bryan: Well, that's the extraordinary thing. *Friendly Fire* sold 17,500 copies in hardcover. And in one night 64 million people saw it. [*laughs*] And you say to yourself, "Why am I writing books? What the hell *is* this?"

The TV version of *Friendly Fire* was very close to the original *New Yorker* piece. The *New Yorker* piece is like a speedboat going across a lake. You go from A to B in a straight line. You're going for drama. In the book, though, you can stop. You can go into the coves and fish. You can spend the time doing what you want. In the *New Yorker* series there was very little family history, for instance, and practically no correspondence. There was that sense in writing the book that I wanted to document what happened. I knew that the entire book was never going to be read by anybody. I don't know of anybody who could read it all without skipping parts. It's set up so that you can skip around.

Schroeder: You mean the book as published?

Bryan: Yeah.

Schroeder: I read it twice.

Bryan: Every letter?

Schroeder: Every letter.

Bryan: That's above and beyond the call of duty. It was set up so that you'd occasionally be confronted with large blocks of type that you could skip. But if fifteen years later somebody wanted to find out how the Army responded or what the government was doing at the time, then they could.

Schroeder: Do you see the book as some sort of reference work, then?

Bryan: I saw it as recording these events as a matter of record. I wanted a record somewhere in the Library of Congress of what the government had done to these people, what the war had done.

Schroeder: Your conception of the book sounds very different, say, from a novelist's conception of his or her work.

Bryan: Yes. Because I never thought that anybody was going to read the book. I really never expected to get either the reviews—front pages of the *New York Times*—or get picked up by the books clubs and finally optioned for television.

Schroeder: So your purpose was political?

Bryan: Oh yes—it was propaganda in the purest sense. Its purpose was to say, "This is what this country did to you."

Schroeder: Isn't it ironic that you would write the book with this purpose but not expect people to read it?

Bryan: I just didn't think that anybody would want to read it. When it was published in '76 the war was over. And it had taken me so long to finish it. The question is even raised in the book, "Is anybody ever going to care, ever going to read this?"

Schroeder: The book did do well in paperback, didn't it?

Bryan: I think it has, yeah. I don't know what sales are, but I think it's in its eighth printing or so. But I always had the hope that it would be a television show. That was how I knew people would be moved by the story. It was very deliberately scheduled to be shown on a Sunday night. Three hours all on one night. People would sit down with their beers and slog through it, and bit by bit they would see what had happened. People who had read the *New Yorker* version already agreed with me politically about what had happened. The same with people who had read the book, so I didn't want to sell it to PBS because the people who watch PBS already agreed with me. So the only chance, really, was to sell it to ABC, the people who brought you *Charlie's Angels*. That's what I wanted. So I admit there was that real political propaganda intent behind it.

Schroeder: You say that you had a political propaganda intent. But in writing nonfiction narrative aren't you equally or more concerned with truth? The issue of truth in reporting ties in, doesn't it, to what we were discussing earlier, objectivity?

Bryan: An example of getting at the truth is the reconstruction of Michael's last mission at the end of *Friendly Fire*. I sent each member of Michael Mullen's unit that I had talked to a transcript of what he had said to me. And then I made a large drawing that placed everybody where they said they were at the time and what they remembered as happening. Then I wrote the draft of "The Mission" chapter and sent each of them a copy to check. I would get back individual responses like "Gee, I didn't know that happened." Suddenly I realized that I knew more about what had happened than anyone who had been there that night. Which is odd, isn't it? Each one of them had a portion of truth. But my truth was a bigger portion of what happened. There are still even bigger portions of truth. The mission, then, is pure objectivity. I obviously wasn't even there. Thank God I wasn't there.

Schroeder: Do you think that books like *Friendly Fire* can have an impact on a public that seems to be dulled to most serious forms of literature? That they can change people's minds and help them from making the same mistakes in the future? I suppose you could even ask the question of the TV version of *Friendly Fire*.

Bryan: Why did Michael Mullen die? He died to keep us out of Angola. He died to keep us out of Lebanon. I think that the Vietnam war has made the American public very cautious about committing American troops, and that's been done because of the media. I think—if you can make a generalization like this—that the American public perceive the media as their enemy; they're not on the media's side. Westmoreland had a lot of public sympathy in his suit against CBS; there was a feeling that CBS ought to get it because General Westmoreland was perceived by the public as a hero, an authentic American hero. I wonder if that isn't largely because of the way that he looks. He looks like somebody Central Casting dressed up as a general. When people see the individual patriotic soldier up against the media, they tend to be sympathetic. I've gotten away from your question, though.

The point is, that had it not been for the journalists (I'm not talking about me; I'm talking about the David Greenways and the other correspondents who were *there*), the American public probably would have been willing to accept the war, to accept what the government was telling them. But in Vietnam, because of the media, people for the first time began to realize that the American government was not necessarily on their side. The government certainly felt no commitment to tell them the truth. If the American people can learn that the American government lies to them—and it does, of course, on a daily basis—then we have accomplished something. And I think that that's very important.

The war didn't end because Nixon decided to end it. The war ended because enough Americans had gotten out and marched and made it clear to their congressmen that they weren't going to get reelected unless they stopped the war. That's where democracy worked. If these guys wanted to stay in Congress, they'd better oppose the war. People also got really fed up with the arrogance of the government. The arrogance of the Nixon administration that "We know best." And Johnson's too. The whole business. There were rumors rampant that Lady Bird Johnson owned the construction company that built the Camranh Bay complex; there were great profits to be made in the war. But people simply got fed up with it. The reason I think the war was allowed to go on for so long was that the people who were being sent to Vietnam were perceived as kids who didn't matter, were kids who could be wasted. They hadn't been "clever" enough to avoid the draft.

Schroeder: In that sense, wasn't Michael Mullen unusual?

Bryan: Yes he was. As soon as the lottery came into effect, a lot of changes occurred.

Schroeder: But most of the other characters in the book—people like Polk and Culpepper—seemed to be among those viewed as expendable by society.

Bryan: Throughout the book is an underlying sense of outrage. It was written out of patriotism, as silly as that may sound. I thought, "God damn it! They can't do this to this country. Somebody's got to do something about it." Writing the book seemed to be the only way that I could do anything.

I think the Mullens acted out of intense patriotism—always—a great love of an ideal country that may not have ever existed, but that's how they perceived their country. One of the ironies is that they had gotten their land because of great-great-grandfather Dobshire's service during the Mexican war, the only other war that the press was really outraged about. The reporting, for instance, that came out of Korea was very supportive of the war.

Schroeder: That fact that we perceive both the Mullens and Schwarzkopf as patriotic only increases our need to have tangible villains, to have people we can blame. But there are very few tangible villains in the book. Certainly Senator Jack Miller from Iowa behaves abominably. But ultimately the villain is the "government," and the government always remains vague—

Bryan: [*on cue*]—vague, yeah. For me the symbol of the government was always the line of buses bumper to bumper to bumper that you couldn't get through to protest at the White House, that you couldn't get through when President Nixon visited Des Moines. That scene with Peg in Des Moines where she was carrying a sign and a plainclothesman rips it out of her hand and hits her was so satisfactory to her because at last there was a face, a figure, a body to strike back at, as opposed to the form letters that the government had been sending her.

Schroeder: Did you share her feelings of frustration at not having tangible bad guys?

Bryan: Well, I thought that the bad guys were the various presidential administrations. Again, that amorphous U.S. government. Of course, anywhere along the line there's people who made mistakes; you can say they're responsible. But I don't know who you ultimately point your finger at except advisors and presidents who didn't get us out of there. I don't think that they got us into it with bad intentions. I think that we were fulfilling our SEATO [Southeast Asia Treaty Organization] treaty obligations. But then there's that passage in *The Pentagon Papers* about why we were in Vietnam; it's such a telling passage that I quote it in *Friendly Fire* [*picks up a copy of* Friendly Fire *and reads*]:

> 70%—To avoid a humiliating U.S. defeat (to our reputation as a guarantor).
> 20%—To keep South Vietnam (and then adjacent) territory from Chinese hands.

10%—To permit the people of South Vietnam to enjoy a better, freer way of life.

ALSO—To emerge from crisis without unacceptable taint from methods used.

NOT—to "help a friend" although it would be hard to stay in if asked out.

That was written in 1965. Let me read what I wrote concerning my reactions to these sorts of disclosures [*again reads*]:

What was so troubling about *The Pentagon Papers* was not so much the disclosures of deceitful and ill-chosen policies, but the obvious contempt with which one presidential administration after another viewed Congress and the American people. As one newsmagazine wrote concerning these papers: "The most instructive revelation may be how little faith the leaders had in those they led—a classic case of the arrogance of the powerful."

When I was writing the book—when, for instance, I was writing about Nixon—I'd get furious; I'd start yelling as I was typing, "God dammit, that son of a bitch!" And then I'd pull the paper out, start again, and be objective. You couldn't let those kind of feelings show. The story told itself.

Photograph by Nancy Crampton
Used by permission of Random House

Norman Mailer:
"The Hubris of the American Vision"

Schroeder: Perhaps we could begin by talking about *The Naked and the Dead*, since it represents not only the first of your books which deal with war but also your first public success. Despite the fact that you were drafted you seemed to view your induction into the Army with a sense of anticipation; you had already written two novels, both of which remained unpublished. Did you see your induction as providing the material which would finally launch your career?

Mailer: I took myself very seriously when I was a kid and wanted to write the great war novel of World War II. I had been in basic training for about two months in North Carolina when the Allies landed on Omaha and Utah Beach, and I remember that I was practically in tears that day, walking around and saying, "God damn it! I'm not going to be in that invasion!" I always wanted to write about the European war and had envisioned myself going there. It was with a sense of shock that I ended up in the Pacific because that was not my number one war; it was definitely my number two war.

Schroeder: It's been suggested—I think by Hilary Mills—that this was, in a sense, intentional on your part because otherwise you'd have to come to grips with the impact of American culture on Europe during the war.

Mailer: No, no, no. If she said that she got it wrong. Looking back on it, I was lucky that I was in the Pacific because the European war would have been too much for me. I realized that when I read *The Young Lions* and saw how much more Shaw knew about Europe than I did—I knew nothing about Europe. So how could I have written about that war? I would have had to take some absurdly small facet of it, whereas the Pacific lent itself to working on a broad canvas. You didn't have to worry about how much you knew. So actually, as far as writing a good novel went, it was luck that I went to the Pacific. But I didn't know that at the time.

Schroeder: Richard Poirier suggests that your fascination with war predates World War II, that as a boy you dreamed of invasion forces and battles. Did war seem an appealing subject, particularly for an American author?

Mailer: I don't know. I really don't know. I saw all the war movies, and kids, particularly in those days, were un-self-conscious about playing war games. There wasn't much pacifism among us; it seemed romantic to us, despite the First World War and all we knew about it.

Schroeder: Don't you feel, then, that the same is true about Vietnam to an even greater extent? That the rash of movies which came out about World War II had a tremendous influence on the generation that went to Vietnam?

Mailer: I really know very little about that. It's funny, but I've never really known many Vietnam veterans. And those whom I have met have never really talked very much about the war with me. What I know about the war in Vietnam is really what I've read about—at least from the point of view of the American soldier in Vietnam.

I always thought that if I had been a soldier there, the war in Vietnam would have been a horrible war to be in, because in the Second World War we did have Hitler, after all—that made it easier. But even with that, there was a general feeling of "Oh, God; the Army's awful; I want to get out of it. This is ridiculous." Most soldiers felt that way. But they didn't feel that way to the point of being openly opposed to the war, of feeling justified for criminal activity. In other words, for some it was almost a point of honor to make money on the black market during the war in Vietnam, whereas it certainly wasn't true during the Second World War. (There were plenty of guys who did make money, but they didn't feel quite right about it.) Most of us didn't even go near the black market.

It was an honorable war in that funny sense because we felt that there was a general, overall purpose to it. On the one hand, Hitler was committing these barbarities, and we all more or less knew it; on the other, the Japanese had attacked Pearl Harbor in the Pacific. So it was a simple war. It wasn't corrupted and polluted and all that, but even so it was god-awful and we hated it. I can't imagine what it would've been like to be in a war which very quickly wears itself out as a meaningful war; when one is fighting communism and the people whose side you're fighting on are irremediably corrupt and awful, and the poor people whom you capture are all skinny and undernourished and have got that look in their eye.

Schroeder: This distinction reminds me of something else that Poirier has said—let me see if I can get it right—that "war is, for Mailer, not essentially good, but good in the present age where and when it proves essential."

Mailer: I think I know what he's trying to get at; I can adapt those remarks to my own thinking. I would say that there are other terrors we have to face besides a third world war—if that happens, it will be the end, one way or another. And that's a pretty god-awful thought. But there's no guarantee that if we avoid war at all costs and keep doing everything else wrong that we're doing, it's perfectly possible we'll just poison ourselves out of existence. There's more than one way to end the world. My feeling has always been that small wars, very often, are safety valves against larger disasters. To use a bodily metaphor, one of my notions for years has been that we'll never find a true panacea for the common cold because the common cold is not an illness but rather a medication, a cure; that is, the cold is a protection against something worse.

Schroeder: This seems related to your views on cancer.

Mailer: Yes, literally. We try to avoid every summer cold that comes along, but I think that if we ever find a medicine to prevent colds, the incidence of cancer will grow because the cold is a way of cleaning out the system, cleaning out the impossible aspects of the system when they first appear. We've all had the experience of avoiding a cold by keeping it away through an act of will and by taking short-term medicines like stress vitamins, so that we don't get a cold for a period of about a week or two, but we also have the experience of feeling this unendurable tension all the time. Finally we either let the cold hit us, or we just don't feel right for a long time.

Using that notion I would say that something like the war in the Falklands, while it was in many aspects a silly and terribly expensive war, was a small war, and it certainly was undeniably good for both England and Argentina. It was good for England because it got some morale back in England, and it was good for the Argentines because it gave them a sense of reality which they had not had before. So both countries may prosper from that war, but there are these ironies.

And if the argument is made that human life is much too valuable to be sacrificed in that fashion, then I think that one could argue that we should stop driving automobiles because that's another way in which human life is sacrificed in brutal fashion. In other words, all of those arguments are hogwash as far as I'm concerned; I've always felt the argument that you must save human lives at all costs is the one liberal shibboleth that gets in the way of everything else.

Schroeder: I have trouble seeing how the benefits of such a war can outweigh its costs. Even if you see such a war as a safety valve, you must admit that it has its attendant side effects. I was in England at the time and witnessed what I would characterize as a collective public hysteria; yes, it certainly engendered morale, but it went far beyond that.

Mailer: Well, it certainly beefed up Maggie Thatcher; no question about that. The Labour Party at that point was intellectually bankrupt and divided. Thatcher doubtless would have won the election in any case—that was her great good luck. But again, this becomes a very large discussion: What is more important, the morale of the country or the people who are leading it? I don't want to get into that because it's finally not answerable.

The point of departure for all of this was the meaning of war—I think that small wars are good, providing there's some meaning to them. I think that small wars between rich boys and poor boys when the rich boys have the advantage of possessing all the weapons are disastrous. They're bad for both the rich countries and the poor countries: they breed unending corruption in the rich countries and unending, unforgiving hatred in the poor countries. They're just awful for the cosmos, if you will. A war between relative equals is not necessarily the worst single thing that can happen.

Schroeder: Then how would you characterize a war like World War II? A big war between relative equals? Wouldn't it qualify as a good war?

Mailer: Well, when I look back on it I see it as a total disaster, but I also think that you can't blame that on the war. The war ended up being the cure for absolutely intolerable insanities in Western culture. Western culture had gotten to the point where, in retrospect, that war was absolutely inevitable because there were historical hatreds that had just simmered for centuries and finally they erupted in that war; there was simply no holding it back. The cost of that war is prodigious. The very style of life was adulterated. Since that war we've had hideous architecture; we've had all sorts of barbarities perpetuated on food. There isn't a major city in the world that hasn't been changed for the worse by it.

If you look at the architecture, for instance, you can blame the Bauhaus movement, you can blame Corbusier, you can blame American architects—you can blame a lot of people for that architecture—but the real horror of the architecture is not the artists who first conceived of it, but rather the cheap contractors who abused it, who discovered that if you put up a building that looks like an envelope or a carton you can get away with it. If you put up a cheap building and call it modern, nobody's going to say, "Hey, we're being ripped off." But in fact the populace of the world has to look at these buildings, and every time you look at one, your mood is deadened slightly. This might just be one-tenth of one percent, but if you start taking the populace at large and deadening their mood by one-tenth of one percent, you'll finally find some economic results coming out of it, less production.

When I look over there [*gesturing out at the Manhattan skyline*], that deadens my mood because I know that those people are running the world, and they have no imagination—that I like, anyway. There's no sense of amelioration. If you compare those new buildings to the older buildings next to them, buildings that were erected by people who were equally powerful and wealthy in their time, at least those buildings show a certain sense of aspiration and a certain sense of the very danger of things, of the danger of ambition. You can look at one of those building which has a spire and start thinking about the nature of power, the nature of hierarchy; you can stimulate your mind, But those other buildings, those corporate buildings, are just absolutely deadening to the eye.

Schroeder: Let's talk about what I am going to refer to as your two war novels and how they were received. Whereas *The Naked and the Dead* was both critically and popularly well received, *Why Are We in Vietnam?* was neither.

Mailer: Well, it wasn't a war novel; I wouldn't put those books together. *Why Are We in Vietnam?* is a kind of a comedy, if you will; it's a no-holds-barred book. But it's not a war novel. If I hadn't put that title on it, no one would have ever called it a war novel. The title may have been a mistake for that reason—it arouses expectations that are not fulfilled in the book.

Schroeder: Would you say the book has little to do with Vietnam?

Mailer: It has a lot to do with Vietnam; if it didn't, I wouldn't have put that title on it. My publisher, Walter Minton, was aghast at the title; he said, "Call it *D.J.*, call it anything, except don't call it *Why Are We in Vietnam?*—nobody wants to read a book with that title." Anyway, I thought that it was perfect: write a book in which the only explanation for the title is the entire book, the entire book is the explanation of why we are in Vietnam. But it had nothing to do with the war, as such.

Schroeder: But isn't the book, on one level at least, a type of allegory?

Mailer: No; what I was saying is that the fevered egos of the men were the explanations for why we were in Vietnam. Vietnam was finally an expression of the hubris of the American vision. This notion that we have to fight communism wherever it appears is an incredible vanity.

It's as if some large country went nominally atheist as Russia did, and they said, "We have to extirpate God wherever we find Him in the world"—we would see that as absolutely ridiculous. Now, in fact, historically the Russians have never been even remotely strong enough to do that, and they don't really even try anymore; they're not interested in extirpating religion as such.

But we've had this canon where we've had to extirpate communism wherever we've gone; it's been a religious crusade, and like all religious crusades it's been just overloaded with hubris. And it's been an absolute disaster because the irony of the thing is that in its simplest geopolitical terms, anyone could see what was going on. I'm not talking now with aftervision—Monday morning quarterbacking—because it was obvious back in 1965 that the best defense we had against communism, if you want to talk that way, would be to let the Chinese Communists and the Vietnamese fight it out because they hated each other. Even the Russians were getting into it—before it was over they all would have been fighting one another. International communism was always cannibalistic. We really don't need to fight them; they'll fight themselves for us.

That war was altogether pointless. If we'd never entered it, we'd be in a much stronger position in the Far East now. And all of the horrible things that happened there after the war would have happened during it. Looking back on it now, Southeast Asia was an area where historically the situation was analogous to Europe. Europe in the 1930s was a place that was going to explode like a volcano and destroy much of itself, and the same thing is true of Southeast Asia.

Schroeder: Would you say, then, that part of your purpose in writing *Why Are We in Vietnam?* was didactic?

Mailer: Well, no. [*pause*] I was just outraged by that war. I've never been outraged as much in the years I've been living as by that war. I thought that everything I cared for about this country was going to get warped by that war, and I must say that an awful lot of it was. I think this country is cheaper since; I think the war hurt us terribly. It corrupted so much, it cheapened values so much, and it brought a profound cynicism into American life afterwards. And it really injured a generation very badly. The one thing that I'll say for that war is that the guys who went to it had more fun than we ever had in the Second World War. But the fun was meaningless. I don't want to be a heavy moralist, but if meaningless fun was the only thing you were getting that was positive from the experience, it could end up having curious and extreme consequences. For instance, no generation of war veterans that I've ever known of were as drug-ridden as that one nor as generally fucked up.

We came out of the Second World War with a real sense of release: we believed that now we were going to start building our lives. But the guys coming out of the war in Vietnam had lost the idea that one had a life that was interesting and purposeful and one wanted to do something with it. In their eyes that was horseshit. The people who were running the country were bonkers. Everything was meaningless.

Schroeder: Don't you think that this was compounded by the fact that society turned on the Vietnam vets and saw them as being silly for having gone in the first place?

Mailer: I certainly never saw them as silly. I know enough about being drafted to know that once you're in the Army you don't have much choice. But no, I never felt that the guys who served in Vietnam were the enemy. In fact, I even went to a Vietnam veterans' dinner in New York—a lot of people were surprised that I was there. I certainly had nothing against the soldiers; what I was against was that idiotic mentality that we are the policeman of the world and that we can control communism. First of all, we can't do this; we're physically not strong enough. It's analogous to me saying that I'm going to wrestle Man Mountain Dean. Furthermore, we were morally and spiritually incapable of it because we just weren't that pure ourselves. And, finally, it just wasn't necessary. So I always felt it was a hideous war in that way. Diem was one of the most corrupt people in the world. What could ever have been more corrupt than that South Vietnamese administration?

Schroeder: You seem to imply that those people who went to Vietnam were corrupted by having been in Vietnam.

Mailer: I don't say this in any judgmental sense, but I think that anybody who went there was corrupted by the experience. If you live in a whorehouse for thirty years, you're going to be corrupted by it. If you live in a filthy war for two or three years, it might be equal to thirty years in a whorehouse. Even the way that people got killed in that war was so damn ugly: they'd step on a mine and get their genitals blown off—that was the symbol of the war. It was such an underhanded and lowdown war on both sides.

Schroeder: What about someone like D.J., who is corrupted before he goes to the war?

Mailer: Well, I never saw him as corrupted; I just see him as wild, as a wild Texas kid who will brook no gods and certainly not his old man and certainly not the world he was raised in. On the other hand, he's so much a product of it that he's caught in the middle of it.

Schroeder: To me he seems a victim as well as a victimizer.

Mailer: Well, I don't ever think of my characters in terms of victims or victimizers because that sort of classification tends to narrow them down too much. Anytime someone is writing a novel and he says, "I'm writing about a victim," that character's not going to be very interesting because in reality very few victims ever see themselves simply as victims. Whenever somebody comes up to me and says, "I am a victim," I'm repelled because I figure that either they're pulling a con job on me or they want to manipulate my sympathies or they're the world's worst sort of victim, which is that they've begun to think of themselves in a totally limited fashion.

Schroeder: But didn't you originally see the characters as victimizers? As you first conceived the book weren't the boys supposed to be killers living in the dunes outside Provincetown?

Mailer: But don't forget that the reason I couldn't write that book about Provincetown is because D.J. just wasn't a killer; he wasn't that kind of bad guy. And he never became that. I thought he'd become that, but he didn't. You know, you write a book and the book doesn't always grow the way that you think it's going to grow. It takes other turns. Part of him remains very sympathetic to me—half sympathetic. I kept getting to the point where I thought that there would be some sort of turn—you do have to have some sort of belief in your characters that they are going to do the actions you've set up for them. But I just never got to the point where I could see him living among the dunes of Provincetown like a wild man and coming into town and killing people. And I also realized that I didn't want to write that book.

Schroeder: Would Vietnam have done that to him?

Mailer: Maybe if he had gone to Vietnam and I had a Vietnam novel in me, yes, Vietnam could have done that to him. Yeah, he could have got into some really heavy horseshit. In that sense, I think that Vietnam did have the potential to make monsters out of wild men and make wild men out of middle-class boys or working-class kids. Vietnam, to the degree that it brought out the best in anybody, enabled them to see sides of themselves that were a little crazier than they had thought.

There's that to be said for Vietnam—I think that people had experiences there they truly would never have had any other way in their lives, which is much more true for Vietnam than for the Second World War. Men really learned in Vietnam what it was like to get shit-faced in a way that they never knew in America. And I think that a certain buddy-principle also came through in Vietnam. You know: your buddy would be even crazier than you were, but the two of you loved each other in a funny way; there was no reason to save each other's lives but you would anyway. This sort of insanity gave a kind of garish but nonetheless an affirmative light to life—I think that was in it. But at such a huge price. It was the most expensive of all wars.

And nothing has been agreeable in America since. Look at our history; there hasn't been a single political figure—some people may love Ronald Reagan (I don't), but leaving him out of it for the time being—every one of those presidents we've had since has been just so ugly and lusterless and graceless and heavy-handed and dull and oppressive in his impact on American styles and American manners. Before Vietnam we had Harry Truman (we didn't like him at the time), who, when you look back on him, had a certain feistiness that was fun. There's nothing wonderful about Eisenhower, but at least he had a sense of calm and balance about him—he was an avuncular figure at least. And then you had Kennedy, who was marvelous. Johnson, however, followed with that demented ego.

Schroeder: What about Carter? Wouldn't you agree that he was perceived as being a real breath of fresh air in American politics?

Mailer: Yes, but he ended up being a real breath of stale air. I think his personality was unhappy. The president is the leading soap-opera character in American life—I don't say this sneeringly—it's just that he occupies the dramatic imagination of America like no one else in American life. And if you've got an interesting character, life gets a little better. Ronald Reagan is more interesting on the whole than Jimmy Carter because he's a little harder to figure out. You just can't figure out what Ronald Reagan is going to say next; he can surprise you with what he says. But Jimmy Carter—you always knew when he was going to sigh, he had this inner sigh and you had to listen to him—it was a little like listening to a high school principal in an auditorium. So although he worked very hard and was a terribly intelligent man and did his best and wanted a good America and all of that—was absolutely a decent man—things deteriorated a little under his four years because he simply couldn't give energy into it.

Jerry Ford was a disaster before Carter. Nixon we don't have to go into—he's been kicked enough. They have not been good presidents or good interesting periods. Watergate was disgusting. The stuff that's followed has not been exciting; television has deteriorated greatly; the mass media in general has deteriorated. The country is less attractive now than it was even in the fifties, which was an awful time but the country then had more of a certain quality, a certain character. So Vietnam had a terrible effect on America. And for the world's best reason: it was an unjust war; we had no right to be there; we didn't save anything from communism; we were just mucking up everything in sight.

Schroeder: Do you foresee America coming out of this?

Mailer: Oh, probably—history is long. We've got to come out of other things too. The world's got to come out of the shadow of mutual assured destruction. If it does, then maybe we'll get somewhere.

Schroeder: You said that you didn't really have a didactic purpose in mind when you were writing *Why Are We in Vietnam?* Is that also true for a nonfiction work like *The Armies of the Night*?

Mailer: Well, where I say that it's not didactic you might say it's didactic and we can both be right. I'm never intentionally didactic. In other words, I never say to myself, "I want to get this idea across to readers." What I try to do is create a state of consciousness that is a fair one, and my hope is that other people will read it and it will change their minds. But I don't have this idea that I want to change everybody's mind in one direction—I hate that; that's propaganda. I don't want to move everybody ten degrees to the left;

I would be happier if as I was moving some people to the left, some people were swinging to the right as a result of what I'm writing because my fundamental belief about a good society is a society in which the cops get better and the crooks also get better. You see, I really am an entrepreneur at heart.

Schroeder: That notion of oppositions seems to run through all of your work—the notion that without tension, without dialectical opposition, things don't get better.

Mailer: Yes, that's the word—"dialectical." Once you get bitten by Marx, you never get over it. I really believe that it's through opposition that creative possibilities arise.

Schroeder: The framing structure of *The Armies of the Night* introduces a dialectic between history and the novel, but ultimately in that book you side in favor of the novel. As early as *Advertisements for Myself* you had said that "only through fictions can we begin to apprehend complex reality."

Mailer: Yes, I believe that.

Schroeder: What, finally, does the novelist have to offer which the historian can't?

Mailer: [*Pause.*] A good style. [*Laughs.*] But for every historian who writes well, there must be twenty novelists who write better. And that's important because though there are people who can read, sometimes the only way that you can perceive reality is through a good style; a bad style's incapable of conveying reality. Even the dullest and most oppressive reality needs to be conveyed through a style that's superior to that reality. A style that's equal to that reality very often won't do it, and a style that's inferior to the reality is hopeless.

Schroeder: Well, let's go back a minute, then. Do you think that your style in *The Naked and the Dead* was suited to your task?

Mailer: Just barely, if it was. I don't think it's a well-written book. I think that it was a popular book at the time because everyone was waiting for a big war novel. Just the way that today if somebody came out with a big, smashing war novel about Vietnam that was pretty damn good, everybody would read it. I'd run to buy it. I've never read a book about Vietnam that really explained it to me. This book wouldn't necessarily be final, but it would give me some huge sense of canvas. Most of the books, because of the shocking nature of that war, tend to focus on specific incidents, on specific characters; there's just been no novel I know of that's been both good and written on a large canvas about Vietnam.

Schroeder: Have you read many of the Vietnam novels?

Mailer: Not a lot. I've glanced at some of them. They come my way and I look at them. When you've been writing as long as I have, you end up (whether for good or bad) going in for the quick taste test—I'll crack a book in two or three places and if it doesn't surprise me in any way, then that's it. The book never gets read. That may be very unfair—I might have hit the three dullest pages of the book—but you work on the law of averages.

Schroeder: I think many people feel as you do—that the really great Vietnam novel is yet to be written.

Mailer: Well, it was more than fifty years after the Napoleonic wars that Tolstoy wrote *War and Peace*.

Schroeder: I'd like to return to *Armies of the Night* for a moment. At the book's outset you state that "one's own literary work was the only answer to the war in Vietnam," but you go on to assert that lacking work which was absorbing and a "happy status with oneself," you would be not only content to write about Vietnam but, in a sense, forced to. Does the novelist, then, have a political responsibility?

Mailer: I think you're right. It's very hard to write good books out of an act of will. They are written from time to time but depend upon other factors—will alone, no. But I think that the main source of energy for writing a good book is preoccupation with the subject. And anger is a very good motive for writing a book. If you're really angry or upset about something but at the same time haven't lost your power to think paradoxically about it, then you've got all you need to write a book.

And obviously, Vietnam was just exercising the hell out of me all those years. It's such a peculiar position to be in—to be hating a war so much that you're truly opposed to your own country, that you live in this odd relation to your own country. It's your country and yet you know that you may be in jail in a year or two because of this war and your opposition to it. I remember there was one period when a bunch of us swore allegiance to those who tore up their draft cards. In other words, if any of them went to jail, we'd go with them; there were over a hundred of us writers who did this one night at the town hall—we all stood up and took the pledge. And that was a funny moment because it was an open-ended action—maybe in a year or two one's life could be changed completely if one went to jail. We didn't know, but our hope was that the size of our group would inhibit the government from doing anything, and it probably did. But we were, technically at that point, guilty of encouraging sedition. The threat of jail was very real. And as you know there were a lot of timid people in that gang who had no taste for jail. That war was the oddest phenomenon; there's been no period of my life quite like it. But the one thing to be said for it was that it gave us a great sense of purpose; we were fighting against something that we felt right about fighting.

Schroeder: But you seemed also to have learned a great deal about yourself and your own relationship with America in writing the book, because those things and those people whom you might have been originally repelled by (I'm thinking very specifically of the turnkey whom you describe in a way that recalls the farmer in Grant Wood's "American Gothic"), you manage to find an affection for. You picture the turnkey, for instance, as a classic American type, and you find yourself admiring those qualities in him, even though in a sense he represents the "enemy."

Mailer: Well, I've always had this sort of half-assed love affair with America. If you grow up in Brooklyn and you're Jewish (which means, in effect, that you're ethnic), then you're out of it—you're out of it, but you're still a part of it. For anyone who's ethnic in America, however, it's also possible not to have a love affair with America. It's something like the love affair a man has when he's married to a woman who's richer than himself or vastly more beautiful; it's not a marriage of equality, it's not a comfortable marriage. But it could be a very important marriage. I think most ethnics in America do end up with that peculiarly enraged but passionate commitment to America. I know that when I'm in foreign countries I feel so American that it's comic to me.

Schroeder: At the end of *The Armies of the Night* you set up this dialectic opposition between history and the novel, but the open-ended nature of history seems in part responsible for your election of the novel over history as a means to "apprehend complex reality." Isn't a sense of closure something which history mitigates against? By the end of the book nothing has been reconciled; you don't know how things are going to turn out.

Mailer: But you can still capture the period—you don't have to know how things are going to turn out to capture the period. For instance, the hardest thing for professional actors to do is to give a feeling of spontaneity to lines that they've memorized. If the next line's going to be "I've had enough of this. I'm going to leave; I refuse to sign this contract," it's very hard for them to say it as if it's coming word by word, because they know that the end of it is "I refuse to sign this contract" and when they've said it, the director's going to have them stand up and move out and slam the door. So it takes great skill to do that naturally.

Now when you're writing about a period that has not finished itself, you don't know the end, and this keeps you open. It bears the same relationship to history that improvisation does to stage performance. Now you have to have improvisatory gifts, to be able to live with the uneasy sensation that you've given no answers at all, that maybe you've deepened confusion rather than alleviated it. It's just a chance you take. No one ever writes a good book without taking some kind of chance.

Schroeder: Well, you end *Armies of the Night* not with a sense of resolution but with a question, with a metaphor, the metaphor of America.

Mailer: Some people had a lot of trouble with that, it was a little bit too passionate I think [*laughing*]. But I think the real end of the book is not that ending, but that ending was an an attempt to have a little bit of Götterdämmerung at that point. But, in fact, I think that there are two ends of the book—the first part, "History as a Novel," which many people think of as being essentially the book, ends really with a set of cheerful ironies. So that even though the events themselves are potentially terribly worrisome, the feeling is similar to that of a Victorian novel—there's the feeling of Thackeray there: "Oh, well, we'll have plenty to laugh about in the times to come." I think one of the reasons the book is popular is that considering what it's all about, it remains fairly cheerful. The ironies are cheerful.

Schroeder: And the second ending?

Mailer: The second ending is less certain of itself precisely because it is closer to history. "The Novel as History." I remember that I had an argument about why it was a novel and not history, but that really what we are talking about here is history. And as history, I ran into this problem that we were talking about, that I did not know the end, so the very end was a bit hortatory.

Schroeder: That question you ask at the end, "Will America, now a beauty with leprous skin and heavy with child, give birth to the most fearful totalitarianism that the world has ever known, or will a new world, brave and tender, artful and wild appear?"—has that child been born?

Mailer: No, not yet. Not yet. But it gives every promise of being a monster. I'm somewhat gloomy about this. There's such idiocy loose in the country now, such a deterioration of nuances, of upper faculties, it's as if all of the heavy thinking is now going to be done for us by computers. This part of the world is becoming immensely narcissistic.

Schroeder: Will things get worse before they get better?

Mailer: Not only do I not know the answer to that, I'm not even sure that one has the right to try to make an answer to it. What we're all dealing with is terribly partial information. To answer a question like that you've got to be able to extrapolate, which means that the beginning of your curve has got to be pretty well founded. Nobody can ever do it. The economists, for instance, are always wrong. Their models are always simpler than reality. So is mine, for that matter. I also think it depends on the inner states of one's body. If one feels things slowly sickening within oneself, then there's a tendency to think the world is like that. And, conversely, if one is slowly mending in some part of himself that's been relatively ill, there's a tendency to get optimistic. So for what it's worth, I'm slightly optimistic now.

Schroeder: Can literature make things better?

Mailer: Well, I hope so, otherwise I've misspent my life. [*Laughs*] I think that you can't point to how literature does this, but to the degree that literature keeps people thinking in ways that are not amenable to the computer, literature performs a vital service. Whatever can't be put into the computer is probably the gold that we're panning out of our culture these days. If it does go into the computer, then maybe it has no value.

Photograph by Miriam Berkley

Robert Stone:
"Keep the Levels of Consciousness Sharp"

Schroeder: Can you start by giving me a bit of your background? What got you over to Vietnam, and how did you manage to get involved as a journalist?

Stone: I was living in London at that time—this was 1971. I was trying to begin a book, and I kept running into the Vietnam situation late in the war. I had been away from the United States for a couple of years. I couldn't get this book written. It seemed to me that these people—my characters—must have been in Vietnam, even though I didn't know quite who they were. I thought, "What is their relationship to this Vietnam situation that is filling everybody's life now, that is so much on everybody's mind?" It's all anybody would talk about when I was with other Americans. It was so present, looming large in everybody's consciousness. And I began to wonder suddenly if I couldn't get some work over there, go and have a look firsthand at what was going on, because it was such an abstraction—the idea of Vietnam as a place and as more than a place.

At that time, an English publication called *INK*, a London imitation of the *Village Voice*, was opening up. And they were ready to have someone go over there. They were started by Ed Victor, who had been an editor at Cape. They wrote me the form letter, and I got myself a cheap flight to Kuala Lumpur and from Kuala Lumpur to Bangkok and then on to Saigon. I spent something under two months there in May of 1971. Most of it in Saigon, looking into the drug trade. I had made some very, very far-out contacts in Saigon. I spent a large part of my time in Saigon itself. Sometimes I went out on Route One in the direction of Bien Ho. (I can't remember now the villages.) The part of the line I saw wasn't terribly active—'71 was the year American forces were being withdrawn from the line in order to keep the casualty rate down. There wasn't a lot of fighting going on involving American troops, but there was quite a bit about thirty kilometers northeast of the city that involved Vietnamese troops. (At first I was only accredited to the Vietnamese government and not to JUSPAO.)

So I was in that area on a number of different occasions, for short periods. Most of the time I was in the city, and I wasn't there very long. It wasn't quite two months. While I was there, actually, *INK* had folded, my putative employers were no more, so what I wrote was finally published in the *Guardian* (what was formerly the *Manchester Guardian*) sometime during the summer of 1971 on two different Saturdays. And that's the extent of my Vietnam career.

Schroeder: Didn't you publish a Vietnam piece in the *Atlantic*?

Stone: Yes, that's true. I had a piece in the *Atlantic*, too. It's been anthologized in a collection of Vietnam pieces. The book with that article is called *Who We Are*. The piece is about deserters, and it's boring. It is me trying to be a good supporter of the movement. It's boring and it's pretentious and (in my opinion) it's essentially false. I haven't read it in years, but that's the way I remember it; it seemed to be excrutiating.

Schroeder: Your position seems to be analogous to Michael Herr's, who told me he originally went to Vietnam thinking to do something like a monthly column for *Esquire*. He got there and after only a week realized that the idea was futile. He called Harold Hayes and told him that. Hayes said, "Well, you're there; do what you like." Michael said that he had always had the idea of a book in the back of his mind, and that anyway the understanding with Hayes was that he was there to write a book. Hayes pretty much turned him loose and said do what you like. Was your position somewhat similar?

Stone: My position was a little different because I stayed a lot longer than I had intended. I was ready just to go and have a look around and then get back to work. I had also promised my wife that I wasn't going to stay there. So she was on my case to come back immediately. When I did finally go home, I felt guilty about leaving. I had a very strong feeling of guilt, which I continue to have about being there such a short time and then turning around and coming home. It was impossible not to feel guilty and flaky about such a lightning visit.

Schroeder: Did you go with the notion that you were going to be writing journalism, or did you always have the novel in the back of your mind?

Stone: I wasn't sure what I had in the back of my mind. I was ready to do journalistic pieces. I hadn't done much work lately. I had been free-lancing in Europe. I wasn't getting a book written. I wasn't getting anything written. It was a dead time in my life. The trip turned out to be the right thing to do. I really was ready to work there as a journalist. I wasn't absolutely certain what the hell was on my mind. I just wanted to go there. That's more or less all the situation.

Schroeder: In that sense, when writing *Dog Soldiers*, did you feel that you yourself were a role model for Converse?

Stone: Yes, as a marginal journalist, sure, and to that degree. Not that Converse is me (I guess obviously). But yes, certainly.

Schroeder: Could you comment on marginal journalism in Vietnam?

Stone: There was just an enormous number of people who were accredited—there was even a high school paper represented. It was not particularly difficult for all sorts of adventurers and wanderers and hippies and whatnot of all sorts to blow into town, coming from Katmandu or from India. It wasn't that difficult to get in. Nineteen seventy-one was probably the baroque period of Saigon. You could run into anybody on the streets of Saigon. There was a whole antiwar contingent of people. And this was true on several levels. There were the Harvard lawyers, the Harvard Law Project people, who were basically antiwar movement types. There were Quakers, the American Friends Service Committee. Saigon was just full of Americans and Europeans of any possible description. It was a real carnival. There were a lot of people with marginal accreditations: stringers from quasi-papers, people with forged accreditation letters that they had written for themselves. A lot of people were dealing dope. There were a lot of marginal people around, a lot of people only nominally press. There were reporters who allegedly dealt with the black market. There certainly were such reporters who dabbled in gold or cinnamon or dope—not reporters from the major papers but marginal people, people with more secondary credentials.

Schroeder: I want to return to Converse for a moment. He is an interesting character for a number of reasons. Philip Roth wrote an article—I think in

1960 or 1961—in which he talked about the plight of American fiction. In it he claims the trouble with American fiction is that everthing in our society is so wacky that when you try to write fiction it comes off as dull in comparison to journalism. Converse is interesting because in our age he is so believable; the whole plot to bring the drugs back to the United States— all of these things seem commonplace. He comes across as very convincing for this reason. It's easy to imagine him living in Saigon and doing what he does and then coming back here. I think that the horror of the book—and here I'd like to see if you agree or not—is that Vietnam appears to follow him back to the United States. Everyone always calls *Dog Soldiers* a great Vietnam book, but Vietnam is only sixty pages of *Dog Soldiers*. The remaining 280 pages are set in the United States. And yet I think Vietnam is the center of *Dog Soldiers*. To get to Vietnam you have to leave it.

Stone: I think that is right. I think I did absolutely the right thing to begin in Vietnam and then to take the story across the ocean. I am pretty well satisfied with the Vietnam scenes. They are more naturalistic than I am often given to. They follow the rhythm of events during my time in Saigon pretty closely. (Obviously I was not dealing or smuggling heroin, but I knew people who were involved with heroin. Certainly not on the international level, but there was a lot of heroin being used by people whom I was acquainted with while I was there.) I describe restaurants and make composites of people. Those people are like the people I knew; they are not individuals, but they resemble a number of types of people who were around. The streets of Saigon described are actual streets; the hotels and restaurants are actual hotels and restaurants. I did what I could to make that presence of Saigon, the presence of Vietnam, a recollection behind the events that unfold later in the book. You have that sense of Vietnam—the antipersonnel tactic which Converse remembers, those different things.

I wanted Vietnam almost literally in the background of the mind's eye while the rest of the story happened. I think that's quite right, that to approach the situation in Vietnam it's necessary to leave it, to get back and see what was happening in California at that particular time, which was, of course, the time of the dying dream of the sixties in California and also the dying dream of the Great Society—all sorts of little bills were coming up due for payment in the early seventies.

Schroeder: A literary analogue that comes to mind is Norman Mailer's *Why Are We in Vietnam?*, which many critics say has nothing to do with Vietnam; and yet, if you read the last page carefully, it has everything to do with

Vietnam. His hero plans to enlist after coming back from the hunting expedition. John Sack has said much the opposite—that all good war stories begin in the United States and go to Vietnam. But you start yours in Vietnam and bring it back to America. I think that in some ways the implications of this are more horrific for the American people because most Americans seem to think that Vietnam began and ended in Vietnam.

Stone: You're right; it didn't end over there. What it meant, its significance, didn't stop there. Vietnam was a terribly important thing for this country. It's like a wound covered with scar tissue or like a foreign body, a piece of shrapnel that the organism has built up a protective wall around, but it is embedded in our history; it is embedded in our definition of who we are. We will never get it out of there. I don't think it is a mortal wound for this society, but I think it is a very, very painful one. I would never write off the pliability of American society. America is really a very tough, endurable thing, and I would be very surprised if it was actually laid low by this kind of thing. We as Americans tend to be rather apocalyptic. Our history is short. You see a country like France, which has been totally destroyed, utterly discredited, has lost its soul eighteen times, and keeps coming back. When we use these terms like "America has betrayed its origin, lost its soul," and so forth, we forget that France does this every twenty years. It's complete with the idea of France—"the French nation is disgraced beyond redemption" and so forth; they lose entire generations, and they keep coming back. They probably always will. For all I know, we probably will too. But it was a very devastating and painful experience for us.

Schroeder: You went to Vietnam as a journalist, and you ended up contributing more significantly by your fiction. What do you see as the benefits of journalism as compared to fiction and vice versa?

Stone: I myself prefer fiction. The best fiction usually endures better than even the best journalism or even historiography. (It is true, for example, that what we know of the Napoleonic wars is what we know from Tolstoy.) I think that the function which fiction performs is that it refines reality and refracts it into something like a dream. It serves to mythologize in a positive way a series of facts which of themselves have no particular meaning. It is a deliberate, shameless, and open effort to make events mean something. When you use the mode of fiction, you are manipulating events deliberately in order to impose a meaning. Reality as a phenomenology, as a primary process, does not have any meaning. So you create a kind of artificial phenomenology. You create artificial events. You make up things that didn't happen about people who never were in order to render in a way more truly events that did happen to people who really did exist. Fiction performs the same function for history or for life that dreaming performs for the mind.

Schroeder: How would you comment, then, on the New Journalism and its impulse to do these types of things within a journalistic framework?

Stone: I think that all writing is ultimately justified by its quality and by its insight. If you have a good, insightful writer like Michael Herr, for example, or Tom Wolfe (who is also in his way, in his altogether different way, a good insightful writer—I don't think that he is as serious as Michael, and he certainly never paid his dues like Michael, but he is also a writer whose work I do not despise), I think that New Journalism in their hands and in the hands of some others works very well because they are as good and as perceptive as they are. It's not a form for me because I would rather have the freedom of being able to approach the "truth" without being bound by facts. In their situations they have an advantage in that their work has subjectivity: they have the freedom of the fiction writer and the authority of the journalist, which is a nice way to have it both ways. But that cuts the other way, too; they have responsibilities to what actually happened.

Schroeder: For you, then, fiction is the best way to convey this "truth." But when you look at Vietnam, it seems to me very curious that most of the books that have come out of the war, books which we would call literature (including the subdivisions of fiction and nonfiction), are in the fiction category, and yet it seems (to me, anyway) that most of the better books have been in the nonfiction category. Although fewer in number, the quality of nonfiction books has been better. It seems that there has been a real failure of realistic fiction to come to terms with Vietnam. I think that the two best works of fiction about Vietnam are *Dog Soldiers*—which as I say leaves Vietnam in order to get to it—and Tim O'Brien's *Going After Cacciato*, which is not cast in a realistic mode at all but is more like García Marquez's work.

Stone: Right. I think that, on the one hand, realism in fiction—a realism of sorts, obviously it's not the old style of realism—has been making an amazing comeback in America during the past fifteen or twenty years. It's almost as if that tradition which people were ready to write off in the fifties and sixties suddenly came back in a big way. Of course, strict realism, the realism of the thirties, is very difficult to apply to Vietnam. It's one of those situations where you have to extend. You're going to miss a great deal if you're bound by simple realism because in a way it's an instrument that has been played out. You just cannot get the effects that Hemingway got by his kind of stoic understatement. It just doesn't ring true anymore; it doesn't have the impact. Nor can you pile horror on horror in a kind of deadpan way because people are desensitized to that. You've got to be able to bring to bear other states of consciousness, even if only because so many people take so many drugs. Who knows, but that may be something subverting traditional realism. But yes, I do think it is true that the best writing about Vietnam, the best fiction, goes beyond the realistic mode. I think that is certainly the case.

Schroeder: Do you think that part of the reason for this is due to cultural factors which the media reinforced? Herr talks about this in his book: how people went to Vietnam with various preconceived ideas and fantasies that they then played out. Thus when these people came back and wrote books, they went through the same sort of things in their books that they went through in their minds. Even though they may have learned a different reality, they are unable to convey that because of the influence not only of other literary stereotypes that they may have encountered but of film and television as well.

Stone: Yes. I think that there is definitely something in that. If you want, it's kind of McLuhanesque jargon to call it a nonlinear war; it sound like Charles Reich. But there is a grain of truth in that. It's bullshit, but there's a grain of truth.

Schroeder: Maybe we could start talking about *Dog Soldiers* itself. Converse is interesting because he engages the reader's sympathy (at least initially) and throughout the course of the book commands more sympathy than Hicks does. He is certainly presented more sympathetically. And yet it is hard to feel sorry for a character who says something like, "I've been waiting my whole life to fuck up like this." It seems that he has an impression of himself as a loser, and in his own mind he sees himself as a victim of fate. Is there a danger within this characterization?

Stone: You always have a danger with a charater who is not admirable. In a way, for self-preservation, the reader has to deny the Converse within him, just as I have to deny the Converse within me in order to be Stone the writer. I can hardly be Converse, nor can any reader be Converse. Yes, you run a great risk with a character who is so spiritually slovenly and so unsympathetic in so many different ways. Certainly you risk alienating your reader, but if you can bring the reader into a certain degree of sympathy or identification with Converse, you gain much more. It is one of those risks that if you get away with it, you have a richer engagement with the reader, you have a greater commitment from the reader.

Schroeder: Hicks seems to be just the opposite. You start out hating Hicks, but you end up admiring many things about him.

Stone: That's the intention. I want to bring a reader into that very situation. You have to be able to see that Hicks is really disturbed in very deep ways. He is almost a psychopath—the term that Converse is always using about him. Yet he is not anything totally alien to people of principle. He is in his own way a person of principle; he isn't a monster at all, but in fact a kind of fellow traveler, another human being. I hope that I can bring people to that realization. I'm taking a risk there, too, with a quirky character like Hicks. I'm unsympathetic. I'm brutal, brutal to the point of being murderous, although I didn't really mean him to kill Gerald. Gerald, the writer who ODs, is not supposed to die. I didn't make that clear enough. I left it open. I should have been more specific. In my mind, anyway, Gerald doesn't die.

Schroeder: I think that Marge is certainly convinced that he is dead.

Stone: Yes, she thinks he's dead.

Schroeder: I think that even Hicks seemed to think that he's dead. Hicks says that he got what he deserved. There's a wonderful quote from Hicks where he says, "I'm a Christian American who fought for my flag. I don't take shit from Martians." This is his view of Gerald. Gerald does come across that way. I find an interesting parallel in Michael Herr's book. The two characters Converse and Hicks—the soldier and the journalist—are mirrored in an early scene in *Dispatches* where Herr recounts a conversation he has with a young grunt who says, "All the propaganda is just a load, man; we're here to kill gooks. Period." Herr then editorializes, saying, "Which was not at all true about me; I was there to watch." There's a similar scene in *Dog Soldiers* where Hicks has just alluded to the fact that Converse has called him a psychopath; Hicks responds by asking, "What does that make you?" And Converse replies, "I'm a writer, and I'm here to watch." You're obviously conscious of this dichotomy between the two viewpoints here.

Stone: You ran into people—it happened more than once; it happened more than once to everybody—who said, "I hope you get killed, you fucking asshole. You don't have to be here. What are you doing here? You guys are really sick. You have homes you live in. You don't have to fuckin' be here. You like this shit? I hope you get killed." It didn't happen once; it happened a lot. You do get very aware of it.

Schroeder: Hicks finally does come across a bit better because it seems that at least he has a clearer view of what he is doing—not only at the end but throughout his life. He has been trying to live his life by principles. You may not always agree with those principles, but you feel that he has some sort of order in his life, whereas just about everyone else in the novel—except the really bad guys—is floating. Hicks is interesting for another reason. In some ways he seems larger than himself, and that feeling is reinforced by Pablo in *A Flag for Sunrise*. Both of them emerge as warrior figures. Are you conscious of this sort of mythic structuring in creating these figures?

Stone: Yes, though in Pablo I'm after something different than in Hicks. There are ways in which they resemble each other, but Hicks and Pablo are not really alike. I think Hicks is really extending—he is actually having a shot at greatness, at power, at true virtue, the old Roman *virtus*. He really is trying for that. He thinks of it as being a samurai because that's his Kurosawa-conditioned Marine Corps orientalism. But he is really after this classic *virtus*, this classical male virtue. Pablo is coming from the opposite direction. Pablo is a real little rat who is almost ennobled by his addled mysticism. I want people finally to feel sorry for the guy. Yet I don't want to fudge on how awful he really is. The guy is complete bad news. Ideally, you should be able to understand why Holliwell kills him, to understand that and not to condemn Holliwell too much. At the same time, you should feel sorry for Pablo.

Schroeder: We wait throughout the whole book for their two tracks to intersect. When they finally do, it's wonderful—the two end up in a boat together. You know that one of them has to go; it's a question of which one. And just as Pablo seems to be a spin-off of Hicks, so, too, does Holliwell seem to derive his literary being from Converse. Holliwell is another figure who seems to be a bit of a bumbler; he's not really clear where his moral and ethical priorities lie.

Stone: Not so much, perhaps, because I think he really regards himself as an honest person. He worries. He's much more securely located. He abstains from the vote by the American Association of Anthropologists and doesn't cooperate with the Intelligence Committee because he's done it in the past. He does this as an act of honesty. He has every reason to think of himself as a humane and decent person. He is more securely located. He's not as wild and crazy. He's not as young as Converse. He's not as much of a Bohemian. He is in some ways a more conventional, a more solid figure. He comes a bit unstuck under the pressures of Tecan, but Converse starts out unstuck. Converse is really all over the place. Maybe it is that Holliwell is simply older, but I mean it to be other things beyond that.

Schroeder: Do you, though, see Hicks and Pablo on one hand and Converse and Holliwell on the other as being representative of certain American "types"?

Stone: That's one way of saying it. But I mean them above all to be individuals. I also mean them to be recognizable. There isn't really a Hicks type. I haven't met many people that good. If you meet one Hicks in your life, that's enough. And if you meet one Pablo in your life, that's more than enough. You couldn't say they are types because they are too special in their individual makeups.

Schroeder: Children play an interesting role in all of your books. They seem to be not only symbols of innocence but also victims of the world around them, of forces larger than they.

Stone: One of the reasons that they are in there is to make the action of the book represent the larger world, which has a lot of children in it. Getting the kids out of the way so that all the bad stuff can happen is unrealistic. There are children in the world. They do also represent, I think, innocence. They represent an aspect of the human condition in that they are people who are in the world, a world they haven't made, a world they dimly comprehend, and their situation stands for the situation of the adult characters, too. I think that comes out in the area in my own mind, in my own sensibility, that I'm not in complete control of. I know roughly what the kids are doing there, but my putting them in was not total premeditation—I know what they're doing there after the fact, after I put them in. First I think, "Well, there should be a kid here because in real life there would be," and then the kid takes on that dimension that you were referring to, which I believe is really there, but it is not something that I had control of; it's something that I'm doing and am not altogether conscious of.

Schroeder: What's disturbing about the children in the books is that they all seem so helpless. You talk about how they mirror the adults in the book, and I suppose it is true of the mirrored adults as well—Converse in particular is certainly helpless in that way.

Stone: That's true. The people in these books do a lot of things. They're always performing acts—they perform more acts to determine their own situation than most people do—but they're still helpless in spite of all the acts they perform. As you say, look at Converse. They do things like decide to sell heroin. Go to Vietnam. Escape with other people's dope across deserts. They perform a lot of actions, but they are still finally helpless in spite of all the actions that determine the actions that they are able to perform.

Schroeder: The whole question of action in the books is pertinent because of the structures of your books, especially *Dog Soldiers* and *A Flag for Sunrise*: their structure is really that of a thriller. You have two or three strands of action that converge and finally intersect toward the end of the book. The denouement of both of these books reflects the thriller's structure. Are you consciously using this formula and manipulating it?

Stone: Yes. I want to exploit what there is of the mythic in that kind of popular melodramatic form. When I started doing *Dog Soldiers*, I vaguely had the Ramayana in my mind, which must sound totally blasphemous to Hindus. I soon cast off from it, but the Ramayana is about the theft of Rama's bride by a demigod. At the center of the story is the pursuit of the demigod and the bride by Rama through all these worlds that are peopled by monkeys and elephants and strange beings and creatures. I vaguely have that kind of form in mind—*Dog Soldiers* is, of course, full of great battles and ends in great battle. I got into that—the sort of shopworn thriller form—as a kind of irreverent echo of the epic. But it also created the necessity to make the thriller work as a thriller, which is rather fun but also a pain in the neck because I'm not very turned on by plot. I don't believe in it, and yet I do have lots of plotting in my books.

Schroeder: Most publishers would argue that it is plot that sells books.

Stone: [*laughing*] It doesn't seem to sell mine!

Schroeder: But your publisher doesn't market your books as thrillers. You seem to be doing two very different, almost mutually exclusive, things. You seem to be writing this thriller, and at the same time you are writing a very serious book as well. I think that your publisher's choice to have your book marketed as serious is a compliment to you, but, on the other hand, do you resent the loss of a larger reading audience?

Stone: I think that if I had started out commanding a large audience and had somehow been deprived of it, it would bother me more than it does. I'm getting larger audiences than I really had expected. I've always thought of myself as a serious writer, and I have never expected huge sales. I'm at the stage where I'm not in the position of a really massively selling writer, where if I don't sell fifteen million copies in the first month, I'm in big trouble. Everything from my point of view is gravy. I never know how the book is going to sell. But, no, I certainly don't resent my publisher offering the book that way. I think they are being straight with the reading public.

Schroeder: I want to ask a question that ties in with what we were talking about earlier, the notion of fiction versus nonfiction. You talked about how we remember the lessons of history through literature. Is this part of your intention in your writing, to lay down the lessons of history?

Stone: Absolutely. I've no modesty as a writer. I'm ready to interpret history if I can get away with it.

Schroeder: What does fiction have to teach that television, traditional journalism, and films can't teach?

Stone: You are not bound by the structure of events. You can get at the nature of events and the nature of humankind in a very direct way because you can manipulate events so that patterns of causality are made clearer. These patterns of motive can be examined more thoroughly than they can in a real-life situation, something that is bound by the circumstances of its actual occurrence. You can present ambiguities of motive in a fiction which correspond to the ambiguities of motive in life. But if you are writing about a situation that actually happened, you cannot present the reader with this much ambiguity of motive—you've got to pretend to detect the real motive, give the reader the sense of why they did that, why they made the expedition, why they killed a person, why they did whatever they did.

Schroeder: It seems to me that another thing you are able to do is to take other types of experience and to plug them into different situations. What

I'm referring to specifically here happens in *Dog Soldiers*. In rereading *Dog Soldiers* it occurred to me that the last section of the book was a rewriting of Ken Kesey's and the Merry Pranksters' experience at La Honda.

Stone: Sort of, yes. Absolutely. You can conveniently mix different experiences, take the experience in one context and move it into a totally different one. There's a way in which that whole mountain situation obviously resembles La Honda.

Schroeder: Is there a danger, then, of the reader who is familiar with Tom Wolfe's version of La Honda picking up your book, reading it , and saying, "Isn't there a parallel here; isn't this character supposed to be Ken Kesey dressed up?"

Stone: I would hope not because Dieter is so totally un-Kesey. That is, whatever Kesey is, he is not a Central European intellectual. Perhaps there is a danger. I don't really paint from life. My tendency is the opposite. If I base something on actuality, it will be unrecognizable, or nearly so by that time. I don't try to render; there're no *romans à clef* in me. I just don't work that way.

Schroeder: I interpret the point of view in the novel as being that the experience on the hill is a failed experience whose time has come and gone. I wonder if you feel that way about the real-life analogue; is your view of the La Honda experience nearly as cynical as *Dog Soldiers*'s rendering of the situation on the hill?

Stone: It's a lost paradise, in a way, but a paradise that was something of a false paradise, too. I don't know if one can speak of being cynical about the events at La Honda because one was never really reverent about them. I don't think that anybody felt reverently. As far as I'm concerned, what was going on was a lot of extremely pleasant goofing. It was just a crazy time.

Schroeder: "Goofing" was one of the words used in *The Electric Kool-Aid Acid Test.*

Stone: It probably was. That's basically what it was. I wouldn't have missed it for the world, but it isn't something you want to spend your whole life doing. When I look at the old movies of those days, the fact is that what it looks like now is a Stanford fraternity party. There are all these very young people—people in their twenties—carrying on. They're loaded, and they're carrying on. If you look a little closer, maybe they would look a few years older—Beta members at Stanford—but not that much older. Just a bunch of kids carrying on. If we were all behaving like that in our forties, we'd be cases of arrested development. It was fine; we were just young and partying all the time.

Schroeder: The other thing of interest here is that while this was going on at La Honda, we were just getting involved in Vietnam. Where did those two experiences intersect?

Stone: The funny place where they intersect in La Honda is in the person of Ken Babbs, who in 1962 or 1963 returned from Vietnam, where he had been a helicopter pilot. There he was, returning in what was a literal intersection of those two. If you read Richard Tregaskis's book, *Vietnam Diary*, which was written about 1961 or '62 (it's Tregaskis who wrote *Guadalcanal Diary*, one of the great books about World War II), you'll find him quoting this Marine pilot, Ken Babbs, as saying what we really ought to do is get in there and win it; let's take over the war from the ARVN and get in there and straighten things out ourselves. Ken Babbs said that. You can't hold him responsible twenty years later. But strangely enough it's Babbs, this merry prankster. This guy is going to appear later—not a merry prankster who went and became a Marine but a Marine who went and became a merry prankster, reversing all logic, the logic of life. So there's a real intersection.

Schroeder: In the novel, do these two worlds come together on the hill?

Stone: They do.

Schroeder: We seem to see an extreme version of La Honda in *Dog Soldiers*; we get the drug experience pushed to an extreme and then gone sour.

Stone: The drug experience didn't particularly go sour for us. There comes a time when you just don't want to take any more acid. I think it goes sour for everybody to that degree. Some people lost their minds over it, and I think it went sour for the country and for that generation generally and for my friends individually. With one exception—there's one person I know who still takes acid, and he's a judge. He's the only person I know out of that whole bunch I knew in those days who still takes acid. Everybody else has quit because finally you figure, "I'm just not up for eight or nine hours of that craziness. I don't have the physical energy; I don't have the emotional energy. I think I'll just listen to a few Beethoven quartets and have a couple of brandies. I'm not going to take one of those pills and go nuts for nine hours."

Schroeder: Along the same lines, one of the phrases I found haunting me in *Dog Soldiers* was this notion of "those who are." It's one of the mysteries in the book. You get the feeling that it's something tied in to the hilltop experience, although it is never articulated. It seems like the same sort of fraternity as "those who were" that I suppose existed at La Honda (you certainly get that impression from Tom Wolfe), except that on the hill we sense a more dangerous aspect of this fellowship. What is the reader supposed to infer from that?

Stone: The presence of wheels within wheels in a secret society. It's the kind of thing that in drug investigations on a large scale you do run into—the Church of Naturalness, or the Brotherhood of Eternal Life, or whatever. People call themselves different things at different times. Basically it's been about dope. So you could say that "those who are" is one of those weird organizations that has to do with dope. And it also relates to the Greek *esthlos*, which Hicks has tattooed on his arm. It was an old form of the verb "to be," a Homeric form which signaled "the aristocracy."

Schroeder: This is one of the loose ends in the book. *Dog Soldiers* breaks away from the traditional format of the thriller or mystery in which everything is tied up neatly at the end. *A Flag for Sunrise* displays the same sort of thing with "the deep"—what Holliwell sees in "the deep."

Stone: I certainly don't want to pin that down at the end, but what is down there we don't really know. It could be (probably is) that right over the reef where he is diving is where Egan dumped the body in the beginning. More than this, though, just what's down there is awful. It's unknown. It's things themselves.

Schroeder: What's down there seems to be tied in with what's on the surface in Tecan itself. Later we meet the operative who is lounging by the swimming pool.

Stone: Yes, he says he's the shark at the bottom of the lagoon. Aside from any metaphorical meaning these scenes may have, there's a very practical reason for their presence in the book. Somebody once wrote a paper called "The Undersea World of Robert Stone"; that was even before I wrote *A Flag for Sunrise*. I have apparently always included those images because I'm a diver. *A Hall of Mirrors* actually had a lot of stuff about fish and the bottom of the ocean. I apparently have a thing about doing this.

Schroeder: Certainly this layering effect is something unique to literature, especially fiction. I know, for instance, that you aren't very pleased with the film versions of either *Dog Soldiers* or *A Hall of Mirrors*. In fact, you disassociated yourself from the latter project. What happens when you turn books into films?

Stone: It's like a book in translation, but much worse because it is in a different medium. It's a fish out of water. If you rely on the power you associate with levels of language, you build your structure basically with language, with sound, and pictures aren't the same as sound. So that it flattens out rather badly. All your possibilities are swept away with tremendous precision. You have one face, one actor. You don't have all this blurry space between events where people move through the murk of the mind's eye, charged with all sorts of dimensions. When images are out there upon the screen in good color and good clear outlines, your structure loses an awful lot of magic. It flattens out. Motive flattens out; characters flatten out; dialogue flattens out.

Schroeder: Do you think it is possible for a film to do justice to Vietnam?

Stone: A feature film would be difficult. You just look at those pictures and you see the kind of thing you would have to do. A documentary might do it.

Schroeder: Returning to literature, I think it is quite easy to read *Dog Soldiers* as an antiwar novel because of the things that happen to the people in the novel. Most of the characters lose. The fact that they are alive at the end of the book means something, yet they have lost an awful lot by the time we get there, and I'm not sure what they gain is worth the losses. *A Flag for Sunrise* is a cautionary tale. This is a book that is really written before the fact. Do you think that books like this can have any influence on what we as a people are going to decide to do?

Stone: I hope so. I don't know how seriously I should take my own hopes. But I'm preaching in a way. I'm not ashamed to say that. I mean, the secretary of state isn't going to read it and say, "Okay, I'm not going to do whatever nasty thing I was going to do." That's not going to happen. But you have to be given something; you have to begin the assaults; you have to keep the levels of consciousness sharp. Somebody has got to do it. It's a small thing, but we're small people in a big world. So I'm writing a piece of fiction that a couple thousand people read; it's no big thing, but it's worth doing.

Schroeder: Have we learned anything from Vietnam?

Stone: I hope so. It's hard to learn. It's hard for a society to absorb an experience. I don't know whether we have. I sure hope so.

Schroeder: When will we know?

Stone: I think if we could ask somebody in fifty years, "What's America like? What's it like to be an American?" then we might know. At this point we don't know. Maybe by the turn of the century we will. Not much before that, I'm afraid.

Photograph by Miriam Berkley

Tim O'Brien:

"Maybe So"

Schroeder: I want to start out with your first book because I think it raises the issue of fiction versus nonfiction and how the two begin to merge in Vietnam literature. On first reading, *If I Die in a Combat Zone* strikes one as a straight autobiography. Yet the impulse was obviously there for you to fictionalize. How much did you fictionalize, or why was there the impulse to fictionalize that experience when so many other writers obviously resisted it?

O'Brien: Well, most of *If I Die* is straight autobiography. All of the events in the book really happened; in one sense it is a kind of war memoir and was never intended to be fiction. It's not fiction. But you're right that I tried to cast the scenes in fictional form. Dialogue, for example. Often I couldn't remember the exact words people said, and yet to give it a dramatic intensity and immediacy I'd make up dialogue that seemed true to the spirit of what was said.

Schroeder: That's what Gay Talese says he does in writing his New Journalistic pieces.

O'Brien: I think it's probably not very new. I think it's old. Any memoir has it, going back to anybody. Unless you're sitting with a tape recorder or taking precise notes every time something happens, obviously you have an imperfect recollection. Things like ordering chronologies, that's made up. I didn't follow the chronology of the events; I switched events around for the purpose of drama. And drawing characters and descriptions and so on. It's not even sewn, just a little vignette and another vignette and another vignette. I'm not even sure what *that is*, but it's a fictional technique. It doesn't really matter.

What's odd about it, though, is that a book which I published and intended to be a straight autobiography or war memoir is now called a novel by everyone, and everyone writes about it as a novel. That goes to your point, which is that for some reason (I'm not even sure what it was; it must have been largely subconscious) the book was written as a novel; that is, the form of the book is fictional.

Schroeder: When I first read the book, I assumed it was straight autobiography, and I was not aware that it might be something else until I read an annotated bibliography that described it as fiction. Then I went and examined my copy—sure enough, on the spine of the book it says "Fiction."

O'Brien: I never noticed that.

Schroeder: So I thought, "I wonder how much is fictionalized and how much is autobiographical; if the publisher is going to put the stamp on it, it's for a reason."

O'Brien: It's not on any of the other editions. That's really odd. Well, there's another reason people think it's fiction. Even my own publisher can't tell. I'm not sure it matters, to be honest. It is what it is, clearly, no matter what kind of label you put on it. It never bothered me when people began calling it a novel. I think Gloria Emerson was the first to do so. I tell them it's not a novel, but really it doesn't bother me one way or the other.

Schroeder: Do you think, then, that this perception has more to do with the book's structure than its content? As you say, its episodic method?

O'Brien: I think it's the dialogue and that sense of drawing scene. When we think of nonfiction, we think of someone telling us, "And here's what happened when they went on like this," without stopping to give us dialogue and characters and so on. If I were to tell you a story about something that happened yesterday, I wouldn't go on for four or five pages without a "scene drawing," that "he said, she said." This creates the illusion of "happiness" which usually isn't there in nonfiction. Nonfiction is usually cast in the language of political science or history or sociology or whatever. And this is not. It's cast in an entirely different language.

Schroeder: Why did you omit your college years from *If I Die* ? You're rather detailed about your early childhood and adolescence, then at the end of Chapter 2 you begin college. At the beginning of Chapter 3 it's summer, and you've finished college and have received your induction notice.

O'Brien: This I did in the interest of selectivity. There wasn't much that happened in college that seemed to reflect on what was important. I tried to pay attention to those antecedents or seeds that bloomed in Vietnam during the course of the experience. And there was nothing in college that was there to really grow. Hence, I just didn't put anything in about it. Little references here and there—I was called "College Joe." I mention that. But there was nothing in college that seemed critical to the experience.

Schroeder: Do you think your experience was atypical in that you were a college graduate who became an infantryman and saw combat? It seems that most college graduates who went to Vietnam got out of front-line duty.

O'Brien: Most did. I never quite understood why I didn't. There were some in my platoon, probably three of us.

Schroeder: Did that in any way alienate you from the younger GIs?

O'Brien: Most didn't know I had been to college. Those who did looked at it the same way that I looked at anybody else who was sort of unusual: "You're a bartender, huh? You were a cop? I didn't know that." It was something unusual. No; there was no alienation that I can remember. I noticed that everybody seemed quite young. But I was young too. I think I was twenty-one. So I was only a couple of years older than the average soldier. I felt young there. I didn't feel that much older than anyone else, though of course I was older than many. There's no question that most of us were kids.

Schroeder: Getting back to this distinction between fiction and nonfiction, we might locate *If I Die* in a mean position between the two, or a bit more toward nonfiction than fiction. But you can clearly see it partaking of both. With *Going After Cacciato* it seems that you've gone to a much further extreme in your fictionalization; the operative word there might be a mythmaking. I see this much more in tune with something of that order than with a fictional work in a realistic mode, such as the books that came out of World War II—*The Naked and the Dead*, for instance. What was your motivation for adopting this mode?

O'Brien: A whole bunch of them. It's so complicated that it's even hard to talk about. On one level I think of it as strict realism; that is, even the so-called surreal sections are very real in a way: one's imagination and daydreams are real. Things actually happen in daydreams. There's a reality you can't deny. It's not happening in the physical world, but it's certainly happening in the sense data of the brain. There's a reality to imaginative experience that's critical to the book. The life of the imagination is half of war, half of *any* kind of experience.

We live in our heads a lot, but especially during situations of stress and great peril. It's a means of escape in part, but it's also a means of dealing with the real world—not just escaping it, but dealing with it. And so I chose to render about half of the book in a naturalistic mode, but I also treated fantasy as fully real. Early on in the book I try to blur the distinctions between what's real and what's imagined, so that the reader thinks that all these things are actually happening. For instance, there's this peculiar falling into a tunnel. It's written as if it were really happening. Odd things happen. What's this guy doing living in a hole? The reader has the same sensation that a person has when he slips into a daydream and then out, slipping into it and out; he doesn't treat the fantasy section as *Alice in Wonderland*–ish, as if filled with goblins and hobbits and fantasy creatures, but instead treats it very realistically, as straight declarative prose.

And there's more to it than that. One of the important themes of the book is how one's memory and imagination interpenetrate, interlock. Paul Berlin will be remembering guys dying in the tunnel, for example, and these memories will set off his imagination, and suddenly he'll start imagining that the trek to Paris has fallen into a tunnel. Hence it's the way those two things interact that seems to me important. Beyond that, one's imagination is also a way of goal setting or objective setting, of figuring out purposes. For example, before wanting to become a doctor, one would have first to imagine giving shots to people. Could you stand it? What would it feel like and look like? If you couldn't imagine being happy sticking a needle into someone, the odds are that in the real world you wouldn't become a doctor. You'd be something else. If you could imagine yourself happy as a professor, getting up in the morning and putting on a tie, having office hours, going to class, preparing lectures—if you can imagine being happy in that sort of situation, then you might go to graduate school in the real world.

Paul Berlin is engaged in the same process. We think of the imagination as kind of a flighty thing when, in fact, it's an essential component of our daily lives. Paul Berlin is using his imagination to figure out whether he would be happy running from a war or not, if he'd be happy living in exile.

Would he find peace of mind and contentment, would he feel that he had betrayed his country, that his reputation has been undermined, his family? And this imagined journey is a way of asking himself the question, "Could I really do it in this other world, this world of physical reality? Could I physically do it?" It's a test of how to behave and what to do.

The imagined journey after Cacciato isn't just a way of escaping from the war in his head—it's that, too, I'm sure—but it's also a way of asking the questions, "Should I go after Cacciato, *really*? Should I follow him off into the jungle toward Paris? Could I live with myself doing that?" See what I'm getting at? How the imagination is a heuristic tool that we can use to help ourselves set goals. We use the outcomes of our imaginings. We do this all the time in the real world. You imagine yourself picking up the phone to call this girl. You imagine yourself dialing. What will she say? Okay, I'll say this, and she'll say that. What if she says no? What shall I do? What if you start sweating? What if she says *yes* ? You really want to go out with her, and you imagine being in the car with her at the drive-in movie, and you imagine putting your arm around her, and you imagine what *she* will do. Somehow the outcome of that long mental process will determine whether you're going to pick the phone up and actually make the call. The central theme of the novel has to do with how we use our imaginations to deal with situations around us, not just to cope with them psychologically but, more importantly, to deal with them philosophically and morally.

Schroeder: This process of imagining is similar to what happens in *One Hundred Years of Solitude*. Were you influenced by García Marquez?

O'Brien: I haven't read him.

Schroeder: Really?

O'Brien: No. Wasn't that the *New York Times*'s "magical realism" thing? I hadn't read any of those guys. I've since read Borges, but I haven't even read much Borges. I was a political science major, so it's hard to be influenced by what you haven't read.

Schroeder: And you still haven't read *One Hundred Years*?

O'Brien: I started it once. I just hated it. My wife read it and loved it, but I got through about three pages; I just couldn't take it. I don't even know what it was about it that I didn't like. I remember the paragraphs were extraordinarily long, and I don't like wending my way through long paragraphs. I looked at another book of his, *Autumn of the Patriarch*. I tried to read that, too, but I got about halfway through that one and couldn't finish it. Borges I've really come to respect and admire. I'd feel good if that magical realism quote were directed toward Borges. But García Marquez—I'm afraid that I still haven't finished anything he's written. Maybe I'll give *One Hundred Years of Solitude* another shot. Everybody says it's a real modern classic.

Schroeder: In an early chapter of *If I Die* you talk about the role of the soldier. You ask what it is that the soldier can teach. Will we learn from the soldier? You answer your question, "Well, the soldier can't really teach anything. The only thing he can do is tell war stories." This is what Michael Herr says in *Dispatches*. *Cacciato* seems to be doing exactly that, telling war stories, but telling them according to the older sense of the term "story," where the story had meaning for the community. Perhaps we've come to devalue the word "story."

O'Brien: It's hard for me to pin down what I mean by that because my friend Erik Hansen, to whom *Cacciato* was dedicated (he appears in *If I Die* and helped me edit it), didn't like that line in the book. He said, "It's not just storytelling; you're doing more than that," but what he doesn't understand—what I'm not communicating—is what I mean by the fullness of the word "story." How do you gather a lesson from *The Iliad* or *The Odyssey*? They're stories. They have no single moral, no single lesson. Not even a set of lessons or morals. The word you used was "myth." The story should have a *mythic* quality to it, even a short story that isn't reducible to a parable from the Bible. You can't say, "Now be kind to your neighbor and don't go to war," that sort of thing; rather, it's like the imaginative process which I was talking about earlier—where you read a story as a kind of imagined event. It *is* an imagined event—I've imagined the events of *Cacciato* just as Berlin imagines them. He doesn't draw any single moral out of the story, and I don't expect the reader to draw any single moral out of it either; but rather, by going through the process of having imagined something, one gathers a sense of the *stuff* that's being imagined, a sense of what a war is and what escape from war is. And that sense can't be pinned down to a message or a moral. It's a story, and you finish a story with a whole cluster, a constellation, of emotions and yearnings and whimsies.

There's also a tentativeness to it as there is in real life—for example, if you go through a cancer experience, you don't come out of it with the lesson,

"Don't get cancer." You come out of it with a sense of exaltation that you've conquered it, a sense of knowledge of your fears—cowardices perhaps—the memory of trauma and tears and all that sort of thing. And it's not one thing; it's an experience. My point is that you can't use literature as a signpost saying, "Do this" or "Don't do that."

Schroeder: The word that keeps coming up is "imagination," and it seems that this is what really set fiction apart from nonfiction. In fiction you have so much more freedom. Do you think that this is what makes us conceive of fiction as the greater art?

O'Brien: In a way, yes. You've done this yourself. Everybody does it. You start telling someone a true-life story and at some point you find yourself embellishing it just a bit—instead of there being four guys coming at you with crowbars, suddenly there're twelve of these fuckers, and they're six feet eight each of them (instead of six feet), because you want to hype up the story's intensity to make your story equal to what you felt personally. And so you rev up detail, heighten it, so as to create an emotion in the listener equivalent to the emotion you felt, this great fear. To say the guy was only six feet tall doesn't sound very impressive, even though it was very impressive at the time.

The sense of embellishment, letting one's imagination heighten detail, is part of what fiction writing is about. It's not lying. It's trying to produce story detail which will somehow get at a felt experience.

Schroeder: Don't you see Vietnam in particular as a subject which shouldn't need embellishment?

O'Brien: It does though. I think it does. Maybe "embellishment" isn't quite the right word. I was using an example to get at what I really mean about a sense of heightened drama. I guess drama is the important element. If you were actually to record an individual's daily experience in Vietnam, it would be boring, monotonous, because 90 percent of the time you're sitting on your butt, swatting mosquitos, putting on mosquito repellent, eating chow, walking, walking, walking. (In reality that's *not* so boring as it sounds in the telling because there's an undercurrent of impending doom always there—the next second could be broken by a mortar shell, a booby-trap could be stepped on.) Yet fiction—good writing of *any* kind—can't employ this imitative fallacy. You don't try to get at boredom by being boring in your writing. Rather you hint at these days going by, which is what the basketball scenes in *Cacciato* do—not much happens but basketball, basketball—but underneath it there's this feeling that something's about to happen.

So the novelistic trick is to hint at the boredom without *being* boring. When a writer simply apes events, when he simply holds a mirror up to the real world, it gets boring: "We sat down. Two hours later we ate chow. We played this game. We did this. And we walked." It'd be really monotonous. So you compress the monotony down. In a way, of course, it's a kind of lie, a kind of embellishing, but you're trying to get at a deeper truth. Truth doesn't reside on the surface of events. Truth resides in those deeper moments of punctuation, when things explode. So you compress the boredom down, hinting at it but always going for drama—because the essence of the experience was dramatic. You tell lies to get at the truth.

Schroeder: There are many passages in *If I Die* that presage *Cacciato*.

O'Brien: Oh, I know. Not only that, but there's a lot of events which I use in both books. You're right.

Schroeder: And the sense of embellishment does come through in *Cacciato*. The same events become a bit stranger, or maybe more significant is a better way to put it.

O'Brien: True. Yes, I did this at least three or four times. I can remember one: shooting the water buffalo. In *If I Die* the guys shoot this water buffalo, and they all watch the bullets ripping huge chunks of flesh from it. There's a similar scene in *Cacciato*. But it's not a whole bunch of guys; it's just one guy, Stink Harris, in the scene in which they meet the women. There are three or four other places where I used a real experience, a real event, and tried to turn it into something more emblematic than it was. I think those passages are probably some of the more successful in *Cacciato*.

Schroeder: The water buffalo scene is interesting because it's based on something that you actually saw.

O'Brien: Oh, yes. I did see it. It happened.

Schroeder: The difference, then, between the two passages is significant because the first is a mere retelling of something that you witnessed whereas in *Cacciato* that action becomes functional; it becomes symbolic of something larger than itself, than a simple historic event.

O'Brien: In *If I Die* the passage is cast as a lesson of sorts, the kind of message thing that doesn't work in fiction. The lesson is that we had gone through all these frustrating days and couldn't find the enemy and had lost more and more and more men. One day we were walking along this rice paddy and saw a buffalo, and for no reason the whole company started blasting the buffalo. There's a lesson there, and it's told in this "lessony" sort of way: "Here's what happens to men who get frustrated. They blow away a buffalo. Guess what else they blow away."

Cacciato, however, is not framed in that kind of "here's Tim O'Brien's view of what happened" mode. Rather, the scene is just an event which happens on the route to Paris, and it's not framed in any kind of moral way. No one makes judgments about Stink Harris blowing away the buffalo. There's no sense of frustration in his doing it. I don't think there's any reason for his doing it. He just does it. He just blows it away. He brags about it— "Lash L. LaRue, fastest gun in the West"—that sort of thing. And it takes on a quality of its own; you remove the preaching, the moralizing, and it becomes its own event. The reader has to figure out what it means, if anything: how it fits into the whole fabric of the book. That's one of those big distinctions, one of the reasons I wrote *Cacciato*—so I could free myself from making authorial judgments and instead present a story. Let the reader make the judgments. It *does* finally take on a symbolic quality—that's the whole idea of what a symbol is, I think, that it represents something beyond that which it is.

Schroeder: Another difference illustrated in the two treatments of the water buffalo scene is a shift in point of view from the first-person in *If I Die* to this detached third-person point of view in *Cacciato*. In that sense, how closely related are the "I" in *If I Die* and Paul Berlin in *Cacciato*?

O'Brien: Not too. There are some similarities, but more differences. The Paul Berlin in the book isn't me. There are parts of him that are, but more parts that aren't. It's not a composite in any way; he's a made-up character.

Schroeder: He seems much more naïve than the "I," and yet for all of his lack of intellectualizing he is, in some way, more philosophical.

O'Brien: He's more of a dreamer than I was, I think. He spends much more of his time in dream. He takes the war and the possibility of running from war more seriously than I did. Hence his concern is more revved up than my own. He's more frightened than I was—and I was very, very frightened.

He's more sensitive, I think, than I was, more aware of the nuances of his surroundings and of his fellow soldiers. And I think he noticed more. *Cacciato* is filled with more noticings, more odd detail, than I was able to render in *If I Die* because there I had to stick to exactly what I saw, and I simply didn't see as much as Paul Berlin did.

Schroeder: It seems, though, that in the long run Paul Berlin is actually out-dreamed by Sarkin Aung Wan in the scene at the conference table, where something becomes more important to Paul Berlin than his dreams. This, I think, is what you try to catch in *If I Die* as well, this notion of one's sense of duty to—not only to one's country because that seems too big—but to one's immediate experience, one's family.

O'Brien: That's true. But, remember, *he* dreams *her*. He's made her up out of thin air. She's his fantasy. His alter ego, perhaps. He's at war with himself. In that Paris peace-table scene when she's talking, part of his personality is represented by her viewpoint when she says, "Go for happiness. Leave this silly war behind. You must live in Paris and be happy. You *can* live in exile. I'm more worried about death, about grotesque happenings. March into your own dream." Part of Paul Berlin is saying all that to himself at the observation post. The other part is arguing another position: "I can't run. I've got an obligation to my family, my reputation, my friends, my town, my fellow soldiers. Besides, it scares me—running away from a war is frightening." And that peace-table scene represents a schizophrenia of sorts. He's arguing with himself, and I don't judge the debate.

I try to make both sides of it as convincing as I can, roughly because that's how it was in my own experience. On the one hand, "God, I sure should walk away from this war—hey, it's a wrong war; it's evil." I felt guilty. But the other half was saying, "God, you can't do that; you've got everything else to think about: what if I am a coward, what about my family? You've gone this far; you're obliged to go the rest of the way." It's this sense of war that I'm trying to get at in that concluding scene. Internal war, personal war.

Schroeder: I'm reminded of something Michael Herr said to me: that *Dispatches* ultimately wasn't a book about war, but a book about writing a book. He went on to talk about *Cacciato*, comparing it to *Dispatches* , and said that he didn't see *Cacciato* as a book about war either.

O'Brien: I agree completely. I don't see it as a book about war either. In part it's a book about writing a book in the same way perhaps as his. Maybe mine is even more obviously that way; clearly, when I talk about imagination and memory, I'm talking about the two key ingredients that go into writing fiction. You work with your memories—those events which are critical to you—and you work with your imagination. Memory by itself is the province of nonfiction—you write what you remember, you remember what you take in notes or on a tape recorder. This is strictly memory—what really happened. The fiction writer combines memory with imaginative skills. And the outcome—the book, the novel—is part memory, part imagination—who knows what? You can't put percentages on it because it's all mixed together, but that's what it is. The very themes of the book are imagination and memory. In that sense it's about how one goes about writing fiction, the fictional process. But for me it's also about how life itself operates. I think our lives are largely, maybe totally, determined by what we remember and by what we imagine—it's a part of that goal-setting thing I talked about earlier. Whom we marry is determined partly by memory, partly by imagination. If you marry a blonde, it's perhaps because you remember this gorgeous blonde cheerleader you were hot for. But your fantasies also come into play. You imagine her as someone new. You imagine being her husband.

Memory and imagination as devices of survival apply to all of us whether we are in a war situation or not. It's a tricky question. Obviously the book is set in a war, and a large part of the subject matter has to do with war. But then you ask the question, "What is war?" It has to do with big philosophical and moral issues. Right and wrong. Being brave. How does one go about doing the proper thing? Is it right to run from the war or right to stay there? Courage and justice. Those are issues that are embedded in our daily lives. I think that as an outside reader, if I were to pick up my book and read it, my feeling would be that I wasn't really reading a war novel; I would perhaps feel that a trick had been played on me. Here's a book passing as a war novel, but it's not really that: it's not like *The Naked and the Dead*, it's not like Quentin Reynolds, it's not like Hemingway's war stuff. It's quirky. It goes somewhere else; it goes *away* from the war. It starts there and goes to Paris. A *peace* novel, in a sense.

One of the things that I worried about in writing it was that I was disobeying the conventions of war literature, the "war genre." But then I thought it's maybe just enough writing a book. It's a war novel on the surface, but it's about lots of other things too.

Schroeder: As you say, it does seem to be really a book more about peace than war, about coming to peace with oneself, making those decisions that are going to make one a man. Thus it's significant that Cacciato and Paul Berlin are running to Paris; after all, Paris was the center of the peace talks. Was that a conscious choice?

O'Brien: Yes, that was. That's largely why I chose Paris as a destination. I knew that I wanted to finish the book with a peace-table scene. In every novel there has to be a central tension if the story's going to be any good—what's going to happen to Ahab? Is he going to get the whale or not?—that kind of central, driving impetus. In *Cacciato* this has to do with how Paul Berlin's going to resolve his philosophical dilemma. Is he going to run, or is he going to stay? What's he going to decide?

There is this sense of moral decision making; the book is one long decision. And so I chose Paris not only because the peace talks were in progress there, but for all kinds of metaphorical reasons—the City of Light and Justice, the symbol of civilization, the Golden City—and also because the Peace of Paris was signed there. For all kinds of reasons it was the ideal site.

But also it makes psychological sense. For a guy like Cacciato or Berlin it would be the obvious choice of destination. I mean, where else would they go? Someone else might choose Albania or some such place if he thought there was an esoteric reason for it, though it would represent the same thing. But not those guys; they aren't the type. As you say, they aren't highly intellectual. They're naïve in a lot of ways. For a naïve person Paris is the obvious choice.

Schroeder: In the same way that Paul Berlin must come to terms with himself, must come to peace within himself, is there a larger purpose behind the book, which is to assess the American experience in Vietnam: America coming to terms with its sense of duty on the one hand and its actual purposes in Vietnam on the other?

O'Brien: I don't think so. In any case I didn't think of it that way when I was writing it. One of the things about fiction is that the writer has to be careful in assigning meaning to his own work. If we were on some kind of public forum and somebody asked that type of question, all I would say is "maybe," because you can't make decisions like that. I try to rinse away any kind of authorial moralizing, whether it's directed toward the country (as you suggested) or toward personal decision making.

Schroeder: Do you think, though, that a book like *Cacciato* does have a didactic force in bringing people back to terms with Vietnam? In recalling

Vietnam to them, does it somehow make Americans aware of the experience, and in making them aware of the *issues* can it help them come to a personal peace over Vietnam?

O'Brien: Yes, that's probably true. All my work has been somewhat political in that it's been directed at big issues. It's not this sort of contemporary tendency to examine purely personal daily concerns—the minutia of life. My concerns have to do with abstractions: what's courage and how do you get it? What's justice and how do you achieve it? How does one do right in an evil situation? There's a didactic quality to the book. It's not the answer to those questions; it's simply their posing in literature which gives them the importance that I think they deserve. Too much contemporary literature seems to me trivial and aimed at rather frivolous objectives. It's not tackling big stuff. This has become a waste of talent and technique and craft and all the rest. If one's going to spend time writing anything, it makes sense to tackle big, important stuff. Not that I even try to provide answers. My aim is just to give those issues a dramatic importance. See what I'm getting at? You don't try to answer questions. You simply pose them in human terms and make them important to readers so that they end up caring about some guy who's trying to decide what to do. "Am I going to stay in the war?" By caring about the issues maybe the reader will carry that concern over to his or her own life. I'm not trying to answer questions but to dramatize the impact of moral philosophy on human life.

Schroeder: Do you think that Americans are coming to terms with questions about Vietnam?

O'Brien: No, not with Vietnam. I think that most Americans are too comfortable. One of the reasons that I write (and one of the goals of literature in general) is to jar people into looking at important things. Much of our lives is spent thinking about clothing ourselves and our families and feeding ourselves and so on, so that we rarely try to grapple with philosophical issues. A good novel will seduce you into caring about those things—maybe only temporarily—but for the three hours it takes to read *Cacciato*, you have to pay attention to that stuff because that's what the book's about. For the average soap-opera watcher, the book isn't going to have much appeal unless the reader can somehow be seduced into the drama of the dream, of the story.

It's not really Vietnam that I was concerned about when I wrote *Cacciato*; rather, it was to have readers care about what's right and wrong and about the difficulty of doing right, the difficulty of saying no to a war. There are all these pressures on you to go to war. In my latest book, *The Nuclear Age,* I'm dealing with the difficulties of confronting the obvious: that the bombs are out there. Until very recently no one even noticed them. I look at literature (at what I do as literature, in any case) as a way of jarring people into paying attention to things—not just the war but your personal stake in the political world.

Schroeder: Vietnam nonfiction often seems much more potent than the fiction. A book like *Dispatches* has a much more powerful impact than almost all of the novels that have been written. One of Herr's constant concerns is to demonstrate the "reality" of the war's *un*reality. Your work is different; *Cacciato* is clearly more reflective than *If I Die*, raising as it does questions of imagination and of the nature of reality. Do you think that the failure of some of these fictional works has something to do with the realistic mode many of them are couched in? That perhaps Vietnam's "unreality" defies this particular mode?

O'Brien: No, I don't think so. I think it's just very hard to articulate. Vietnam was an experience that many people in America had felt that they had gone through because of television; they felt that they were veterans of the war. If you watch people die on television night after night, you begin to think that you are an eyewitness—maybe even in a sense a subconscious participant in that conflict. Subsequently, they are unwilling to understand that they weren't participants, that no matter how many hours you watch people dying on television, you don't have to stay up at night on guard duty, you don't worry about being killed, you don't have any personal jeopardy, and so on. I think that in that sense television made people more open to realistic nonfiction—televisionlike things—as a way of reliving or revalidating what they perceived as a personal experience. That's the only thing that I can think of.

For me Vietnam wasn't an unreal experience; it wasn't absurd. It was a cold-blooded, calculated war. Most of the movies about it have been done with this kind of black humorish, *Apocalypse Now* absurdity: the world's crazy; madman Martin Sheen is out to kill madman Marlon Brando; Robert Duvall is a surfing nut. There's that sense of "well, we're all innocent by reason of insanity; the war was crazy, and therefore we're innocent." That doesn't go down too well.

Schroeder: Well, this seems to be a rather recent development because many of the early novels don't come across that way. Many of the novels

come across in what we characterized earlier as this World War II fashion—
you charge up the hill, fire your weapons, and the enemy falls down dead.

O'Brien: Yes, tick 'em off. Gustav Hasford's book is one I think of, and
Jim Webb's certainly is. But when it comes to your original question, I really
don't know the answer to it. I don't know why novels haven't succeeded as
well as nonfiction in gaining a general widespread popularity. One possibility is that they aren't as good, that they aren't as well written. For many
novels, that's true; many published novels should have been written as
nonfiction because their *content* is nonfiction: the authors are not trying to
imagine; they're writing purely from memory. They'll give fictitious names
to characters, but you're actually seeing a home movie of what really
happened to somebody. Good novels don't work on that principle. Novels
will fail if you do that. Too many fail for the very reason that they should
have been nonfiction; they should have been cast as war memoirs. They
don't do what novels ought to do, which is to let your imagination add to
memories. That's all I can think of that explains it. Personally, I don't like
most of the novels nearly as well as the nonfiction.

Schroeder: Have you read *Dog Soldiers*?

O'Brien: Yes. I loved that book. I'm not sure it's about Vietnam, but of
course mine isn't either.

Schroeder: I was going to say that *Dog Soldiers* seems to do the same sort
of thing that both you and Micheal Herr do: it's a book that uses Vietnam as
a point of departure for discussing other issues and ideas.

O'Brien: It's one of my favorite books. It's a wonderful novel. I just
finished *A Flag for Sunrise*—it's just a real blowout. Of the contemporary
writers I admire, Stone and Herr are at the top of the list. They're it. They
write literature; they do work that goes beyond the mundane. They
transform their material into something that's going to last. It has resonance,
vividness. It grabs your emotions and squeezes them.
   Both *Dog Soldiers* and *A Flag for Sunrise* are works of a lasting writer.
Dog Soldiers is a Vietnam book in a sense, though I don't know if Bob thinks
so or not. But I suspect he does. I suspect that he looks at it as I do at
Cacciato. It's not a war novel, exactly, but it is clearly anchored in the events
and in the moral concerns and evils of that era. There is a sense of evil out
there that one's trying to battle against, but always with a sense of futility.

This is coupled with an impulse to try to run from it and to escape it; it's clearly there in *Dog Soldiers*, that frantic racing. After the stash, up to those mountains. What do you find when you get there? You find war. A real battle scene. The same kind of principle holds in *Cacciato* —despite that long-imagined trek to get to Paris, they end up doing barbarous things. You can't outrun it. I think that's why I admire Stone's work: he doesn't shy from evil; he really tackles it in a nice dramatic way.

Schroeder: When did you first realize or feel that you would be writing a book about Vietnam? When you first went to Vietnam, did you have *If I Die* in mind, or was it something that evolved?

O'Brien: It happened while I was there. Partly I began writing little anecdotes, four or five pages. Not stories but vignettes. But I didn't think of them as a book. I thought of them as little vignettes. I wasn't sure what they were or why I was doing it. But having got back a year later, I had accumulated a stack of them. Some of them were terrible, and some of them were pretty good. I never seriously thought it was going to be a book until it was done. At no point did I think I was writing a book. At no point did I think of even sending it to a publisher. I was in grad school, and my concerns were academic. I wanted to get through my doctoral program. I wanted to pass the orals and get the dissertation written. Writing was kind of a sidelight. At night, when I was tired of studying, I would hack out a chapter. I didn't call them chapters, just little things. Then I began putting them roughly in chronological order, but not exactly. At some point I thought, "Why not?" And then, very quickly—I mean in a month or so— I stitched it together into a book and sent it off. After sending it off, I forgot about it. And when the publisher called to say he'd accepted it, I couldn't remember sending it to him. I mean that particular guy. I knew it was someplace. I remember one of the odd things that happened was that I sent it to Knopf (this was in '72) and had a letter saying, "We like it very much, but we have a book under contract called *Dispatches*." This was about five years before Herr even finished his book.

Schroeder: And you hadn't published anything before that?

O'Brien: No books. I had published in *Playboy* a chapter of *If I Die*—or what became a chapter; also a couple of pieces that I had sent from Vietnam were published in the *Minneapolis Tribune* and in my hometown newspaper. But the *Playboy* thing was the only major piece that had been published.

Schroeder: Do you feel that *If I Die* really paved the way for *Cacciato*?

O'Brien: Yes. I'm glad I got it out of my system. Otherwise I would have ended up writing one of these books that we were just talking about, autobiography cast as fiction. The power of *If I Die* is the same sort that one gets from a book like Ron Kovic's. It's just there as a document. It's not art. I didn't know what literature was. *If I Die* is just a straightforward telling: "Here's what happened to me." But these little things that we talked about— adding dialogue, for instance—these made *Cacciato* possible. Otherwise I'd have written a *Cacciato* which wasn't *Cacciato*: it wouldn't have been nearly so good. I look at those two books, and one of them I think of as my effort at literature and one as my effort at just relating an experience that happened to me, as I would tell a friend.

Schroeder: You've made the distinction that those who write simply from memory write nonfiction, whereas those who write fiction use memory but additionally use imagination to compress and intensify experience. What if you want to write about a particular experience, though, and you have no memory, no personal experience to begin with? I'm thinking in particular of those sections of *Cacciato* set outside Vietnam.

O'Brien: In the Paris section, for example, I don't want to sound like a tourist, but I do want to describe with an informing eye, a kind of tourist's eye—what the city was like—because I figured that would be more or less what the characters in the book would have, a surface knowledge of the city. It was the only part of the book that I researched in any way at all. I figured I should know at least as much as Berlin would know—the general layout of the city—and not much more. The sections on Tehran and Afghanistan were entirely made up. That's the best way to write a novel. Again, I wasn't tied to real stuff. I made up names for things: the courthouse, for instance. A lot of language is made up. In the Mandalay section, I made up the name for the monks and so on. That's what I'm getting at. There's a sense of playfulness to it that isn't possible in nonfiction. Where you don't have to have such a sense of fidelity to fact and reality, you're not going to know all the names of things; you're going to imagine things. When I looked at it as Paul Berlin's imagination, I thought that I may as well imagine it myself, sometimes anchoring it in stuff that he might know. He might know that the SAVAK was a police agency in Tehran, and he might imagine the jail cell, and he might imagine being beheaded. But while some of that will come from what he might know of the real world—his knowledge of the SAVAK, perhaps—much of it—people being beheaded and the fly on the nose—is imagined. It's that kind of combination which couldn't happen if I had to write a book about really going to Iran; those things just wouldn't happen.

Schroeder: While surface detail is a necessary ingredient in fiction, sometimes a lack of detail can be equally effective. For instance, the character who is really the most fascinating in *Cacciato* is Cacciato himself.

O'Brien: Yes, he is, isn't he?   That suggests that the less said about someone, the more compelling. It's something that every novelist should remember. Something I tend to forget. People have the feeling that the way to make character is by trying to nail down every little specific of mannerism, dress, and physical appearance—how tall? what's the exact shade of the hair?—when, in fact, some of the more memorable characters (for me, all memorable characters) are remembered for one thing. All I can remember about Ahab is that he chased the whale, that he was obsessed by it. That's why I have Cacciato obsessed about going to Paris. Or I think of Huck Finn. Does he have red hair and freckles, or is that just on the cover of my book? I can't remember if Twain gave him red hair or not. I know in the movie Huck's hair was red. But I really can't remember if he *actually* had it. All I remember is his quest, the lighting off for the West, getting on that raft. This is something that for a novelist is so easy to forget, because you think that the way to get your readers to believe in your characters is to supply a lot of detail. But a reader doesn't remember it all; he can't process it all. The best way to get at characters is through a single *idea* of a character: the idea of chasing a whale, of getting on a raft. This is half "plottish"—chasing a whale—but it's also half idea, the idea of lighting out or of being obsessed by something. As a character, Cacciato is memorable because the reader can fasten on this idea of a guy who's run away from the war. The reader doesn't have to worry about a lot of physical stuff.

Schroeder: For me Cacciato is memorable precisely because he is so vague. He's more of a symbol than a person; when I think of Cacciato, I think of the scene where Paul Berlin dreams that "Cacciato's round face became the moon."

O'Brien: That's exactly how I think of him.

Schroeder: That's the characteristic I remember most vividly.

O'Brien: As another example of this fiction/nonfiction split, there's a character like Cacciato in *If I Die*. In fact, Cacciato has his genesis in this fellow from my own basic training whose name was Kline. Kline was this klutzy guy with tiny beady eyes. A *complete* klutz. He came to reveille one morning wearing two left boots. Erik Hansen and I were always looking at each other and thinking, "Is he *really* this klutzy?" Or was it an incredible act that he was using to get out of Vietnam? Because if he's really that klutzy, he could be recycled through basic training to infinity. And it was this notion of a character who from the surface evidence was stupid that gave rise to Cacciato. Is Cacciato naïve, an innocent? Is he a cipher who acts purely on animal instinct? Or, as Berlin asks, is Cacciato smart? Has he got more going for him than everybody thinks? It's one of the mysteries of the book. I keep the reader off guard, thinking, "When am I going to meet Cacciato? When am I going to find out what his motives were? I'd like to pin this guy down." I never let this happen. Even though Berlin sees him. I stop the scene so that the reader never gets to grab the guy. If you *were* to grab him and to examine him in minute detail, then you would run the risk of being mundane-Cacciato would be ordinary. His dialogue, the explication of his character, would undercut the mystery of the guy. This again is the distinction between fiction and nonfiction. In *If I Die* I treat the character in detail. I describe him, what he did, and so on, and remove the mystery: "Maybe he's really a smart kid who's acting dumb." But by describing him in such detail, I make it clear to the reader that this guy really *is* dumb. In Cacciato, though, I can let the mystery stand.

Schroeder: The other image of Cacciato that is so memorable occurs in the chapter "World's Greatest Lake Country." Cacciato is fishing, and everybody knows there are no fish in those craters. Yet he persists. It's as if he knows something no one else knows, or that by a sheer act of will he can *will* fish into those craters.

O'Brien: That's the feeling I'm trying to evoke. That's exactly it. It's the sense that "maybe there is something there that nobody else knows about." A sense that "well, it's not very likely, and yet maybe—" It's the sense of "maybe" that I really like about his character. And it is this sense that runs thoughout the book. "Maybe so."

Photograph by Jerry Bauer

Larry Heinemann:
"Novels Are More Polite than a Simple 'Fuck You'"

Schroeder: You grew up in a working-class family and none of your brothers went to college. Were you interested in writing when you were growing up?

Heinemann: No, I grew up in a house where there were no books. Of four brothers, I'm the only one that graduated from college. One other brother went to college; two of my brothers never graduated from high school. The jive in our house was "Finish high school, get a job." My old man came through the Depression with the belief that you get a job for food, a real sort of Depression-survivor mentality. I hadn't the least interest in writing or literature, although when I was in high school I took four years of English. I took a lot of history and humanities courses because they were just interesting. But it never occurred to me to get into writing until after I came out of the Army.

Schroeder: You were partly using college to avoid the war for a while.

Heinemann: Yeah, I was just like everybody else. I went three years to a junior college. It was a place called Kendall College in Evanston, right across the street from Northwestern University. I wanted my 2-S deferment, just like everybody else. I graduated in January '66—graduated and ran out of money at the same time. I was going to take a semester off to make some money and then go out to San Francisco State. I was interested in theater more than anything else, and San Francisco State at that time had a good reputation.

I got drafted, just like that; got scarfed up, just picked up real quick, because a lot of kids on the North Shore had more money than I did, and iron-clad deferments. It's a very affluent part of the country. So they were picking up everybody they could. It was mostly guys like me.

I came out of the Army very highly motivated. All of a sudden I became a very highly motivated student. I went to a small arts college here in Chicago, called Columbia College, and just sort of bumped into writers. There was the fellow who was the chairman of the fiction department, not the English department, the fiction department. He had been a medic in Korea during the Korean war, although not a combat medic. He was also a contributing editor for *Evergreen Review*, which, just for the record, back then was one of the leading left, liberal, radical journals of the country, connected somehow very strangely with Grove Press. Maybe they just shared the same offices or something, I don't know. But this guy was more than curious about what was going on overseas, more than just "tell us a war story." You see, a lot of the kids I went to school with were very active in the antiwar movement, very active in the peace movement in Chicago and around the country, and were seriously committed to ending the war. A number of them thought that the Army was just full of shit and being drafted was stupid. But, beyond that, they understood that the war was really a bad thing. I didn't have the kind of ambivalent welcome that a lot of GIs were treated to when they came back. I know guys who said that when they went back to school they didn't say anything about having been overseas. But I wasn't one of those guys. Part of it had to do with the fact that this teacher I had, this writing teacher, gave my war experience and the time I spent in the Army a tremendous validity in front of the other students, and I think that had a lot to do with them sort of sitting back and listening in a way that was more than serious: it was curiosity, and it was sort of a recognition of "There but for the grace of God go I." I got into writing that way.

Schroeder: You didn't write at all when you were overseas?

Heinemann: Oh, God, no. It never occurred to me to take a journal. I wrote letters to my wife before we were married (we didn't get married until after I came back). Her letters to me are much more interesting than my letters to her; my letters are just gibberish. If someone ever wanted to publish those letters, I would say no. Not because I won't let any secrets out, but because they're so poorly written. They're junk; they're just not worth reading. I reread them—she kept mine, and I kept hers—and when I was writing *Close Quarters* I remember at one point sitting down and going through all the letters and saying this is just total bullshit. I don't understand why this woman ever thought I was worth anything; the letters were just so poor.

Schroeder: When you came back and started writing in those classes, was it also partly therapy?

Heinemann: At the beginning, yeah. The first couple of years it was. When I came home, it took about two years to sit down and tell my wife everything.

Schroeder: Like Dozier in *Close Quarters.*

Heinemann: Yeah. But then to go over it and go over it and go over it and go over it and go over it—it's not cathartic. And *Paco's Story* was not catharsis in the least.

I started from a dead stop. I had never been a good student. I was reading dictionaries and bonehead English books, and I graduated in '71 and started teaching there part-time, teaching English, teaching freshman English. It began to dawn on me that I was writing a novel, and so I started reading other war stories, *The Iliad* and *The Odyssey*, *War and Peace*, and every war story I could get my hands on. Just to find out what the war story genre was.

Schroeder: At that point, were you reading any Vietnam stuff? There hadn't been much published at that point.

Heinemann: There hadn't been much published. There was almost nothing published.

Schroeder: This was around '69? '68?

Heinemann: Well, '68, '69, '70, '71. In 1972, Michael Casey was named the Yale Younger Poet, and a volume of his work came out—

Schroeder: *Obscenities*?

Heinemann: Yeah. That was in '72. And that was the first imaginative writing I had seen out of the war; Michael Herr had had several articles published, which later were collected into *Dispatches*, and his writing—well, I didn't know what to think of his writing. But I wanted to see what the other soldiers were writing about, the other guys that were going to school. When I began teaching I taught a writing class somewhat facetiously

called "The Psychology of War: The Combat Experience." The class was
for veterans only; I think the most students we ever had was five people.

Schroeder: Where was this?

Heinemann: This was at Columbia. Columbia College here in Chicago, not
the Columbia in New York.

Schroeder: That must have been a tremendous class, though.

Heinemann: It was. We learned an awful lot. Two books came out of that.
One, *The Five Man War* by Charles Bellinger, who had been a helicopter
pilot, was published as a paperback a number of years later by Playboy Press,
and the other was *Close Quarters*. Some good writing came out of that class;
I got a great deal out of it.

Schroeder: When did you start working on *Close Quarters*? It came out in
'77, right?

Heinemann: I started working on it in '68.

Schroeder: Was your experience similar to Michael Herr's in writing
Dispatches in that it took you a long time to see how the material was going
to come together?

Heinemann: Well, partly I didn't know what writing was, and I didn't know
what writing a novel was going to be like. Part of it was simply finding a way
to tell the story, to find a language and a wherewithal beyond the craft,
beyond all the rhetoric and technicalities. The other thing, too, I understood
perfectly well without having anybody tell me was that there was no fiction
being published, so I could take my time. I didn't even bother sending
anything out until '74.
  Penthouse magazine had been doing a monthly series of Vietnam
nonfiction, and I sent them a forty-page chapter from *Close Quarters*,
"Coming Home High," about the plane ride home. The editor called me and
said, "We'll take it, but you have to cut it." So I cut it about in half. Then
the next year, I sold them another piece, and then got an agent. The year after
that I finished the first draft of the novel that I would show anybody. That
was in '75, and we sent it around to maybe a dozen places. The editor at
Farrar Straus wrote this very nice rejection letter and gave me some good

advice. The draft was only about 188 pages; it was just this little bitty pile of paper. Basically, the book was about a hundred pages short. So I took the manuscript back and took another year and rewrote it, and in '76, resubmitted it. Farrar Straus took it in two weeks, which was very nice. Then we went through what is called the rewrite of the final manuscript. I can't remember how many pages we started with, it was over 250; by the time I got through rewriting the final, edited manuscript, it was 420 pages.

Schroeder: The other thing that had changed in that period, though, was the political climate in terms of these novels. Fiction was starting to get published. When you talk about how quickly they snatched it up, do you think part of that had to do with literary fashion, that all of a sudden it was okay to publish Vietnam novels?

Heinemann: At Farrar Straus, a woman named Pat Strachan was my editor for twelve years. She and I talked about this many times. She was an editor's assistant at that time, and she said that *Close Quarters* was the first Vietnam novel that she saw. Her take on it was that people simply weren't ready to read about the war. And all of a sudden—I guess in '76—*Born on the Fourth of July* was published and then in '77 came *Close Quarters* and *A Rumor of War*, which were published the same week, and then *Dispatches* that fall. Before 1975, you could count the good books written by grunts on the fingers of one hand: there's David Rabe's plays, *The Basic Training of Pavlo Hummel* and *Sticks and Bones*; there was Michael Casey's collection of poetry, *Obscenities*; and a novel that no one has ever heard of by Robert Roth called *Sand in the Wind*. A superb, really sterling book, and I've never seen anything by him since. I would really like to sit down and buy that man a drink, because I thought it was just a dynamite story. I learned a lot from him and really learned a lot from Michael Herr.

Schroeder: There were a few other early books, but you're right, they weren't by grunts. They were novels by journalists, like David Halberstam's first novel, *One Very Hot Day*, and John Sack's *M*.

Heinemann: And that's the difference between the films before *Platoon* and the films since *Platoon* because Stone and these other guys are people who have direct experience of war. That's the difference in the quality of the films; there's just some extra jive there that you don't get even with *Apocalypse Now*, or *The Deer Hunter*, which were superb films. It's interesting that David Rabe's *Streamers* was taken by Robert Altman and made into a film. That is a powerful, powerful film. I think it's a powerful film because it's a piece of film adapted from literature, and not an original screenplay. Sometimes I get the idea that filmmakers don't know how to write. I was amazed to find out that screenplays are rarely beyond a hundred pages. I'm one of those guys that thinks there's no such thing as a short story. There just aren't any.

Schroeder: I've heard you say this.

Heinemann: It's a great gag. I don't see how you could make a decent film in under three hours. I'm sure a lot of filmmakers agree with me, but nobody will sit still for that long.

Schroeder: The short story is undergoing a tremendous rebirth right now, but I haven't seen any collections of Vietnam stuff. There were some collections that came out years ago, but they were collections by various people.

Heinemann: The VVAW [Vietnam Veterans Against the War] did a collection of short stories and a collection of poetry. Tim O'Brien's new book, *The Things They Carry*, is supposed to be a collection of sorts.

O'Brien and Caputo and Yusef Komunyakaa and Bruce Weigl and W. D. Ehrhart and Larry Rottman and I are going to Vietnam for three weeks in June as a delegation of writers at the invitation of the Writers' Union in Vietnam. We're going to Hanoi, the DMZ, Hue City, Danang, My Lai, Ho Chi Minh City (which Tim Page calls "Ho'ville"). All of this makes it sound like I know everybody, but I really don't.

Schroeder: Have you seen Page recently?

Heinemann: No, no, I just got a postcard from him. He's in Hanoi now; he was in Laos and Cambodia, looking for Sean Flynn's grave. When he was there in '85, somebody finally told him that Flynn had been captured, taken to a POW camp in Cambodia, and killed in a B-52 airstrike. So he's back looking for Flynn's grave, which is a very cool thing to do.

Schroeder: Was Dana Stone killed in that strike as well?

Heinemann: Yeah, he and Stone got captured together. I haven't seen a copy of *The Things They Carried*. I'm interested to see it. I'm eager to see it. Actually, I'm obliged to read it because he and I are going to be traveling together. I better go with my shit together.

Schroeder: Some of the most successful Vietnam novels were the ones that weren't realistic. In many ways, isn't it harder to write realistic novels about Vietnam? I think this may be so for two reasons: first, because the war did have that surreal quality; second, because the war novel as a genre has become almost formulaic, and I think that's due to the nature of the experience itself. If you look at realistic novels, people start in boot camp, and then they go where *Close Quarters* starts: they show up in Vietnam, and they're inexperienced, they don't know anything, and then they gradually go through this process where they become aware of what's going on around them. And then they go back home. So that there is this real life experience which is the same for most people.

Heinemann: There's a couple notable things here. When I read Paul Fussell's book, *The Great War in Modern Memory*, he really ran down what the war story genre was. I had never thought about it particularly until I read the book, and he's really right: it's the first literary effort by the person, since most war novels are fictionalized memoirs. I used to be sort of embarrassed by that, but I don't see any other way to do it. For a young writer any undeniable, remarkable event is going have such a powerful imaginative pull that the only way to tell the story is just tell it flat out straight. I think that you could go back in literature a considerable way and find realistic fiction emerging from a war.

I think the difference with Vietnam really has to do with the fact of just where literature was going. You have the examples of *Catch-22* and *Slaughterhouse Five*. I didn't read *Catch-22* until I was at Fort Knox just ready to ship over, and I refused to leave the barracks. I had about a month to go before I was going to ship over, and I said, "Fuck this. I'm going to just read this fucking book in my bunk, and everybody else can go take a squat." I just couldn't believe it. What a dynamite book. Fuckin' Yossarian, I mean, everybody is nuts but him. Were you in the Army?

Schroeder: No.

Heinemann: There's nothing more nutty. If you're an intelligent person, you have to deal with the military mind—being told what to do twenty-four hours a day by lifers, people that in any other circumstance would be shoveling shit in Louisiana somewhere, who don't have the brains, who just don't have it. The guys who think that the Army is just great. And the Army is just a piece of shit. I don't know if anybody else has discussed the military mind with you, but there are people who are running the military, including the Joint Chiefs, who are stone fucking crazy. I think James Webb is stone fucking crazy. Guys like Oliver North—stone fucking crazy. If he had to go out and get a real fucking job, he would be out in the fucking cold. Just trying to explain that kind of insanity in fiction is difficult.

Schroeder: You even see this in nonfiction. You get it in Herr.

Heinemann: That's one of the beauties of that book. He's one of the few journalists who really got the joke. He really understood what he was looking at. That's why that book is so brilliant because the whole military is just bullshit. He had enough detachment, as well as enough intimate connection with the guys in the field. So it's both at once. It must have driven him crazy.

But I don't think the psychology of the war was necessarily any more bizarre in Vietnam than it was in Korea or in World War II. I think it was more concentrated. I think a lot more people were watching and taking film, and the film was being shown a lot. We were doing such strangely bizarre things. But no more bizarre than breaking the Enigma code or the 82nd and 101st Airborne doing a jump the night before the Normandy invasion. Eighteen thousand troops jumped; ten thousand were never seen again. Just disappeared. Jumped out of planes and gone. I don't think the psychology of being a soldier of an industrial nation has changed all that much since the Civil War. Trying to make that clear to people took on kind of a dreamlike aspect. Plus there's a whole movement of literature. You're trying to explain it to yourself at the same time you're trying to explain it to everybody else. Gustav Hasford's *Short Timers* was the first really sort of galloping, leaping kind of hysterical narrative. I shouldn't say hysterical, sort of breathless. I guess there have been others; I really haven't read all that much lately.

The thing that I learned—talking to the other students at Columbia, and reading other war novels and also the fact that in Vietnam I was in tracks [armored tracked vehicles], a sort of peculiar, esoteric experience—was that basically you're trying to explain an alien experience to people. I felt it was really important that people understand what the work was. War as a job, this is work. Everybody has an experience of a really shitty job. *Moby Dick* is about a lot of things, but it's really about the fact that Melville at one time in his life for a couple of months had this really shitty job. There's a lot of literature that comes out of that—good jobs, too, but lots of shitty jobs. I felt it was important that people understand just what happened and why things happened in this way or that way or the other. Explaining the war as work will start with that, and the story will build on that experience. So there's all the description about what a track is, and how to do an ambush, and how firefights work—that sort of detail.

Schroeder: Yeah, you are anticipating something I wanted to ask you about. In *Paco's Story*, the opening chapter, the ghost says some disparaging things about reporters. Was part of your purpose in writing both of the novels something other than purely artistic? It sounds like that's what you're saying now. In other words, it wasn't simply just to get at the truth we find in a novel, but was to explain how things were.

Heinemann: Hmmm.

Schroeder: It seems to me that's one thing that realistic fiction does; one thing it has in common with the nonfiction is that it tries to present a picture of what the war was all about, what happened, and the real details of that experience.

Heinemann: The odd thing about literature is, particularly in this half of the twentieth century, that nonfiction is probably more successful at that than fiction. The reason I like to write fiction rather than nonfiction is first of all you can make it up, you can just bullshit.

Schroeder: But with a book like *Close Quarters* the temptation on the part of the reader is to say that it's very thinly veiled autobiography.

Heinemann: OK. Take me away. [*Extending his hands for the handcuffs, he laughs, though with some exasperation.*] In my reading of nineteenth-century nonfiction, history, and biography, things like *The Voyage of the Beagle*, *Life on the Mississippi*, I see similar instances where the authors are trying to describe the details of their work. In *Life on the Mississippi*, for example, Twain is elaborate in his explanation of how much he loved that work and how much he regretted that the work couldn't continue. You get sort of the same thing in fiction, but it isn't reportage in my fiction; it's first this happened and then this happened and then this happened and then this happened and then this happened. I've had people tell me the big firefight scene in *Close Quarters* is probably the best firefight scene they've read; you really get a sense of the space and the noise and the aftermath and all that. It didn't matter to me that I was going to be accused of stealing all of this from nonfiction because I think that storytellers, fiction writers, can steal that stuff back.

Schroeder: But wasn't that particular scene taken from your own experience?

Heinemann: Yeah, as a matter of fact, Oliver Stone's battalion and my battalion were there. Why bother to make it up? His battalion and my battalion and two batteries of artillery were involved, and in one night we killed five hundred guys. And when I saw *Platoon*, I was positively astonished to see the scene where the camp is overrun, because there were just too many coincidences, coincidental images. I wrote to him (we have friends in common), and I said, "Were you at such and such a place at such and such a time?" He said yeah. He was in the Third Battalion of the 22nd Infantry, and I was in the Second Battalion of the 22nd. It didn't exactly happen like in the movie, but it was clear this was an event that had made a tremendous impression. It certainly was the worst night of my life. I wanted just to explain that. Tolstoy wrote about the Battle of Bordino, and he wasn't even born then. He went to guys that were there and had them tell him. But that's just what kind of a good writer he was.

Schroeder: It's like Crane and *Red Badge of Courage*.

Heinemann: Yeah. Like that. That firefight was as close to a set-piece battle I ever saw. And it was the worst night of my life. I really wanted to explain that in the morning the woodline looked like ruined drapes. There was meat all over everything and everybody was pissed off and tired and thirsty and hungry and the first thing we did was smoke a joint. I wanted to get out of there. We had airstrikes for three days and there was the smell of all these corpses. It was in our mustaches and the water and our food. I can't remember ever feeling that poorly, just pissed off and depressed. One guy in our platoon was killed, and I was the one who found his corpse. The guy's corpse was about the size of a burnt turkey carcass. Fuck this, I just want to get stoned, I just wanted to sit there and sweat and be pissed off all by myself.

And all of a sudden, there was this Chinook helicopter full of reporters, journalists; these guys are climbing all over everything and asking all these asshole questions. Fuck you, you know. If you want to know what it's like, stick around. Stay the night, Jack. This television guy had his camera guy stand on the track and take photographs down into this ditch where they were burying all the corpses. Don't you fucking people have any idea what's going on here at all? And these guys all looked like a million bucks. So I really had the rag on for journalists. I felt that for everything that was being written about the war and all the film that was being broadcast, there were still these extraordinary distortions about what was going on overseas.

Schroeder: That was exactly what Michael Herr said. He didn't feel that the truth was being told in any way.

Heinemann: Yeah. When I got home, I would watch the news just to find out what was going on, and it was gibberish. The images that I knew were not being seen—the spirit of the troops and the gut feeling of the people in the field, and just the whole madness of it, the psychotic madness, because the psychologists have a word for battle-hardened soldiers, "combat psychosis." That means you're stone fucking crazy. You accept this madness. None of that was coming through at all. It was all bullshit rhetoric and body count. They put a lot of jive into body count. That's one of the things that convinced me when I finally discovered I was writing a novel to go ahead and write the novel because there were a lot of things that were just not coming through. I think Herr and Page and Halberstam, Neil Sheehan, Gloria Emerson—people like that who really worked hard and understood what was going on—I think that they were trying to argue, but nobody was listening. But I didn't have a lot of respect for journalists and photographers generally. I never ran into Page; I suppose that Page would've come to the platoon with a film can full of dope. "Yeah, we got something to trade you here for it, sure." That's pretty hip; what an entrée. "Here, have some dope." "Thanks, because we don't get much of it out here." Interesting man.

But the experimental fiction that I was kind of horsing around with, it just didn't fit. The closest I came to it, I think, is one scene where they're smoking dope and playing cards in the back of the track, and Dozier picks up the red-filtered flashlight and has this sort of wet-dream reverie. This kind of masturbation reverie that he gets into later. That's about as close as any of that comes. But just to tell the story straight was so bizarre. For instance, I think I'm one of the first writers to talk about what actually happens on R&R. You take a thousand dollars and spend a week in a Tokyo whorehouse. My editor, Pat Strachan, is a very tall elegant woman, went to Duke University, and I'm sure she and I would not have met in a million years if she hadn't been my editor. She would call me up every couple days and say, "Is this right? Did you actually do this?" "Well, some of it's bullshit, but yeah." When she got to the R&R chapter, she was positively mortified. She said, "They've been making love all night. Is that possible?" I said, "Well, Pat, you've probably never been on R&R." And I tried to explain to her just how fucking horny I was. And this is the woman who edited *Paco's Story* with her eighteen-month-old daughter sitting on her lap, and so was reading *Paco's Story* from a very particular point of view.

Schroeder: I think one of the things which *Close Quarters* does so successfully is render interior states in a way that a lot of the realistic novels don't. Rather than try to paint your canvas really broad and have a cast of hundreds of characters, you've got a smaller cast of characters, but we really get to know Dozier well. We see a lot of what's going on in his mind, and he talks a lot.

Heinemann: The story is told from Dosier's personal, physical point of view, so the "canvas" will be small—the human voice is inaudible at two hundred feet—and the characters are few to keep the story simple and manageable for me. The title *is Close Quarters*, which conveys many levels of claustrophobia.

I discovered right away (and my writing instructor had taught me) that when you're writing something that, imaginatively, is just compelling—a year out of my life that was so vivid in my mind—the story just can't be denied. To retell the story is basically to relive it. It's fun and it's not fun because you remember all of the things. There wasn't a round-eyed white woman within a thousand miles of us, but we had great parties, just these get down, squat naked, higher than a fucking kite, just puking drunk, shitfaced drunk, parties. In these little bitty tents, with these two-dollar stereos and all these dusty tapes, just everybody having a hell of a good time, juxtaposed with this mean, mean ugliness that you couldn't deny, to be honest with yourself, you just couldn't deny it. Being a grunt was the meanest, ugliest, most grueling, ball-breaking work I have ever done—*and* for thirteen cents an hour.

So, on one level, I was seeing it vividly; on the next level, I was actually reliving the experience. Then, at another level which gave me more distance, I was quite aware of being very reflective about the whole event. And not just this one event, but the whole thing. A year's tour is dramatically, utterly pat. It begins here and ends here. I didn't want to do anything with basic training because everybody's told basic training stories to death. And basic training stories are just puppy shit compared to everything else. There's a reason why James Jones stops *From Here to Eternity* at the beginning of the Second World War: because the rest of it is a whole other story.

I was very much aware of the fact that there was this ongoing reflection as if, after all, the story was happening all at once. I do think that's the one thing in the story that made it possible to tell it in that way. If this is a fictionalized memoir, then there is a great deal of reminiscence, and kind of a puzzling along. Early on in the story, Dozier is talking about growing up— he was raised with a leather strap—and I can't remember exactly what he says, but it's something like "What did I ever do to deserve this?" That's something that informs the whole story all the way along. I realized very quickly that there were these levels of distance, notches of distance, and as a writer you could bounce from one to the other, so that some scenes are very immediate and other scenes seem to be a little more removed.

Schroeder: *Paco's Story* begins with "the first clean fact" and with the ghost saying, "This is not a war story." The irony is that it *is* a war story and contains lots of war stories. Tim O'Brien in *If I Die in a Combat Zone* says that the only thing the soldier can do is to tell war stories. We don't necessarily learn anything from hearing them, but that this is the soldier's responsibility. Does this sound right?

Heinemann: Yes, it does—is "responsibility" your word or his word?

Schroeder: It's probably mine. [*Checks notes.*] What he said exactly is that "What can the soldier do? The soldier can tell stories." The implication is that's all he can do.

Heinemann: I think that he's right, but that there's more to it. He's compressing a great deal. It's interesting that you would mention the word "responsibility," because that's one of the things that has struck me about writing and storytelling. When you tell someone a story, basically you are passing it on to them, and you make them responsible for it. You can see this most dramatically in pre-literate societies, where all the wisdom of the people, all the ways to do things, the creation stories, the mythology of the people, the history of the people, is transmitted orally, and the people who listen become responsible for all of this sheer information. When it comes time for them to turn around and tell someone else, they'd better get it right. Hunting is a perfect example. Sioux Indians, before they had Spanish horses, would somehow get a buffalo herd to leap off a buffalo jump. How do you do that? How do you get people to cooperate in that way? How do you transmit any urgent skill: how to fish for salmon, how to string a bow, where to look for certain kinds of herbs? If I'm the medicine man, and you come to me and say you want to be a medicine man, and I can't explain to you, out loud, and make you remember what's what and what to leave alone, you're not going to amount to much.

It seems to me that storytelling is the same way. I have a lousy background in literature, it's not very organized at all. But it seemed to me the stories which really touched me in a visceral way and the stories that allowed me to participate imaginatively were this kind of really compelling work. I don't know that you can read something like *All Quiet on the Western Front* and not feel this tremendous sort of horror; or read *Mrs. Dalloway* and not get a real fellow feeling for this upper-class British lady; or *Moby Dick* and not walk away with some connection with all of the characters, Queequeg and Ahab, particularly, but also the whale, as well as the ship and the work. So there's something about telling a story in such a way, and it does have to do with the quality of writing, I think, because nobody's going to read writing on strong subjects that's not well-written. *Mein Kampf*, for instance—we probably would have saved ourselves all sorts of trouble if Hitler had been a better writer because people would have read it and understood what the fuck he was talking about. They didn't really believe that he was talking about all of this shit. I mean, he actually did what he said he was going to do.

Passing on this responsibility is important. My daughter, who's twelve, and my son, who's nine, have begun to ask me particular questions. They've seen my writing—I make no secret of it, and I'm not dishonest with them at all. I'm passing on this experience that really made an impression on me. The weird thing that happens is the people who listen to you get this sense of their own responsibility for this story, to turn around and retell it. It works another way too: one of the things I puzzled about, and one of the things this guy who was my instructor just flat out told me, was "Don't worry about exposing yourself." Because a lot of young writers have this thing about, well, should I tell everything? That kind of self-censorship is a disservice to the story; you are not taking responsibility for this story. He just flat out said—and I think it's true—that when you go ahead and take full responsibility for telling a story, including this considerable risk of self-exposure, an interesting thing happens: it's the reader who feels exposed, it's the person listening to the story who feels this exposure. When that happens you can also tell the writing is good because the person who is reading the story has been allowed to imaginatively participate.

Schroeder: Isn't that why a lot of people don't want to read Vietnam fiction?

Heinemann: Yes, that's true. I was once accused of violating good taste because there was a time when I thought I just wanted to take the war and shove it up everybody's ass. The night I won the National Book Award, this guy asked me why I wrote novels, and I said, "Well, it's more polite than a simple fuck you." I told this woman that taste is one of the reasons why the war dragged on for twenty years. That was at one of those idiot summer writing conferences in New England, the first and last time I ever blew two weeks at a writing conference.

There is this matter of seeing the story and telling the story in such a way that what is compelling to you is immediately compelling to the person who is reading or listening. And that's one of the things that Tim means (I shouldn't put words in his mouth), but also it's this matter of testifying once. It's like a woman who's been raped. It's important for her mental health to tell somebody and tell somebody she trusts.

Schroeder: There's another point in common that I've noticed between your writing and O'Brien's. When I was talking to Tim, he said something which struck me as curious at the time. We were talking about Paul Berlin in _Going After Cacciato_, and he said, "I was a little like Berlin, but quite different in many ways, because he noticed a lot of things I didn't see, and I noticed a lot of things that he didn't see." This struck me as odd because the character seems to assume a real life—he's talking about Paul Berlin as if Paul Berlin was a real person. I heard an interview you did in which you said about Dozier that you knew a lot about him, but he knew nothing about you.

Heinemann: That's right. I think it's critical for the authority of the story to conceive characters so they seem to have a life outside the story, even if you don't tell about that.

Schroeder: I'm wondering with Paco, if you knew as much about Paco as you knew about Dozier.

Heinemann: No. I admit I did cheat some.

Schroeder: Because he seems to be a much harder person to get to know.

Heinemann: No, I think Paco was much more mysterious. In some ways Paco grew out of the character Atevo in _Close Quarters_. This kind of mysterious, half-weird person. I originally conceived of Paco as a Mexican Indian from Arizona or New Mexico, but I don't know anymore. That might well be it. He was a man who did things that I wouldn't do. He had this utter confidence, like Crazy Horse, who was utterly convinced, he knew that when he went into battle he was invisible, and therefore could not be killed by a bullet. Well, son of a bitch, he wasn't. They had to knife him in the back from behind, so who's to say that that wasn't true?

Paco is one of these guys who is absolutely utterly firm that he's not going to die. When he's by himself, and he's stuck in all this shit—the shit that's the corpses of the ninety-three guys—and he's stuck in this shit, the only thing he can think to do is to repeat over and over, "I must not die. I must not die." And he doesn't. At a certain level, you have to accept that: Yes, he's not dead because he said, "I'm not going to die." That's the brilliance of his spirit. And he's willing to take all these shit jobs because of something that's utterly foreign to everybody he meets. I never did get to that, to explain what that is: it's really one of the weaknesses of the novel.

Schroeder: When we see him after Fire Base Harriette, he seems to be the living dead. One wonders, what did he live for, because the life that he's living seems void of any meaning.

Heinemann: Well, that's kind of odd. I went in wondering what's left for this guy, but believing if he didn't die when everybody else died, he has no business giving up. He's one of those guys who'll drink themselves to death by the time they're forty. He's not about to put a bullet in his head or give up that way.

One of the things I learned when I was overseas was that I had this superb concentration. When I was writing *Close Quarters*, there came a time when I was really cranking on the story, when I thought I could remember every moment. Just go through the thing moment by moment and get it right. To go back to this matter of the realistic novel, I think one of the other impulses to write *Close Quarters* was that I really wanted to be able to get it straight in my own mind, to validate in my own imagination what I had just been through. A general whisper in the country was denying the validity of an experience that was very vivid to me—no one else was agreeing with it. Nevertheless, I knew what I did, and I knew what I saw, and I knew what I became and that's what I was going to write about. I was going to set the record straight; I was going to straighten everybody out. Whether I did or not is another matter.

But a guy like Paco can't stand to have more money than he can keep in his pocket, maybe two hundred bucks altogether. He's one of those guys that's waiting to be woken up. And it really isn't going to happen. He's one of those guys that's been so devastated that there's this exquisite distance between him and everybody else. I think a lot of that has to do with the ghosts that move around with him and keep everybody at an arm's distance. Here's a guy who's not going to have any kind of intimate contact with anybody, ever. He's lost. So he's as good as a ghost.

Schroeder: In the opening chapter of *Paco's Story* you describe a scene in which a Filipino band is putting on their show, and everybody's around, slathering, watching the show. You make the statement, "Let's tell the truth, James, do you ever expect you'll see that scene in a movie?" The implication being, well, of course not. I'm wondering if things have changed, and if you think maybe we will see that scene. Can movies do the things that fiction does? Can they tell us the things we need to know in the way fiction can?

Heinemann: Well, they can, and they can't. There are some things that fiction does that just takes longer. There is an undeniable vividness about film that's just compelling. It's a different kind of storytelling, and it really depends on the intelligence of the person making the film, and in what they leave in. The one thing film has always had trouble with is point of view. Right now we're talking to a filmmaker about the movie rights for *Paco's Story*, and I'm intrigued, really curious, how he's going to represent on film the voice of the story, or how he's going to film the first twenty pages. If he does it to my satisfaction, I'd be tempted to give him his fucking money back.

You get a sense of the possibilities with a film like *Streamers*, it's just very, very, very tightly constructed; and you get a sense of it in a very rich story like *Apocalypse Now*—whereas the premise of the story is somewhat flat, the filmmaking is just dynamite. I'm not a big film goer, but I know that there are other examples of film as story that just can't be beat. I also know that there are other examples of fiction as story that are just unfilmable because the human voice can do more than film can. You have the restriction of time, of film width, of a certain spectrum of color—all these technical things that come into it, including sensual imagery. How do you film smell? Or touch? I think it must be just agonizingly difficult to make a superb film.

It's agonizingly difficult to write a good novel in a whole other way. It's certainly cheaper, but it takes longer, and it's only you. A perfect example would be *Born on the Fourth of July* the memoir and *Born on the Fourth of July* the film. Each is rich in its own way. When I was out in L.A. for the first time in my life last week I got to spend a long afternoon with Ron Kovic and a couple of friends of ours. He just waxed eloquent about the material they added to the film that is not in the book. I think, if somebody came to me and said they wanted to make a film of *Close Quarters*, I could think of a million things that have been left out. So, in a sense, he got to rewrite the story. And Stone, for all of his shortcomings, is a superb film maker. He knows what a story image is; he's one of those guys that's not capable of a subtle image, but that's okay, there's a lot of guys who aren't capable of a subtle image. I don't think William Burroughs is capable of a subtle image, and no one bitched at him because *Naked Lunch* is just a dynamite book. Reading the book makes you want to see the film, and seeing the film makes you want to read the book. I don't know how else to say it.

Schroeder: Do you worry about being labeled a "Vietnam writer"? You've done two novels and aren't you doing a nonfiction book on PTSD [Post Traumatic Stress Disorder]?

Heinemann: No, I put that aside about a year ago, because it just got to be too much. It's a very depressing subject. I got a Guggenheim fellowship last year and I worked on a Chicago novel some, and then on the first of the year we signed a book contract with Farrar, Straus. I'm finishing it up now, and it's called *Cooler by the Lake*. Vietnam is not mentioned once, and nobody dies, everybody gets laid.

Schroeder: Are you happy about that?

Heinemann: Yeah. I used every Chicago joke I know. The joke about the title is that it's the quintessential Chicago summertime weather report. It's always cooler by the lake. So every time the weather report comes on in the summer they're going to be plugging the book. That's the first joke. I'll be finished with that soon, and after I come back from this Vietnam trip, I'll pick up the nonfiction book.

Schroeder: So there's life after Vietnam?

Heinemann: Yes. I used to worry that there wasn't. I know Caputo used to be really firm about this: no more, no more. I got the same sense from Tim O'Brien: no more, no more. But they keep writing about it. Finally, it just occurred to me that right now that's okay, because those of us who know about it and can be articulate about it ought not just walk away from it because we have a responsibility. But the minute I get done with this nonfiction, I will have written three books on the subject, and cross my heart,

I'll have had my say. Anyone wants to talk to me about it, I'll refer them to a bibliography. The war has been like a nail in my head. The war has been like a corpse in my house, and I want it out.

But that won't happen until I finish the nonfiction book. If you are in a position to talk about something that's very important to you and you feel strongly about, you ought not deny it. Some friends of mine have said that the PTSD book is so upsetting it's just depressing. "Why don't you buy back your advance and just let it go?" they ask. The only way I know how to respond to that is, first of all, it offends my sense of completeness. If I didn't write the book, thirty or forty or fifty years from now, would I regret it? If writing the book drives me nuts, ruins my marriage, burns my house down to the ground, I will still have had twenty-two years of wonderful luck. Because I came back from overseas without a scratch. We're not rich, but we're not sleeping in the park. I've been very lucky, and if it drives me crazy, well, OK. Right now, though, I feel a tremendous sense of responsibility to tell the story. Also, as a writer, anything that you can conceive and experience imaginatively with this kind of undeniable energy, you can't deny. You really have to give out until you're done with it, go to the last mile, right down to the very end; otherwise you're shunning something that makes a person a human being, that makes me a masculine man. But I want to get it done as quick as I can. I'm not afraid to be a Vietnam writer in the same way that I am not ashamed to be called a Chicago writer. I've lived here all my fucking life. So, you can't deny it, you just have to make the best of it. What you have to do is to explain Chicago to everyone else so that they wished they lived here. There's a great song, it's a blues song—I can't remember the title of it—but one of the lines is "I'm going to Chicago, sorry, but I can't take you."

Photograph by Thomas Victor
Used by permission of HarperCollins

Bobbie Ann Mason:
"Eventually I Had to Confront the Subject"

Schroeder: You didn't set out to be a writer. You got your doctorate from University of Connecticut having written your dissertation on Nabokov. Had you planned on being an academic?

Mason: No; I *did* set out to be a writer, but I got sidetracked into those lines, which seemed to be the only thing I could find to do. There weren't many writing programs at the time. I graduated from college and just drifted into graduate school because I wanted to read and write, and the only place I could read and write was in school. I had no intention of being a teacher or a scholar.

Schroeder: Did graduate school in any way help you with that, practically speaking?

Mason: Well, it gave me some time to learn how to read. I hadn't had much of a literary education. I feel that I had a very sheltered background. Graduate school— academic pursuits and the style of speaking and writing—never took with me. I never understood what was going on or how to do it. I never understood politically what the issues were. I just like to read and write.

Schroeder: Did you have much time to write when you were in graduate school?

Mason: No. I wrote a lot of term papers. I would try to write, but I didn't have any encouragement anywhere, and I didn't have the right perspective on my material. I didn't know what my material was. It took me a long time to grow up, to see what there was to write about, and how to do it, and so on. I tried from time to time, but then I would give up. It took a while to find my way.

Schroeder: When you were young, you had a fantasy of being a writer, but did you have an idea of the sorts of things you wanted to write about then?

Mason: I started out writing mystery stories, like the children's mysteries I read when I was eleven. And then, when I was in high school and college, I was more interested in writing satire and funny essays, and I picked up on writing fiction in college—short stories. I think from the time I was in college, I knew I wanted to write fiction.

Schroeder: Initially you chose the short story as your form; it wasn't until after you published *Shiloh* that you wrote *In Country.* Do you have a preference for one form over the other?

Mason: Writing a novel is a lot more gratifying than writing a short story. Because it's a lot longer, you spend more time with it and the characters, and you can go further with it. The short story has its own virtues, though, which are different. A short story can be very—it's more like a diamond: concentrated and having many facets to it.

Schroeder: Did you begin writing fiction immediately after finishing your dissertation?

Mason: Off and on. It took me a long time to find out what I was doing. You can go to graduate school and read *The Great Gatsby* and *Moby Dick* and *For Whom the Bell Tolls* and all the great works, and you can find out how they're structured and what the themes are and what the issues are, and all those things. But then you try to write one, and none of what you learned seems to apply because it is backwards. *The Great Gatsby* is a finished work, so you can tell what the themes are. But when you start writing your own fiction, you don't have anything; it's a process of discovery. So it may take a long time to find your way around the material.

When you read a book in school, you're taking what's there and you're analyzing it. But there's nothing to analyze when you're creating. You don't have anything there yet. You have to write it before you can analyze it. So you can't say, "I'm going to write a novel about the quest for the father." You can say it, but whose quest? Where? And why?

Schroeder: *In Country* started as a short story, didn't it?

Mason: Yes. I did have that set of characters in the story, and they and their relationships came rather quickly. The story was entirely different, but the situation, the family relationships, was there. I couldn't make it work as a story, but I was interested in the characters. I had Sam living with her uncle, Emmett, and I had her mother, Irene, being off in Lexington with a little baby, and I had Sam and her boyfriend, Lonnie. The focus was on Sam and her boyfriend.

To back up a little bit: The inspiration for the story was a couple of kids I saw on a street corner in Allenstown, Pennsylvania, selling flowers to passing motorists. I noticed them, and thought that if a couple of kids were doing that in my home town in Kentucky, it would be really unusual. I was trying to imagine a couple of kids in Kentucky selling flowers, and that's what started it. I imagined Sam and her boyfriend being unconventional kids, because selling flowers is an entrepreneurial thing to do; it's not like getting a job. I was fooling around with that, and thinking about them just having graduated from high school and not being able to get jobs and needing something to make money. Unemployment was very high at the time, and so I began developing this story about how they were selling flowers out of Lonnie's van and trying to drum up business. But Sam was living with her strange uncle, who seemed eccentric.

Another of the initial inspirations was that Emmett wore this skirt. I don't know where it came from; I may have seen a Phil Donahue program where some men were wearing skirts: they had a notion that men should wear skirts. So Emmett was wearing this skirt, and Sam didn't have a job. I knew Sam's father wasn't there, but I didn't know where he was. I thought maybe her parents were divorced or maybe he died, but I didn't know what. I couldn't make this work as a story, but I had this interest in the characters, so I thought, "I'm just going to keep writing, I'll just write a novella. I'll write for eighty pages and see what happens."

I wrote and wrote, and Emmett died of cancer. He was this mysterious character that I was really interested in, but I was afraid to get into him, so I just had him die of cancer. I didn't know what the center of the story was, and I said, "This doesn't work." But at some point, when I was trying to figure out where Sam's father was, it just hit me like a ton of bricks: her father died in Vietnam. She was at an age where this was practically the first time in our history when this could have been written about the Vietnam war, when there's a young person coming of age whoese father had been killed in Vietnam. There had been just enough time since the earliest soldiers died over there. Then I knew that I had a novel. I guess in the meantime I had figured out Emmett was a veteran. It all clicked. All those years in graduate school studying about the quest for the father had meaning. The quest for the father was a powerful theme, but when I had studied those things, they were all intellectual and abstract.

I had no relationship to that concept; I didn't understand it personally at all. In *The Odyssey* I could see Telemachus searching for Odysseus, but it didn't have any meaning for me. Finally, in the act of creating it, it had personal meaning, it had reality. Then I knew I had a novel because I knew it was a significant subject and a universal theme.

Schroeder: Did Vietnam start taking over at that point?

Mason: It took a while. By this time my editor at Harper & Row was encouraging me. I told him about my ideas for this novel and about Vietnam. He was really behind it. I wrote almost a draft of it. And it was about Sam and Lonnie trying to sell flowers. Meanwhile Emmett was being a very eccentric Vietnam vet and Sam's father had been killed.

I didn't know where it was going. My editor, Ted Solotaroff, who liked all the main notions about it, told me that the novel was very boring. It had these two kids selling flowers, and it avoided the issue. He encouraged me to come face to face with the subject of Vietnam; he said I was avoiding it, which I was. I was scared of the topic. What did I know? I was a girl, I had never been to Vietnam. I felt intimidated writing about the subject. And questioning a little bit whether I had the right to get into that. I guess I knew I did, but still it's not easy to make that leap.

So I ditched those flowers and tried to get into the relationships more: what Emmett was going through and what Sam was also going through. I started to develop Emmett as sort of the surrogate father for her. I don't think I ever thought of it much in very broad terms. It really is amazing how the story is pieced together inch by inch, a little bit here and a little bit there, until it finally adds up, and you can shift it around and finally can see it.

Schroeder: The issue you raise about privilege, who can write about Vietnam, is very interesting. Some veterans think you had to be there to write about it. What was it that allowed you to make that leap?

Mason: I think you had to be there to know certain things about it in certain ways, to actually know the reality of it. The imagination can do other sorts of things. It's actually easier to imagine something than to experience it. It's easier to send Sam out to the swamp than for me to go there. I didn't go to the swamp.

Schroeder: But part of your point in the scene is that the swamp situation will only take you so far, imagining the war isn't the same as experiencing it.

Mason: That's right. That illustrates what I felt about it. I felt that even the creative imagination can only go so far; beyond that, you had to be there. But what I thought a writer could do is to suggest and imply how much more there was. In a way, the restraint of standing back can be more powerful than directly showing the thing itself. Just like horror is often greater in your imagination than when you're actually seeing something horrible. There are uses of the imagination and techniques of writing to suggest things in powerful ways.

Schroeder: Sam's very good at that, isn't she?

Mason: She has a really gory imagination, and she thinks she can face anything. But there's a limit to what she can take.

Schroeder: For instance, when she reads her father's diary and finds out how his experience in Vietnam shaped him.

Mason: Yeah, she can't take it. Early in the story she begs Emmett to tell her something about Vietnam and he says no, and she says, "Well, I'll just imagine it worse than it was." He says, "No, you can't." That was a very clear statement of the whole idea.

But you also asked what made me feel like I had the right to write about the war. I was writing this story for quite some time and had written two or three drafts before I went to the Vietnam Memorial. I didn't know until that time that the characters were going to go there, that the book was going to end there. When I did go there in the spring of '83, it was raining that day. I walked all the way from the Capitol down the Mall to the Memorial. I could hear them talking. I could imagine them driving that Volkswagen all the way to Washington. And the characters that came to mind were Mamaw and Emmett and Sam. I just felt like I was living this scene, and they were with me. So when I saw the Memorial, I saw it through their eyes. I saw all the other people there, all the family members. I hadn't had any personal experience myself with anyone who went to Vietnam, but there were all these people around me who did, and I was coming at it through the imagination. I guess this event was a turning point for me because then I felt it was something that touched every American, and I was an American, and I had the right to tell our story. You see all those names. Sam felt that all the names in America had been used to decorate this wall.

Schroeder: And she sees her own name on the wall.

Mason: She saw her own name. Well, the reason that happened is that when I went there in the rain, I hadn't been there five minutes when I saw my own name. So then I felt—I *had* to feel—that we were all involved with it. And we are. The name was Bobby G. Mason. I've always been fascinated by thinking of someone else with the same name, and so to see that—I have a very common name, so I've always been aware that there are other people with the name. I always thought that was an interesting thing to imagine. But anyway there it was.

I had been afraid to tackle the subject initially. It was like America had tried not to think about Vietnam, tried to forget it. I didn't have any particular motivating force to make me write a novel about Vietnam. I mean, I could have forgotten about it. I wasn't trying to forget about it, but there wasn't anything to force me to think about it, either. These little things happened, and I discovered these things about the characters. So eventually I had to confront the subject, and I felt good about doing it. I felt like it was important. Also, I feel like it wasn't at all original. I was able to do it, I was able to have it surface in my consciousness at the same time it was starting to come out in everyone else's. The finishing of the wall was a sign of this, and everywhere you started to see people getting concerned. The book became a mirror; it became possible to do this.

Schroeder: Were you reading Vietnam stuff?

Mason: I started once I realized I was writing about Vietnam and my editor began urging me to face the subject more. Yeah, I read. I didn't read extensively into the history of the war; I just read stuff that would help me to understand what veterans were going through, and what the guys had gone through in Vietnam. I read oral histories—Mark Baker's *Nam,* Al Santoli's *Everything We Had* , and *Charlie Company*—and things like Caputo's *A Rumor of War* and Michael Herr's *Dispatches.*

Schroeder: Were you reading any fiction?

Mason: I read *The Thirteenth Valley*. All together, just a basic collection of books that were published in the late seventies and early eighties. I felt like I saturated myself in a very short period with the world of an American soldier in Vietnam and his return to America. So, after a while I couldn't read anymore, because I couldn't read them without crying, it was so overwhelming. Also, every person's story was individual and different, but yet they all had a common ground, and all of them were very eloquent, it seemed to me. The people telling their stories in those oral histories had a very distinctive voice. That was what I felt I was trying to pick up: they had a distinct language.

For a writer, I think the imagination is activated by words and by language, so the terminology they used, the term "in country" itself, became important to me. Those terms just reverberate in your mind and evoke things, and the language becomes your way of understanding their world. There was such a common ground in their stories that I felt I could grasp some of that and use it. There were some things that occurred in every story; like when the recruits landed in Vietnam, the first thing they noticed was the heat and the smell—they all said that—and they all talked about walking point, and the rations, and how the canned peaches were the prize. They all said the same things about certain things. Even though every guy had a different past and a different fate and a different set of circumstances, there were just certain things about their world that I could pick up on. Also, a lot of them shared the same tone in discussing their experience when they came back. Many of them said they got spit on and called baby-killer at the San Francisco airport.

Schroeder: In creating Sam Hughes it seems that you're not only able to create the consciousness of a seventeen-year-old, but at the same time there is another consciousness that runs through the book: we experience the consciousness of the seventeen-year-old, and then we're given distance on that; we're able to step back from her and see not only her charm, but also her silliness and the inexperience of her youth. Are you conscious of creating this double perspective?

Mason: I don't remember thinking of it that way. There's so much of Sam that comes from me. People ask me how I can write about a teenager, since it's been such a long time since I've been a teenager and since I don't have any teenaged children. But once you've been through your teenage years, if you can maintain some kind of connection to that experience then you understand what the teenaged mind is like. It was just a matter of making her come to life and finding what her point of view was. Once I felt I really understood how she saw things, then I could have put her in any situation whatsoever and know her attitude, what she'd say, and the tone of what she'd say. So once I got that center, then the character was consistent, and I could do anything.

But before that it was trial and error. She was easier than some of the others. The hardest character in the book was Lonnie because I took him through several different types. He started out being rebellious and unconventional like Sam, so they were two lost kids out on their own. I also had his mother being really wild. But at some point he got transformed into a foil for her, a contrast, because I realized that all my characters were eccentric, and I kept saying that the town was so constrained and dull and everybody was so conventional. But I didn't have anybody in the story who was actually like that, so I finally realized that Lonnie had to represent that kind of solid conventional aspect of the town. He went through a lot of transformations.

Schroeder: Your characters—in your short stories as well as in your longer fiction—always strike me as being labors of love on your part. One critic called your characters desperate and dreary. I don't see them that way at all.

Mason: Oh, good, thank you. People have said that they find them desperate and dreary because they would hate to find themselves in their shoes. It's not their life, and they're threatened by them. My characters don't see themselves that way at all.

Schroeder: In an interview you once mentioned how all the heroes in the books you read in graduate school were artists or writers. And you wondered why not have some ordinary people as heroes? Even in a lot of the Vietnam literature the protagonist is the guy who went to college or had two years of college education or wants to be a writer. The person who embodies the central consciousness in the story is somebody who isn't average. You do a tremendous job of representing typical people, people who went and fought in Vietnam. I think Emmett and all of his friends are well cast. You mentioned earlier that you didn't know people who had been in Vietnam. What did you have to do to get those people so right? Was it just from reading the books?

Mason: Yeah. I tried to absorb all those experiences I read about, and then tried to transpose that onto people like the characters I knew.

Schroeder: Then were they like people you grew up with?

Mason: I didn't base them on anyone in particular. Temperamentally, Emmett's probably closer to my father than anyone else. So I took it from there. If somebody like my father went to Vietnam, how would he behave when he came back?

Schroeder: I thought it was a tribute to the powers of the imagination earlier this evening when that veteran at the movie asked you about your father, where his name was on the wall. He was obviously identifying you with Sam. Has that happened to you before?

Mason: I've heard that a couple of times.

Schroeder: People are always willing to undersell the powers of the imagination.

Mason: When you were asking about Sam and the two levels, I should have said that I found the characters so personal that putting them together, creating them out of little scraps, makes it's hard for me to see them in broad, analytical terms.

Schroeder: Who did you see as your audience when you were writing *In Country*? Was it the same audience that you had been writing your stories for? Did you think high school kids were going to read it?

Mason: I don't know if I ever thought about it.

Schroeder: While reading reviews, I noticed that *The Book Review Index* put a "J" for juvenile publication by their listing of *In Country*. Reviewers seemed aware that this might be a book that would appeal to people like Sam.

Mason: I find that interesting because there are some schools, such as many schools in Kentucky, where they wouldn't teach a book like *In Country*.

Schroeder: Because of the language?

Mason: The language and such sex scenes as there are. They have a real hard time with the language. If the people who saw the movie in Western Kentucky had any complaint, it was the language.

Schroeder: Isn't the language in the book so true to the people you're describing (who, after all, are from Western Kentucky)? I don't think you're exaggerating.

Mason: It's pretty mild.

Schroeder: Did you think teenagers would read *In Country*?

Mason: I don't remember thinking that.

Schroeder: Do you ever think about your audience at all?

Mason: No, I don't think so.

Schroeder: How do teenagers learn about Vietnam?

Mason: Apparently not in their history books. Perhaps there's a paragraph in their history books. So their knowledge of Vietnam is probably pretty spotty; maybe some schools or some isolated teachers bring in materials.

Schroeder: Even someone like Sam Hughes, who wants to learn about Vietnam, encounters all sorts of road blocks. Even her uncle, whom she lives with, won't tell her. Can fiction do what our schools don't seem capable of and teach our kids about Vietnam in any real way?

Mason: Sure. I would think that teenagers would learn more about Vietnam from my novel than from a little chapter in their history book. Vietnam would be more real.

Schroeder: Did you ever have any intention like that for the book? That the book was presenting an experience that a lot of Americans went through that a lot of other Americans aren't paying enough attention to?

Mason: When I was writing I didn't have a very strong vision of the whole or even enough of a sense of confidence in what I was doing or what I was dealing with even to think about those things. What was on my mind was so particular and so detailed—I worried about questions like "How am I going to make this scene interesting?" or "Does this follow that, what happens when she goes to Tom's?" I wasn't thinking about the subject in any broad way, and so I wasn't thinking about who was going to read it. I don't remember having enough confidence in it to impose myself onto it; I was just trying to feel my way along to see what would happen, to see how it would become coherent.

It's so awfully hard to make something come clear and coherent and for it to be interesting. It has to be interesting first of all, then once something comes clear you can start to shape it. I wouldn't have said, "Here I am writing a Vietnam war novel that kids might read"—I just wouldn't have thought that. I finished the first draft and I finally wrote a complete draft of the story as it more or less is (it had a few more drafts and revisions), but the basic story had Mamaw climbing the ladder at the end. (I had it structured a little differently, with the trip broken up and spread throughout the story.) Anyway, I sent it to my editor.

I had no idea if it was any good, if it was interesting, if it held up as a story, if it had any significance, if it was moving—I had no idea. My editor was really very moved by it, and that was enough to give me a little confidence in it, to send me back to it, to start to see it and revise it in a way that would accentuate it, to let the emotion come through. I was so tentative about it; I wasn't even sure of my own emotion, if I was moved by it. I'm far more moved by the characters after the fact than I was when I was writing it.

Schroeder: You were saying how tentative you thought that first draft was and how you weren't sure if it was any good or not. That's probably different than what happens when you're writing short stories. After finishing them, you probably have a much better idea of whether your stories work.

Mason: Oh, I often feel that way about the stories, too. I think the stories take the same process, just in a much shorter way. With the novel I was just as particular about the details as I am in the short stories. In a way, writing a novel is like writing a very complicated short story.

Schroeder: One of the questions that continues to intrigue me is why do you think there haven't been more books like *In Country*? More books about Vietnam, written by women; or more novels about the peace movement? We have this tremendous surge of interest about the experience of the war, but little, I think, about the war at home. Your book seems unique in that sense. There was a lot of journalism at the time. I think of books like Norman Mailer's *Armies of the Night*, a brilliant book about the march on the Pentagon and the antiwar movement in general, but in terms of fiction, there hasn't been much.

Mason: There's a marvelous novel by Jayne Anne Phillips, *Machine Dreams*. I haven't yet read Susan Fromberg Schaffer's *Buffalo Soldier*. It's a Vietnam novel about men in Vietnam and coming home, I think. I don't know that women are often much motivated to write about men's experiences in that way. And I'm not sure what would motivate someone to write a piece of fiction about flower power or the peace movement. I'm not sure.

Schroeder: I guess my feeling is because it's a subject that affected the whole country, there's a lot of dimensions that have just continued to go unexplored.

Mason: I don't know what to say about that. I'm fascinated by the sixties and wish I could write a novel about them. In a way, though, it's too close, and in a way it's just nostalgia, so there's no clear way to get it.

Schroeder: Closeness is perhaps the main problem. With World War II some really great stuff started coming out in the sixties, books like *Catch-22*, for instance.

Mason: It takes a while. One thing I remember from graduate school, a notion that impressed me, a teacher that I had said that in the mid-nineteenth century the New England Renaissance in writing really was all about the Revolutionary War and the discovery and settling of America. It was about American identity. It took almost a century after independence for this surge of creativity focusing on the identity of America to emerge. He also said that the Southern Renaissance in the mid-twentieth century, all the writing that came out of the South, had to do with the Civil War and its aftermath and what it meant to the country and to the South. So it takes a hundred years for a war to have a major literary movement, for people to really come to terms with it. And it's not the people that went through it, but minds that came much later.

Our communications, our technology, make us more inclined towards fads these days. Everything is speeded up. If there's a subject, it's going to be written about now, I think; it's going to be a fad. But it still might take a hundred years to really digest it.

Writers may be reluctant to address the sixties. They don't want to seem to be faddish and flash-in-the-pan. They want to wait until they really know what they want to say about it, and I don't think anybody really knows what to say yet. I feel like I might be embarrassed about it in a way. On the other hand, it's too precious to us to blow it, to do it wrong. I think for people like me, the sixties was a very intense special time, the way the time in Vietnam was for the soldiers, maybe—certainly not as intense—but the sixties had that very special and concentrated energy. Because it was our growing-up time, it's very precious to us. That's why the music is so important.

Schroeder: That's what's so interesting about Sam trying to get back into the war and into the sixties. In some ways, she's more a child of the sixties than the eighties. She knows the music as well if not better than everyone around her.

Mason: Oh, she grew up on it. The movie changed that a bit, but Sam grew up on the music, with her mother and her uncle. I did that very deliberately: I thought, this much time has passed, a generation has passed, and so these hippies had their kids, and the kids would grow up listening to this music. I thought it was a very positive thing that the music would no longer be part of a generation gap; it would be the one thing that united the generations, and it was the thing that united Sam with her father. That rock 'n roll music carried on this tradition. Even though it's not very old, it already has a tradition, and it can bridge these gaps. In Sam's case, the gap was between life and death, her father was dead. But she connected with her father's generation. In lots of other ways, there were communication barriers.

Schroeder: It seems a little ironic, though, because if Dwayne had lived, being a country boy, he would have ended up listening to the music Lonnie listens to, rather than listening to the music that Irene listened to.

Mason: That's an interesting observation. I hadn't thought of that.

Schroeder: The only time we hear Lonnie listening to music, he's listening to country and western.

Mason: "High Rolling"—in the movie, anyway. I didn't stress that in the novel.

Schroeder: You like the treatment of the movie.

Mason: Yeah, real well.

Schroeder: Did you work at all with the screenwriters, or were you there when they were filming?

Mason: I worked a little bit with the screenwriter when he was doing research. There were two screenwriters; they didn't work together, they worked consecutively. They were different scripts. Both of them came to Western Kentucky to scout around, and so I talked to them. I read all the scripts up to a certain point and made notes. So helped out a little bit in development, but didn't do any writing. After the movie started filming, I didn't have anything to do with it.

Schroeder: But you were pleased with your characters in particular? Since you feel so close to them, they were recognizable to you?

Mason: Yes. Particularly considering that it's awfully hard to translate a book into film and especially a book that has a lot of interior qualities, that's not really dramatic or cinematic in any obvious ways. Frank Pearson says it was the most difficult challenge he's ever had in screenwriting, and he's a veteran screenwriter. So considering that it's a difficult transformation, I thought it was an amazing job of distilling the main elements of the book and being faithful to the story. The shooting script was longer, but they edited it down quite a bit. I didn't see the whole long version, but I think it may have lost some of the motivation from the story. I accept it the way it is, and I think they did a remarkable job. Everybody involved with it treated it very respectfully, and they were all very serious. Even the crew members working on very minor jobs were thrilled to be working on the movie because they felt it was a story of substance. I was very gratified because they all felt it was a special project.

The actors treated it very specially. Bruce Willis was so serious about the role; it meant a lot personally to him from what I understand. I think he lost a couple of buddies in Vietnam. I'm not sure, but I think high school friends. Peggy Rae who played Mamaw was just marvelous. She used to play on "The Waltons" and on "Gunsmoke" and "The Dukes of Hazzard." She's a television actress, and she's never had a big movie part like this. She was thrilled, and she was just wonderful. She became friends with my mother; there are a lot of qualities of my mother in the grandmother's character in the novel, so that was good.

Schroeder: What about Emily Lloyd? She must have come to this subject fresh. Did she know anything about the war?

Mason: I don't think she did. But she was determined to get the part, and she was very serious about playing that role. She seemed to identify with it and to recognize what she could do with it. I was so thrilled with her in that role because having created Sam and having identified with Sam, Sam is in fact my child. Seeing Emily playing her, I'll admit that I fused the actress and the character and wanted to know Emily, be very protective toward her. I felt like I knew her, and I think Emily was enough like Sam personally to allow that also. So it was a very complicated emotional experience for me and a very positive one.

Schroeder: Now that the movie is out and the book has been out for five years, are you going to return to Vietnam as a subject? Have you thought about that at all?

Mason: I don't plan to. I mean I may, but I'm working on a novel right now that has nothing to do with Vietnam. I'll be working on it for some time, so at the moment I have no plans to write about Vietnam.

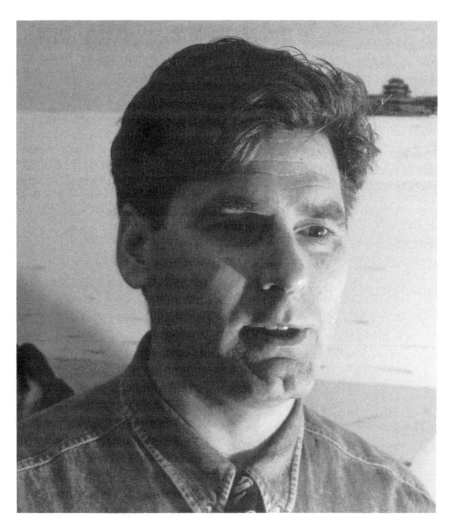

Photograph by Jean Weigl

Bruce Weigl:
"Poetry Grabbed Me by the Throat"

Schroeder: When did you start writing poetry? Did you write in Vietnam?

Weigl: I have a theory about artists, a very simple-minded theory, like most of my theories: that artists are people who don't stop doing the things we all do as children. That dancers are people who don't stop dancing; painters are people who don't stop painting; and writers are people who don't stop writing stories and poems, which we all do as children. On one hand, I've always written; on the other hand, I really didn't become a serious writer until after I got out of the Army and started school at Oberlin in 1971. That's when I really began to think that I wanted to try to be a writer. Not necessarily a poet, but just a writer. When I sat down to write, it was poems that came. After I finished my undergraduate degree, I still didn't think of myself as a writer, although I knew that I was writing, and that I wanted to continue. I did a Master's and thought, well, what am I going to do now? I'll go do a Ph.D.

No. I did not write in Vietnam. I felt pulled towards some kind of expression but I was too afraid of *everything*. Writing would have been too much to add to my rucksack.

Schroeder: Your Master's degree was in English lit, not creative writing, wasn't it?

Weigl: It was both, but it was an M.A. as opposed to an M.F.A., with more emphasis on literature. It's a curious thing: you get to a certain point where you realize that suddenly there's no going back. Poetry chose me; I didn't choose poetry. I have this strong sense that poetry just kind of reached out and grabbed me by the throat and said, "Do this, motherfucker. This is what you're supposed to be doing."

I had about eight different majors at Oberlin. Experimental psych was my initial interest. But my mentor in experimental psych had a sort of a moral epiphany about working experimentally with animals while I was a student and refused to do it any longer and actually became an administrator. I was left with no teacher. This was the guy I was working with and I was modeling my life after. I was also taking a literature course, and I took Stuart Friebert's creative writing class, and my life suddenly changed. For the first time I got encouragement and serious feedback about my work, and I began to write about the war. Suddenly this cornucopia of horror and nightmare opened for me as a writer, and I began to have an inkling of what lay ahead.

Schroeder: It sounds different from a lot of guys who went to the war and wrote poetry as a form of catharsis.

Weigl: I never liked the idea of art as therapy. Maybe it works for some people, but I don't like the idea of poetry as a therapeutic. I never thought of myself as exorcising anything as I wrote the poems because very early on it became an aesthetic struggle for me. The poetry was a formal context. The poetry was always separate from the personal, emotional, psychological issues because I was struggling with text, and that's enough to have to worry about. To get the words right, as Hemingway said. Trying to get the words right. But I will say, and this is very important to me, that my paradox as a writer is that the war both ruined my life and made me be a writer.

Schroeder: Was there somebody who pushed you towards poetry, one of your teachers? Were you encouraged specifically to write about Vietnam?

Weigl: I know exactly the moment it happened. It was an evening very much like this. A young poet by the name of Tom Lux had come to Oberlin to teach. We were the same age, even though I was an undergraduate. I loved him. He wrote a book called *Memory Is a Hand Grenade*, which was important to us all in those days. Anyway, we were sitting in his office one night, drinking, and something reminded me of a story about being in a lift-ship once and seeing this guy, a VC, on a bicycle. I had never written a Vietnam poem up to that point. I told Lux this story of the man on the bicycle, and he gave me a piece of paper and a pencil, and said, "Write it down, just like you told it to me, just like you told it to me, right now." And I did, and he said, "It's a poem there, a wonderful poem. Look at this," and he read it to me. And I thought, "Jesus Christ," and that was it. It's called "Him, on the Bicycle."

It's odd now, but back then it didn't occur to many of us that the war could be a subject for our writing because no one wanted to hear about it. When we tried to talk about it, people would turn away; so who would want to read about it? I literally got letters from editors saying, "We're not interested in this subject anymore," while the war still raged, '74, '75. Levertov, Bly, and other non-vet writers had done their Vietnam schtick, and the publishing world said, "That's enough."

Schroeder: Larry Heinemann talks about your poetry in the context of Wilfred Owen and Robert Graves. Did you see yourself as being part of that tradition? Were you consciously part of a tradition?

Weigl: Not consciously, but over the years I have come to see that I have a lot of affinity with Owen's work in the same way that other Vietnam veteran writers have a lot in common with the soldiers of trench warfare. In Paul Fussell's book *The Great War in Modern Memory*, Fussell argues that trench warfare changed consciousness. No small argument. The meliorist myth died; things were not going to get better again. They had to create a new kind of heroism. They had to create new versions of themselves because they saw in trench warfare that they were capable of doing things they never thought they were capable of. So trench warfare dramatically affected Western Europe; it didn't have that much of an effect on the United States. Vietnam did to the United States what World War I did to Europe. I think that's why Vietnam poets have a lot in common with poets of World War I.

Schroeder: While reading your poems I'm also struck by the fact that the influences on you seem to be legion. In particular there seem to be a lot of contemporary, certainly twentieth-century, influences. When you were beginning as a writer, were you consciously as a critic developing this repertoire?

Weigl: Go to the source of the fire. Get a burning coal from wherever you can. The more I read in school, the more I saw possibilities. The British Romantics were really important to me, especially Wordsworth and Keats. Emily Dickinson is an important influence on my work. I have her *Complete Poems* open on my desk as I write. Once, for two years, I read only Dante. For me postmodernism is an amalgamation of all those traditions, formally and stylistically. That's the great thing about free verse; it's not what the New Formalists want to say it is: formless, shapeless poetry. In fact it can be, when it's done well, more shapely than some of the so-called fixed forms. I saw fairly early on, in a naïve way but nevertheless it served me, that there's lots of different places I could go and bring stuff into my own work from different eras, different literary sensibilities.

Schroeder: I think that's one of the things that sets your work apart from some of the other Vietnam poets. They're so tied in to the experience of Vietnam that they don't have any larger concept of poetry as an art which reflects other art.

Weigl: My very good friend W. D. Ehrhart, who's one of the most important anthologizers of Vietnam war poetry, is going through this right now. And I know it's been a struggle for Tim O'Brien too and for many other Vietnam vet writers. It's a struggle for Ehrhart because he wants to get better, he wants to expand his mind and sensibilities as a poet, but he's thought and written about the war so long in that way, in the way of the foot soldier's, that it's hard for him to see the world differently as a poet.

I've always been interested in other subjects, however powerfully the war has colored the way I see the whole rest of experience. Also, my first subjects as a poet, unlike some other Vietnam poets, were not about the war; I think that's an advantage. I also spent considerable time in the university *after* the war. In those days, as an undergraduate at Oberlin, completing my M.A. at New Hampshire and the Ph.D. at Utah, there was not a great deal of interest in my work about the war; actually, in anyone's work about the war. Most of the people in positions of power in the university had not fought the war and there was some guilt there, some male *angst* I suppose, and they tried to suppress the subject. On one hand that was good for me because it forced me as a writer to go elsewhere for poems and allowed me to be much broader than others who have written about the war in terms of the occasions I find appropriate for poetry. But ultimately, I think we're all in the same boat so to speak. We've all been irrevocably altered by our war experiences and when we sit down to write a poem, almost always, the war looms largely.

Schroeder: Didn't you come out of a working-class background? So you weren't born into a family or community that saw value in poetry.

Weigl: I was not headed in the direction of books at all. There were no books in my house. There was a Bible, which was ill read. My parents didn't read to me. It's not a bookish family, which is not so unusual. There's a community full of people like that. But I always felt different from my family, even though I wasn't a very good student in high school. I always felt drawn toward something else.

Schroeder: If the war hadn't have come along, would you have ended up a poet?

Weigl: I don't think so. I had written some poems earlier: about family, about Lorain, where I grew up, about *angst*. Those poems that we write about the great crisis of the self.

Schroeder: Did the war push you closer to poetry, cause you to mature as an artist?

Weigl: I think so. I found my subject. As dumb as I was I knew that I'd found a subject. There was a little tiny speck of light that said, "Hey, there's something here. You've just been given something." The whole war just opened up then in my mind. I thought, "Jesus Christ, look at all the poems that are there. Am I going to be able to write them?"

Schroeder: We always think of war as alienating—it alienated you from your roots, for instance—but in another sense it put you in touch with a different culture that you might not have had access to otherwise.

Weigl: I started asking questions that the tradition of values I was raised with couldn't answer. So, one of the things I had to do was go inside for answers; and another thing I had to do was to read. I wanted terribly to understand what had happened in Vietnam: to my country and to me. All of that contributed to making me be a writer. It's a strange, strange thing what the war did to me. I'm absolutely convinced that I would not have become a writer, I would not have gone to college, if it hadn't been for the war. That's a powerful paradox in my life.

Schroeder: Were you attracted to other genres at all? Other forms of writing?

Weigl: I write criticism now. I tried fiction, but I always admired poetry's compactness and its ability to do so much in such a short span of time. Early on I also fell in love with the idea of what a line could be. Charles Simic told me when I was a student—I didn't understand what he meant until years later—"As soon as you realize the impossibility of writing poetry, you'll become a poet." It was a great moment when I finally had that recognition.

Schroeder: The prose poems in *A Romance* are almost stories. Short short stories.

Weigl: I wrote those because I had been reading Rimbaud and Russell Edson, people like that, and I was intrigued with the form. I liked the idea of the form; the history of the world on the back of a matchbook, as David Young has said. Frankly, I could not find a form for those poems. No matter how I delineated them (I knew really little about lines then), nothing worked. So I said what the fuck, make them prose poems. Recently I was thinking of going back and writing some more prose poems. Vignettes, call them. James Wright simply called them prose.

Schroeder: Was Wright an early influence, being from Ohio and a working-class background?

Weigl: Jim's son Franz and I were students together at Oberlin. So that's how I got introduced to Jim's work. I was sending my Vietnam poems around, getting no response whatsoever, and getting depressed about it. Franz sent them to James Wright. Jim wrote me a letter back, and at the end of the letter he said, "Out of the horror of your poems there rises a music that is beautiful." I remember thinking, "Fuck those other guys; Jim Wright said this." I met him a few times afterwards.

But you're right: he was also the voice of the working people for me as a poet. Everything seemed right when I read him, everything seemed essential;

there's no fucking around in his poetry. He said he longed to write the poetry of a grown man. I heard that and thought I understood what he meant; it was important to me, and I still love his work. And I'm proud when anyone points out the similarities, even when they do it accusingly. I don't care.

Schroeder: You're probably best known as a Vietnam war poet, and yet you write about lots of other things. You've mentioned how your subjects select you; can you elaborate on that?

Weigl: I think this is true for most poets; I'm not positive that it is, but I think it is. I know it's true for somebody like Simic, for example. Writing for me is an act of discovery. It's not an act of creation. So when I sit down to write, I seldom have something specific in mind. It's just not the way I work. I rail against original intention when I write, and I teach that way too. I think original intention usually gets you into trouble because the unconscious is so involved in this act. You have to allow the poem to write itself. You have to allow the poem to talk to you. When I sit down, even if I have generally something in mind, frequently the poem will go in another direction. Like Simic says, follow your hunches. Trust your instincts. James Wright has a poem which begins, "I'm almost afraid to write down this thing." That's trusting his instincts. That line would have occurred to ninety-nine other people, but only Jim Wright was smart enough to write it down.

There was a time when I stopped trying to write about the war, but it kept coming. When I sat down, that's what came, those images came. Those smells and sounds. Tim O'Brien and I had a long talk about this recently. Tim wrote a book called *The Nuclear Age*, which was really not a very good novel, panned by everybody. Tim knows it wasn't very good. He went through the same thing I went through, "OK, we're not going to write about the war anymore," and then he wrote a bad book. He had turned away from what was in his heart. Now, he went back to it and wrote his greatest book, and maybe the best book about the war yet—*The Things They Carried*. We both had to go through that experience to realize how fortunate we were. Simic once said to me, "You're lucky. There's so many writers who don't have a subject. The world gave you a subject." The business about being identified as a Vietnam poet doesn't bother me at all. It's great. If that's how I'm going to be remembered, it means I'll be remembered. Why should subject matter? It doesn't. All that matters is that you say the thing well.

Schroeder: In your criticism you've written about the necessity of having a subject. You've suggested that perhaps the Formalists don't have one.

Weigl: It's one of my passions lately, attacking those people at every turn. I see the New Formalists—they call themselves Expansionists now—I see them as part of the new conservatism. New Formalism is a neo-classic corruption that asks for an exclusive subject matter and an impersonality of speaking voice. It's cookie-cutter stuff. It's a kind of formalism one sees in the poetry societies of America, not in the great poetry. There's not one so-called perfect sonnet among Shakespeare's sonnets, not one that is consistently numerical. The New Formalists fail to understand a critical point about writing traditionally formal or numerically regular verse: that you never sacrifice language to satisfy the demands of form. The best poets don't have to sacrifice anything. If these guys could write like Wilbur or Frost, then it would be all right. But the work that's coming out, most of it's shit.

I'm not against form. No poetry, even bad poetry, is totally formless. When you break a line, you create a form. I tell my students that free verse is to poetry what jazz is to music. When you first start listening to jazz, the first time you listen to Coltrane, you don't hear anything. You don't hear any shape at all. The closer you get to jazz, you begin to see that there's shape there; it's just more expansive than the forms of a popular, numerically repetitive song, for instance. Free verse has its forms too. In his book *Free Verse: An Essay on Prosody*, Charles Hartman argues this point brilliantly.

Robert Creeley says form is an extension of content. The problem with the New Formalist thinking is that what you should struggle for when you write a poem is to find a form for your experience; that's what form should be about, and if you're so exclusive that you decide beforehand this is absolutely a fixed form, sometimes it's going to work, but sometimes it might not work. Sometimes it might not be the right form for that particular experience, and you're going to lose something. By forcing that last line into a pentameter, you might ruin the whole poem, because sometimes that's all it takes, just one bad turn in a poem and it's gone. It crumbles before your eyes. I tell my students to look at Greek sculpture and then at Roman sculpture. The perfection of beauty, on one hand, and our humanness exposed on the other: the broken noses, the potbellies, the funny ears, as opposed to the ideal beauty of the Greeks. This is a kind of neo-neo-classicism that we're seeing in the New Formalists, a late, corrupted neo-classicism.

My new book has several decasyllabic poems and poems written in other accentual or syllabic forms. I'm a serious student of English prosody. I teach prosody. I know Paul Fussell's book on prosody well. I know Hopkin's *Prosodic Theories*. I have my own prosodic theories. I'm a reader of traditionally formal poetry and I love it. I think the most important thing a young writer can do is study traditionally formal poetry. It's the dogma I'm fighting and arguing against. And it's the exclusivity of the movement.

Schroeder: About Vietnam as a subject: in *A Romance* and *Monkey Wars* Vietnam is woven throughout the books, but the balance seems pretty even between poems about Vietnam and poems not about it. Is Vietnam as a subject diminishing over time?

Weigl: No, it's just changing. There's literally distance on it, because it's been over twenty years now. It's amazing. It could have been yesterday. I'm getting older, and hopefully I'm getting a little smarter. But it will always be here in my work, always. When I look at you, I look at you through those eyes. I sit down the way I sit down because of the war. When I sit in a restaurant, I sit so I can face the door. It's always going to be there for me as a subject, and I'm thankful for it. But the poems change; they've become—[*pause*]—I don't know exactly how to describe the newer poems about the war. They're less concerned with combat and more concerned with people. And, since I've been back to Vietnam twice recently, I'm also now writing about postwar Vietnam.

Schroeder: The other thing I wonder about is the "I," the persona in the poems. Has it changed? Has the persona gotten closer or further away?

Weigl: It's gotten closer. My poems have always appeared to be personal. I've always wanted my poems to appear to be personal, even though they frequently weren't. But now they're actually more personal. I feel more confident writing about my personal experience now that I'm over forty. I feel more at ease calling myself a poet and thinking of myself as a poet, so I feel more comfortable with saying this is my experience, and I'm going to write about it, as it happened, in my terms.

I used to be much more self-conscious about the persona in my poems. For instance, when I used to read "Song of Napalm" I would start by saying this poem is dedicated to the speaker's wife. It was important for me that people understood that the "I" was not necessarily me, that there was a difference between the "I" and me. They're the same, and they're different too, because you revise them, you lie. You find a voice to tell each particular experience. You know, Joyce's description of the artist paring his fingernails? That's where Weigl is in those poems.

Schroeder: In *If I Die in a Combat Zone*, Tim O'Brien says, "Can the footsoldier teach anything important about war merely for having been there? I think not. He can tell war stories." Does that sound right? Does some sort of teaching go on? I guess it's more subtle than that. A poem of yours that I instantly think of is "The Last Lie."

Weigl: I think too often poetry and art in general comes after the fact in this country, as opposed to in other countries where poetry can actually be a political force. In our country, because of the way art is regarded, it doesn't really have the same kind of impact. In the same breath, I know that "Song of Napalm" is read by thousands of high school students. It's a widely anthologized poem. At least once a month I get a letter from some school kid who read the poem and who saw something there. There's proof that I'm wrong about what I just said, on the other hand. All it takes is one person to learn the lesson of that poem, because that person's going to grow up and have kids, and those kids are going to have that lesson, et cetera. Having "been there" allows you at least the opportunity to teach something that others couldn't teach. The most important lesson I learned in the war was the lesson of perspective. Knowing the difference between what's important and what's not. What matters and what's a waste of time. I've tried to raise my son that way, and I hope that ethic is at work in my poems as well.

Schroeder: You dedicated "Song of Napalm" to your wife. When you wrote it, did you have a sense that kids might read it?

Weigl: No, I didn't. I had no idea that the poem would become what it's become. It's really a widely read poem; it has a life of its own.

Many of us have been raised to think that poetry wasn't for us, which is really unfortunate, because it really is, and should be for us, for everyone. I don't really have an audience in mind; I never have had. It's too large an abstraction for me to deal with. I feel that if I'm honest and work hard, I'll have an audience. I'll have readers.

Schroeder: One of the critics faulted *Monkey Wars* for not having many startling turns of phrase. Is your decision to use simplified language purely aesthetic? I'm wondering if perhaps there is a political motivation as well.

Weigl: I have to say I'm sick of these assholes saying that about my work. It's the only thing that gets under my skin because I struggle so hard for that simplicity, that clarity. I work my ass off to make it that way. One of the most important things I've learned from reading poetry is that all great poetry has clarity in common. There's nothing clearer to me than Chaucer or Shakespeare. Or Dante. It's not difficult. It's wrong to tell people great poetry is difficult. Students are afraid because we keep implying it's difficult. It's not elevated language. It's clear, direct language. And I struggle hard for that in my own work. It's the language by which we speak and imagine, curse and bless on a daily basis. It's what Williams called the American idiom, and it's the language I'm in love with.

It's really a fundamental misunderstanding about my work. I don't pay attention to reviews good or bad. You can't. It would be nice to sit down with those reviewers, have a conversation, and say, "Let's talk this out. Let me tell you what I mean by this. This isn't simple because I'm stupid. This diction isn't direct because I'm uneducated or ill-read. I write that way because I *am* educated, because I *am* trained."

You suggested there's a political gesture behind that kind of diction, and you're absolutely right. What "they" want to do is keep poetry, art in general, out of our hands. It's the same thing the New Formalists want. They want that exclusivity, they want art to be the property of the academy, the museums. They don't want the people to have it, because it's dangerous in the hands of the people. They don't want to acknowledge that we too can write poetry. That we can use the language of the steel mill like Wright did so beautifully. Look at Frost's diction, how simple and clear many of his poems are.

You have to have your own diction to tell the war, your own language, because the old diction doesn't work anymore.

Schroeder: Your poetry has been criticized for its bleakness, and at readings you've admitted that there's not a lot of humor in your poems. But though there's not a lot of humor, there is hope in your poetry.

Weigl: Writing a poem is one of the greatest acts of affirmation, of affirming life that I can think of.

Schroeder: I think that comes out in "Song of Napalm."

Weigl: I do too. They're distressing poems in a way, but on the other hand, they *were* written. And I'm still here to write them.

Schroeder: Paul Fussell has said, "Whatever the reasons, it seems undeniable that no one expects interesting poetry to emerge from that sad war. All we can expect is more of what we already have: a few structureless, free verse dribbles of easy irony, or easy sentiment, or easy political anger." Is Vietnam poetry in general as bad as Fussell seems to think?

Weigl: He said that in *Popular Culture* a couple years ago. And in his forthcoming anthology of war literature he includes only two poems from Vietnam; fortunately, one is mine! It seems to me that he just doesn't know where to go. I don't think he must be reading much of the poetry. Although recently he's acknowledged that perhaps some good work did come out of the Vietnam war experience.

Schroeder: I have a theory that the great nonfiction about Vietnam has been written already. But I think the fiction is really still coming, and the best is yet to come. What about the poetry? Is there good stuff still to come?

Weigl: There have always been fewer mainstream poets writing about the war than there have been fiction writers or nonfiction writers. Economics is one obvious reason. I don't mean to be egocentric, but if it's going to come, it's going to come from those few of us who have been doing it for the last fifteen years. I think that it will continue because we're not going to stop; as long as we're around, the poem will be there. Hopefully there will also be an evolution of concerns as expansion of the range of our poetic options.

Schroeder: The war is now being appropriated by film and television. Does it get harder to write seriously about the war with the competition of these other forms? What does poetry offer that these other forms don't?

Weigl: Poetry teaches in a way that no other form can teach. Poetry speaks about the world like only poetry can speak about the world. The commercial aspect of fiction has shaped the kind of fiction we read and write in this country, whereas in poetry there have been many, many more revolutions in style. I don't worry about TV. No one ever remembers what they watch anyway.

Schroeder: What sorts of problems raised by the war do we as Americans still face?

Weigl: The largest issue is the issue of the MIAs. It's become a cottage industry: MIA-izing. It's perfectly clear to anyone with an iota of intelligence that there are no Americans being held prisoner in Vietnam.

It's saddest for the parents and lovers and wives and husbands and children of those men. There may be Americans in Vietnam, but if there are, the Vietnamese don't know where they are, or what they're doing there. The Vietnamese certainly have absolutely nothing to gain by holding anyone prisoner. And they haven't had anything to gain since the end of the war. The Vietnamese have 150,000 MIAs who they haven't even begun to account for. I think people don't realize what happens in a tropical country. When someone falls dead, two weeks later, there's a tree there. And three weeks later, you would never know someone died there. It eats up entire airplanes, the jungle.

The MIA issue has been orchestrated in part by members of our government because it's a way to keep us from normalizing relations with Vietnam.

Schroeder: Your poetry is not only translated into Vietnamese, but you're one of several vet writers who have been back to Vietnam.

Weigl: All my efforts now are towards normalization. That's why I work with the Joiner Center; that's our goal. Our government won't do it, so the writers are doing it. Yes, I've been back to Vietnam twice since the war.

Schroeder: How have Vietnamese writers responded to your interest in the war?

Weigl: Initially, in 1985, I thought they were baffled by our interest in it. They didn't understand why we kept writing about it. I've come to understand that was just party line. Those guys suffered the same things we suffered. We have a lot in common, and now, of course, they're also writing about the war in deeply personal, far less political ways.

Literature is a sacred aspect of their culture and writers are taken very seriously there. They love us. They love the fact that we were soldiers and now we're writers. We're treated like diplomats when we're there.

The opening up of Vietnam has allowed them to admit now that they made mistakes. Li Lu, one of Vietnam's most important novelists, wrote a novel five years ago that was the first published literary document which accused the Hanoi regime of making mistakes in the war. It was a big deal for that book to be published. So now I understand that we have a lot more in common than I thought.

There is this fact, though, that's critical: they don't take the war as personally as we took it. It's easier for them to forgive. Because ours is an egocentric culture whereas theirs is a much more selfless culture. If you're Vietnamese, you're always attached to some larger thing: a family, hamlet, village, et cetera. It's not just "I." That says a lot about their culture. It's something we didn't understand about their culture when we went in there. If we had understood that fact and the cultural implication inherent there, then we may have understood the nature of the revolution and never have invaded their country.

Schroeder: Do you think the artists are going to make a difference in terms of getting things normalized?

Weigl: In Vietnam they will because they're very powerful now. They represent the liberal forces in Vietnam. And the fact that we're having a writers' conference in Vietnam this summer is evidence these people have a lot of power. There were conservative, old-line forces against this conference. But the liberals won out.

Schroeder: But what about our writers? Are our writers going to make a difference with our government? Isn't the biggest obstacle right now to normal relationships with their government, our government?

Weigl: It's the only obstacle. If you remember, during the Paris peace talks, Nixon promised restitution, financial restitution. That was part of the deal. And as soon as the Vietnamese let the POWs go and the war was stopped, Nixon said, Fuck you, you're not getting it. No. There are some specific reasons why this government does not want to normalize. First and foremost, we don't want to take responsibility for what we did to those people and that country. And if we normalize we will assume responsibility; we 're going to have to start paying for that shit. We don't want to pay for it; it's going to cost a lot of money. We ruined their ecosystem. It's ruined because of us. Those chemicals live in the soil for 250 years. They're in the streambeds—Agent Orange and different defoliants. They're in the streambeds, in the food chain, and we don't want responsibility for that. I think that's the single largest reason why we don't want to normalize relations.

In an odd way, Vietnam would be a lot better off right now if they had lost that war. We would be helping them. But because they won, we can't help. Maybe that's part of the cowboy ethic that got us into the war in the first place: you don't help somebody who kicks your ass.

Photograph by Edward Betz

David Rabe:

"A Harrowing Audience Experience"

Schroeder: I've noticed some similarities between Larry Heinemann's background and yours; for instance, you were both studying theater when you were drafted. At that point, were you considering a career as a playwright?

Rabe: I didn't know whether I wanted to be an actor or a writer, and I was trying both at the time. I was headed in that direction, and that's why I was in theater. I had done some creative writing in college. But I still thought I might want to be an actor. Then I quit graduate school. I knocked around for about a year and a half and got drafted.

Like Pavlo in *Pavlo Hummel*, at the time I was drafted, unless you were fairly politically astute, there was no war. It didn't exist. It was about to exist in a big way, but it didn't. Of course, a lot of people knew, but the bulk of people didn't, weren't thinking about it. So when I got drafted, the concern about going or not going was not a specific moral question, and I was certainly not a conscientious objector in any general sense at that point in my life.

Schroeder: Did you expect to be drafted?

Rabe: Yeah, and I tried to avoid it though not because of the war, since there wasn't a war. I tried to avoid it because I didn't want to go away for two years and do this stuff. Then I got sick of trying to avoid it, and I thought, "It'll be an adventure, the hell with this, I'm tired of what I'm doing." I didn't want to go back to graduate school; I was sick of school. I just got tired of coming up with excuses. I thought about getting married in order to avoid being drafted, and I said, "This is nuts. It'll be interesting; I'll go away for two years—so what?" So I let myself give in at that point.

Like in this scene fairly early in *Pavlo*, I remember a sergeant talking about Vietnam, and we were all saying, "What? Where? What's he talking about?" It was literally while we were in the first couple of weeks of basic training that a bunch of people got killed, and the war started to shift very quickly. The kind of issues that a lot of people faced later on—"Should I go into the Army and go to Vietnam?"—really weren't on my mind when the draft happened. So I just went in.

Schroeder: Did you see going into the Army as something that would provide you with material later?

Rabe: I don't know. I didn't really. In the sense that you see your life will provide you with material, I did. But I was never a believer in looking for it, and I'm still not. I've always believed that what you were provided with would just happen; material will come out of your life. So, on some level, yes, but it wasn't a specific thought; it was in the sense of, yeah, it'll be an adventure. But on the other hand, I didn't go airborne once I was in. I almost did—all these younger guys that I was friends with in basic, or even pre-basic, when we were at Fort Jackson, wanted me to go airborne, wanted me to be an officer. I thought about it, but didn't do it. If I had done that, I would have had a different life.

Schroeder: Didn't you end up working in a hospital?

Rabe: Yeah, I was in a hospital unit, but I was not a medic. I guess it was partly my personality, and partly being older, being twenty-five—they couldn't get me to do anything; really, I just did what I had to do. They wanted me to be an officer later, and I wouldn't do that, either. I remember, the NCOs found these choices very peculiar. So I just ended up where they put me finally. When they asked me to volunteer for anything, I basically didn't do it.

There was a period in Vietnam after I was there for about three months when I tried to get transferred. A brief period. This is the naïve part: even though I was older, even though I knew better, I fell into it. I was in a hospital unit, and the NCOs thought I was nuts for trying to get into a combat unit. They were happy to be where they were. I was like Pavlo for a brief period when I thought I had to be out there in the action.

Only after two things happened did I change my mind. Once I was on guard duty at the gate, and a truck came in with two guys from basic who I recognized. I was so happy to see them. They were like ghosts. I didn't know what kind of outfit they were in now, but they were coming to visit one of their buddies in the hospital who was dying. I was thinking, "Hey, we're old buddies," and they didn't know me, they didn't want to look at me. That made me realize that this stuff is real.

Then a couple days later an Australian came in to visit a friend of his, and I was again on guard duty. We were talking, and I said something about trying to get transferred, and he looked at me and said, "Stay the fuck where you are." It was like he gave me permission, like he said it was okay, and he was from it, he was there day in and day out in this shit. Then that was it; I stopped all this stuff. But the truth is they never would have transferred me in a million years, and I wasn't trained to go in an infantry unit anyway.

Schroeder: Why wouldn't they have transferred you?

Rabe: I wasn't equipped to do what they needed. I was equipped to do what I was doing. Basically what we mostly did was prepare the place. For a large part of my tour, it was barely a functioning hospital, because there was nothing there when we got there. A large part of the time we spent building the place.

The only way to get transferred really was to extend, to go back to the States, train in something, and volunteer to go back. It's just an interesting kind of reality. There's a fantasy that you volunteer to go, and then you go. That's not it. They need you where you are, whatever dumb job you're doing.

Even at twenty four, I fell prey to the Pavlo syndrome. It's guilt really. You're there, you know you've got it easy, and you feel guilty. Although a lot of guys with me didn't; it never crossed their minds. The simpler souls were just thrilled to be where we were. It never occurred to them to volunteer to go into this havoc if they had been lucky enough to have been exempted from it to begin with because they could drive a truck or whatever.

Schroeder: In the introduction to *Two Plays*, you talk about how you were unable to write in Vietnam, and you say, "All I knew in Vietnam were facts, nothing more. All simple facts of such complexity that the job of communicating any part of them accurately seemed impossibly beyond my reach." Do you think part of that had to do with being older than most of the people around you? In that you essentially had a different perspective than somebody like Pavlo would have?

Rabe: I think in a strange way, and it's still kind of true, I have a kind of side of me that remains naïve, and then there's a side of me that remains very cautious and very thoughtful. At that time, those two dynamics had less information or less experience to make decisions on. I think that on one hand, I was older; and on the other hand, once I was there and once I was in the hospital, you would be encountering these seventeen- and eighteen-year-old kids who clearly had a whole other level of experience, and in a sense were older, in the sense that having a certain innocence carved out or blown out of you makes you older.

I tried to keep a journal for a while, once I was going to go over. At that point I started to think I should. Once you're going to a war, obviously then if you've ever thought of writing, the idea of material crosses your mind. I started keeping one on the ship going over. (That's another thing: not too many people went over by ship, but in that first buildup, most people went by ship.) Once I got over there, besides being very busy, keeping a journal became impossible, and my efforts eroded. The attempts at it became shorter and shorter, and then they stopped. They stopped pretty quickly, actually.

It did have to do with being older on some level; on another level, it came from a sense of invalidity. Just a sense of not being able to comprehend it. There was no way to write it. It almost felt like a sacrilege to write about it. In a sense, you knew you were not going to get it; it was larger and bloodier than anything you were going to put down. This was true on every level: the social level, the Vietnamese and what you saw them going through, just on a day-to-day basis what was supposed to be safe and good. So I backed right out of it. I didn't even write many letters.

Schroeder: Did you still know you wanted to write about it at some point when you got back?

Rabe: Maybe in some way. I think what happened actually, as my tour started to wind down, I might have started thinking about it again. But in the middle I wasn't thinking about it.

Schroeder: When you came back, you were pretty much at a loose end for about six months. Then at some point weren't you working as a feature writer for a newspaper?

Rabe: That was later. I was regrouped by the time I was doing that. Yeah, I came back, and relatively speaking to what a lot of guys were going through, I had no reason to be upset, because I didn't go through what a lot of people did. But I felt somehow that I absorbed it. I don't know what happened to me, but it was like osmosis or something. I actually came back quite happy, but within a couple of weeks, it was like going to Mars. Because what you walked into was this unbelievable incomprehension and indifference that you just simply couldn't fathom. You thought you were going home, and you came back to something else.

Schroeder: You didn't know how much you'd been changed by the experience.

Rabe: No, and how much everything had stayed the same here, and how people were unchanged. The only kind of allegiance I felt, the only kind of sense of ally or compatriot was other vets. I was against the war ultimately, but I was never comfortable with the antiwar movement. I was never comfortable, obviously, with the other side. I had no allies.

Schroeder: When you came back, the war was still popular with a majority of people. It wasn't really until Tet that things started to change.

Rabe: Right; I came back at the beginning of '67. Tet wasn't for another year. You just felt people didn't know what was going on no matter what their position was. If they were for it, I felt they didn't know what they were talking about. And if they were against it, they didn't either. So you were on your own. But I didn't even have a lot of vet friends. A few—the guys that I had known. I knew two guys from Philadelphia who I could stay in touch with. And there was one guy from Wyoming. I met some new people, but not a lot. It was a weird time. By the end of the six months, I was beginning to think about writing about it.

Schroeder: Didn't you go back to school in there too?

Rabe: Yeah, at the end of the six months. I ended up going back to Villanova to pick up the Master's that I had started and quit. I only needed a few credits. I lived out by Villanova, and after I got those credits I moved into Philadelphia and began bouncing around in rooming houses. By then I had started to write.

Schroeder: Wasn't it during that period that you wanted to write a novel? You've said you wanted to write a novel because you thought theater was "lightweight, all fluff and metaphor, spangle, posture and glitter." And then you got a Rockefeller Grant, and so you started the plays. Your view of the theater must have changed in that period too, because *Pavlo Hummel* isn't like that at all.

Rabe: It changed. It's funny. I still think I hold the novel up as a higher form. The people I grew up admiring as writers and minds were all novelists, except for a couple. Americans, I'm talking about; Europe was different. And I still feel that way. Whether this has to do with some other part of my life, or my father's life or something, I'm not sure. But I still have the feeling that a great novel—[*breaks off*]. It's folly to say it; I have this feeling, but it isn't true. Tolstoy is not better than Shakespeare.

Schroeder: Have you ever actually tried to sit down and do anything with a Vietnam novel? Would you still be tempted to?

Rabe: I have one; I don't know if I'll ever finish it. I might. It's a short one. There's a novella I started once, that I could work on again. It's about being back, but it's very connected to Vietnam and the Vietnamese experience. It's about the way I felt at the time, and I still sort of do. It's a strange thing. I've been asking myself what that feeling is based on, and I don't know the answer. I've been fooling with another novel, actually. But it has nothing to do with Vietnam.

Schroeder: Did you have any models for the theater? People whose work you really admired?

Rabe: I had a mixed bag of people I admired and still do admire. My favorite American playwright is Arthur Miller, and then I became very attached to the work of Ionesco and Genet. And then there was a lot of individual stuff I saw, there was a lot of work going on at that time that was meaningful. But those are the three whose work I had an ongoing sense of. I admired Beckett, but he never got me the same way that Ionesco did. I don't know why exactly. I knew he was a wonderful writer, but for me he didn't really resonate. And he still doesn't whereas the other two still do.

Schroeder: It's interesting you mention Genet and Ionesco because when you were trying to work out some of *Pavlo*'s problems, you talked to Joe Papp about the play's realism. This was your first play and you didn't want its realism to be totally diminished. Why did you feel so strongly about that?

Rabe: I had already set up a framework in the play that *wasn't* realistic, and I had written most of *Sticks and Bones* and knew what *that* was like. I was trying to keep *Pavlo* as close to the facts, so to speak, the literalness of the events, the graphicness of the events, as I could. I was a little afraid of metaphoric solutions or metaphoric explanations. But then I had already set up a framework that provoked this questioning.

Schroeder: For instance, Ardell, Pavlo's ghost-like overseer, was in there throughout.

Rabe: Yeah, that was all organic; the play started with Pavlo's death, that was always there. Ardell's presence was always part of the construction and events were always out of sequence. Not out of sequence—once you were into the death zone or whatever, events were in sequence, but you were already out of sequence—

Schroeder: The whole play's a huge flashback.

Rabe: Right, and then you get back to Pavlo's death again. Things were clearly set up to be metaphoric. I was struggling with something in myself about not wanting to betray or be dishonest about the experience, not to corrupt the experience for the craft, so to speak. This is something I always wrestle with, which is a good thing to wrestle with, but ultimately you have to do something to make things cogent.

Basically there were two major changes. The first was my idea under Joe's provocation, and then the other idea was more his. The first idea was to take a scene in Act II (the scene where Pavlo, after he's drunk and is getting ready to go back to the fort, gets dressed, and Ardell comes in and helps him) and move it to the end of Act I and make it metaphoric, setting it on the tower rather than just in a room. It was the same dialogue and the same scene, but it was a great theatrical maneuver because it gave a great end to the Act, and gave it a lot of lift, and made it not just a literal dressing scene, but a transformation of this guy into a warrior. The other change was to make the killing of the farmer enacted rather than just told, and we came up with a way of staging it so he relived it. There may have been a couple other little things, but those were the big ones.

Schroeder: I also got the impression that in wanting the play to be realistic, you wanted it to be about people, to really focus on people, and the play does that extremely well. For instance, Sergeant Tower is an extremely memorable character. There's been a raft of similar characters since but to the best of my recollection, he's the first of the drill instructors that we've seen in the literature and films about Vietnam. All the other ones seem to follow from him.

Rabe: [*laughs*] I'm sure they all follow from these actual guys, the individual DIs and first sergeants. I know I really loved mine. I was twenty-five years old, and I was amazed by this guy. I really thought he was a great man. There was no questioning his sincerity and his desire to train people to the best he could to survive if possible. He was belligerent sometimes, but he was not a sadistic guy.

Schroeder: It's become popular to portray them that way.

Rabe: There are those guys. There was a guy or two under him, one guy in particular, no question about it. But he wasn't the first sergeant; he was a platoon sergeant under the first sergeant, and there was no question he was nasty. He wasn't my platoon sergeant; my platoon sergeant was okay. This other guy was somebody I was glad didn't have power over me. They were all tough of course, but there was a difference between those who were tough because that was what they were doing and they knew what they were talking about, and then there were these other few who were just mean.

Schroeder: Brad Christie compares your Vietnam plays with Michael Herr's *Dispatches* and says that both books examine what Christie calls the "cultural memory map"; he says, "The works focus on men and their fears rather than the event itself." Does that ring true to what you're trying to do?

Rabe: I would think "men and their responses" would be more accurate. I love Herr's book. I think it's a great book. I don't know, it's a strange statement. What does it mean?

Schroeder: I think he feels that some of the most successful works are those that have tried to focus on individuals, whether they're real or fictional creations, rather than try to deal with the event in any kind of objective way. That perhaps the best way to get at Vietnam is through personal response.

Rabe: It seems to me that I would have to know a book or a play that he felt failed. But if you're writing fiction or in the theater, you have to concentrate on the people. There are books, of course, where the events are too overwhelming. To me, it's a very tricky question because I think there are books about the war where events just take the people over, and that's true, too—that happens. Does he say or can you name any books that were less successful because of this?

Schroeder: I think a lot of the realistic novels are like that, because they try to use large casts of characters. One of the problems with some of the realistic novels is that a lot of the characters seem like types or cut-outs, and you don't really care for them ultimately because you don't empathize with them; you think of them as literary characters.

Rabe: I haven't read a lot of the books; I've read some, but not a lot. But I sort of know what you mean in that case. Although some are very powerful, they're never quite able to find a technical solution or a tone or a structural device that would distinguish them from World War II books.

Schroeder: In *Sticks and Bones* you chose to use the names of the family members from "The Nelson Family" TV show for your characters. Because of the names you choose for them we bring to those characters certain associations. On one hand we feel we know them, but obviously we get to know them in a very different sort of way. Originally, you had thought of calling them something else; you mention in *Two Plays* that you wondered how the play would have turned out.

Rabe: At one point, the names I toyed with were names that we used in the TV show. Because the play was what it was, I wanted a kind of larger-than-life entrance for people. The play didn't think it was a slice of life; it wasn't trying to link up with an earlier tradition of theater. But I felt the need for the play to have a larger canvas—not canvas perhaps, but larger echo. People would have a lot of connotations and references as they saw it.

Schroeder: I don't know about the TV version. When was it done?

Rabe: You don't know about the TV version? Really? That's fascinating. This is something I wondered about, frankly. History seems to have missed it. I think it must be a one-time event in American history of television. After *Sticks and Bones* was done on Broadway, Joe Papp won the Tony for producing it and the same year also won a Tony for his musical version of *Two Gentlemen of Verona*, and so he was suddenly a powerful guy. CBS came to him and wanted to do his shows as TV specials, three or four specials in a year, and they signed a contract. He made it a condition that one of their productions would be one of my plays. CBS started with *Much Ado About Nothing*, and then they read my plays and opted for *Sticks and Bones*.

I remember leaving the office and saying to Joe, "They don't know what they're doing. They've taken this because it doesn't have as many 'shits' and 'fucks' in it. But they really don't know what they've got." Joe hired Bob Downey to direct it; he was an underground director at the time, a very bright guy who made several really great underground movies. I had just seen one of them, called *Greaser's Palace*, and although I was afraid of him on a certain level, I thought part of this movie was brilliant. We trimmed the script down a bit, and then he shot it in five weeks on video, out on location.

CBS was scheduled to show it in late '73 or '74 when the POWs were about to start coming home. They finally screened it and said, "We can't put this on." It was all set to go, and they pulled it. A lot of political stuff was going on at the time: Nixon had a guy named Clay Whitehead who was trying to influence the way the affiliates could affect the network. They were trying to get the affiliates to make their own decisions. There was a lot of intimidation and maneuvering going on. *Sticks and Bones* was canceled, and as a result there was a big brouhaha, and several weeks later CBS decided to put it on and let each affiliate that wanted show it. So it went on that night and literally had no sponsors—this is probably the only time in American history that a network show went on at nine o'clock East Coast time and had no sponsors and had a disclaimer the likes of which you've never seen. It basically said, "Don't watch this."

Schroeder: Did many of the affiliates pick it up?

Rabe: There were affiliates who didn't pick it up, there were affiliates that picked it up, there were affiliates who showed it at three in the morning; there were all kinds of decisions made. But on the East Coast it went on with the disclaimer, and I saw that night. It went dark for fifteen seconds where there was supposed to be commercials, and then there was half an hour of story, and then it went blank again, and that's the way it went.

Schroeder: Did you like the production?

Rabe: I did, and I do. I've got a videotape of it. I don't know if it's available any more. One of the cable stations bought it not too long ago and distributed it for a while. It's a very good production. It's an extreme version. It captures the tone of the play wonderfully, but it's very zany. I thought it might be overkill on television, but it really gets the bizarre tone that you need to make it work It's funny that it's not ever mentioned, as a kind of odd political-social event.

Schroeder: At one point, you said that *Sticks and Bones* wasn't about the war. But obviously while the events of the play take place apart from the war, the war is still the center of the play.

Rabe: Sometimes you say something because you are in a context, and you are reacting to some other statement. I think it is about the war, I think it isn't about the war. It's certainly about coming home from the war, and it certainly makes a political statement about materialistic oblivion in relation to carnage. Because I was in a hospital, I would go through periods where I would feel that I had cheated or something, and I would feel that I hadn't paid the proper dues to claim to make any grand statements about the war. So sometimes you make statements like that, but on the other hand it's about the war in a kind of nonliteral, deeper level. It's more about coming home, and talking to people at home.

Schroeder: Towards the end of *Dispatches*, Michael Herr says there was nothing in Vietnam that wasn't waiting curled up back in the world. He believes that American culture is responsible for what went on in Vietnam and for what has happened since.

Rabe: It's completely responsible.

Schroeder: What I find most troubling about *Sticks and Bones* is that at the end of the play, Ozzie, Harriet, and Rick haven't learned a thing. Did you feel at the time that these characters were typical of Americans coming to grips with Vietnam?

Rabe: There's two ways to look at it: Ozzie is the only one in the play who's capable of understanding what David is saying; the other two are not capable. Ricky is a nemesis, he's a killer—he would rather kill than have this stuff bother him. Harriet thinks if she has to face this stuff she'll fall apart. Ozzie is the only one who really could grasp it. On the other hand, what David's really asking for is a level of insanity.

When the play was first done in '72, the audience who went to the theater wanted desperately to see a play about this nice guy that they could like. It really put them in a quandary because toward the end of the play I think a large part of this audience is feeling, "Kill this fuck." They don't expect him to get killed, but when he does, they're complicit. So it's quite a harrowing audience experience, but it's what I think is right. In other words, I felt at the time that his rage and the rage of a lot of vets was such that they couldn't just come back and explain it; you had to make an experience of it somehow.

People who didn't go were nonetheless complicit and didn't want to admit it. That's the way it is. I'm sure I'm that way now about a lot of things in the world today. I live my life, and I haven't taken the time to understand or do anything about things that I should. In a sense, I probably worry about this more than other people, but that isn't doing anything about it.

But to get back to what you said, David's asking them almost to join him in a kind of anarchy. So can they? The answer is they could (although Ricky never would), but where would they be? At the end Ozzie will be haunted and the other two won't have learned anything. I don't know what Ozzie will have learned, except that he's haunted and there's really nothing that he's capable of doing himself. The whole thing is literally swept under the rug. There's a wonderful image in the TV version: after the girl is killed, they literally put her in a big green garbage bag. (I think in the stage version she was put behind the couch.) In a large sense, I don't think anything has been learned.

I think in many ways, the play was really on the money about the way the vets were going to get treated.

Schroeder: The play certainly seems to have foretold the kind of reception that most vets throughout the seveties experienced.

Rabe: To me the recent welcoming is a very uneasy re-embrace where there is collusion in the reacceptance—we all agreed to have the same amnesia. The vets are welcomed back, but they have to shut up. It's clear that in terms of what are seen as the vets' more excessive demands—for example Agent Orange—the country has been saying, "No, you'd better shut up about that, and then we'll give you a parade. We are not going to admit that we were culpable as a government, as a people in some of these problems of yours. These are your own genetic problems." Which is absurd. There's a kind of collusion. But I am also not part of it anymore. Again, I feel a little like a distant intellectual. Maybe a lot of the guys, the guys who were on the line and in the mud, want that patriotic stamp, that patriotic hug, and that's good enough. That's not something I ever wanted once I came back. But then I'm not a guy from a farm from Tennessee. Even though I grew up in the Midwest in a small town, I have a different outlook and always have had.

Schroeder: Why did you come back to Vietnam as a subject in *Streamers* after having done other things?

Rabe: It was the big experience. But *Boom Boom Room* in a sense was a part of that coming home. I spent a lot of time in those bars. There was a vibe in those bars that was similar to being over there. A kind of sexual edge, danger, whatever. It was part of it. Though in fact *Streamers* had been started before any of the other plays. It had a very strange construction. I started *Streamers* before I started anything else. Then I wrote the other two plays, and *The Orphan* sort of in the same rush. The way they were written was not quite how they got produced, which was *Pavlo, Sticks and Bones, The Orphan, Boom Boom Room, Streamers*. The beginning of *Streamers*, the first half an hour of it, was the very first thing I wrote when I came home. It was a fragment, a kind of one-act play, and I didn't like the idea of one-act plays, so I just kept it. I started writing these plays in '68 or '69, and was finishing *Streamers* by '72, '73. It wasn't a big gap of time.

Schroeder: You also went back to realism in it. Of the three plays, it is the most realistic. Was that a conscious choice?

Rabe: No, it just came out that way. That's the way it started, and again the material itself dictates a lot of that. In other words, if you're going to do *Pavlo* and you're going to try on stage to depict something with the scope of an army, you need a metaphor, or else you end up with fragments that just jump around. So I used the metaphoric unity of basic training.

The material of *Streamers* dictated a fairly confined, or singular, place which is then conducive to a kind of realism. But it isn't really a traditionally realistic play; it's realistic in the sense of having one set and in the way the characters talk. In the terms of the emotions and the way the action develops, it's not realistic. The realistic play develops in a certain kind of mechanistic way. One of the events I struggled with in the production of the play (which to me is what makes it move into another realm, makes it not realistic), was people were forever trying to get me to have Carlyle stab only Billy, not the Sarge, and not have that whole coda at the end. Then it would have been a realistic play. Once you have the Sarge stabbed, and once you then go onto that latter part, you move into a kind of—it's subtle, but it's not realism anymore.

Realism is not about how people speak, it's about how events are constructed. In other words, the realistic play is a play in which cause and effect work in proportion. A realistic play says, "You make me mad, and I'm

mad in proportion to your cause." It's derivative of the Newtonian notion
of the universe. I think it's not true, it's not how life works, because it doesn't
take into account the unconscious. So in *Streamers* when that moment
comes, you don't have just the response that the play has prepared you for,
you have the response that is contained within the characters, in their
unconscious; you get a nuclear response rather than a proportionate cause
and effect. The cause is one thing, but the effect is disproportionate. It
moves into another realm, and I find that it's not realistic in that sense. It's
more real as far as I'm concerned, but if you use the term to mean a certain
kind of theatrical approach, it's not. That approach says, "I cry, and you feel
sad or happy, depending on what you think of me." The cause and effect is
all very clear-cut and in proportion, which is not really true, I don't think, in
life.

Schroeder: It seems appropriate, too, ending with Cokes, because of the
characters in the play, he's the only one who's been in Vietnam.

Rabe: The people who talk about the plays talk about them as a trilogy, and
for me they're not. They are a group of four plays, though *The Orphan* failed
as a production, and maybe it failed as a piece of writing. To me *Pavlo,
Sticks and Bones,* and *The Orphan* are three different approaches to this
experience. *Streamers* embodies them all; it's like an umbrella over them
all. The emotional life, especially in the play's ending, is sort of the finish.
If any one writing session completed the work for me (which may in fact be
finished in terms of writing about Vietnam unless I finish this novel), it was
that: it was writing the Cokes stuff. It was an elegy for the whole sequence.
To me, it's a four-play sequence, not a three-play sequence. It's fascinating
that because *The Orphan* failed, it gets dropped out. Even if it is a failure,
it's still part of it. Oddly enough, *Streamers,* and especially the Cokes's
scenes, is the finale in terms of emotionally trying to find a way to look at
all this stuff. Just simply to mourn it all.

Schroeder: Were you pleased with the screen version?

Rabe: No. I wasn't actually. It's too bad. Bob Altman is a good director
and did his best and was very generous to me in the editing. He had a lot of
financial troubles with the production and a very limited budget to begin
with. I think his concentration got broken. There was a performance that
got out of control, and he didn't catch it. It threw things out of whack. So
the play didn't work well as a film.

Schroeder: You did the screenplay for *Casualties of War*. Were you happy with that?

Rabe: No.

Schroeder: Did you know the book it was based on?

Rabe: Oh, yeah. I knew the book before. I had read it sometime in the early seventies. My problems with *Casualties* were certain things the director did in the script: he added some scenes, little scenes, but crucial scenes that changed the emphasis of things. He cut some key scenes, and he reversed the sequence of some things. I wrote some dialogue under duress that was based on a scene that later got cut. When I wrote the dialogue, there was a dream, you saw a dream, and you saw Eriksson wake up kind of screaming. I begged the director to take that dialogue out and he wouldn't—this was the dialogue at the end with the girl. I always felt that when he gave her the scarf and she turned away, he should simply say, "Chow Co," which is hello or goodbye in Vietnamese. And then she would just look at him and say, "Chao Ong," and leave. All this dialogue about "You had a bad dream, it's over" and all that stuff was put in to make the scene explicit, but it really was heavy-handed. I hated it, I mean I literally begged and wrote letters. I wanted some other changes too that I felt would have made a big difference.

There were also several things added in the beginning and the sequence of events was switched, which made Michael Fox's character much too separate from everybody else. When they kidnap the girl and he stays in the village, he says, "I'm sorry"—that bit was added. To me that was nuts. He shouldn't have known that much at that time. He shouldn't have had such a clear grasp of the moral situation.

Schroeder: He was too new.

Rabe: Yeah. It made everything that followed not dramatic, plus it isolated him from the other characters, and gave him a moral superiority that he shouldn't have had at that point. He should have arrived at that stage late in the script, where he had to struggle through and decide whether he was going to tell. Anyway, I had a lot of complaints about that.

Schroeder: In the introduction to *Two Plays*, James Reston says, "The theater must recapture its proper confrontational role." But you've shunned the phrase "antiwar play" applied to your work. Do you see it as confrontational?

Rabe: Yes. Those plays certainly. There's a relativeness: *Sticks and Bones* is very confrontational, and so is *Streamers*, and I guess *Pavlo* is too to some extent. Lesser than the others, though.

Schroeder: Reston goes on to add, "The playwright becomes more important than the historian, for in no other war of our history was the private word more important than the public pronouncements." It seems to me that he's giving artists a pretty large burden to bear.

Rabe: But you know what he's talking about because there was an immense distance between the public description—not the pictorial description of the war, but the PR governmental description of the war—and the way people experienced it. I think the plays were very confrontational. My rejection of the "antiwar" category was based on two thoughts. First, that the antiwar play was based on the belief that when you write a play, you think you can actually affect the course of events (which I don't believe). The second notion is that you distort your experience in order to make your point, and I feel I tried not to distort the experience, and I also feel that the theater is just not able to deeply affect the course of modern society. The theater's expertise is not developed like the machinery of the media and the facility to use it. You just don't have access—your ideas just don't reach the same numbers of people. The tremendous amount of skill and brainpower that goes into advertising, and governmental advertising, is so huge that a play barely makes a bubble.

Schroeder: One of the things that interests me about your work is that your plays were successful and were winning awards on Broadway in '72, when very few Vietnam novels had been published. The theater was ready to accept this subject and be able to look at it critically long before fiction.

Rabe: I'm talking, I guess, in a larger way. Someone might say, "You're wrong, those plays had a big effect." I think they had a big effect in some ways, but I feel the machinery of ideology is so powerful. I guess I'm talking more about now than then. The TV version of the play did try to reach the larger public. (Finally even Broadway is very small if you compare it to communication in the United States. A negligible number of people see a play in a year compared to the number of people that receive the general propaganda, like "The Ozzie and Harriet Show.") Communications are even more bleak now.

Schroeder: Do you think part of the success of your plays has something to do with the medium of the theater, or if it has to do with the fact that you went to Vietnam as an older person, and you went very early in the war, so you came out and were able to write about it? In one sense, you beat other people to the subject.

Rabe: I think that's partly true. And it was theater as well. For if you have success in the theater, you get a kind of exposure in the media that you don't get for a first novel, unless it's tremendously successful. There is another ingredient here that has to be mentioned, and that's Joe Papp. Every theater on the East Coast had turned me down. It wasn't the theater as a faceless, nameless entity that embraced me, it was Joe Papp, who has a particular bent towards political thought and an aggressiveness as a producer. It wasn't "The Theater"; it was him, and he had his own theater built up to a point where it was great staging area for the plays. Then the plays were good, and he gave them good productions. Plus what you're saying is true, that I was older and capable of writing as quickly as I did when I came back.

Schroeder: Because of the nature of plays themselves and because they're tied to the war, do you think they're going to survive? Will they go on being shown? Unlike movies which will get dragged off the shelves forty years from now, what sort of life does the theater offer your plays?

Rabe: I don't know. Obviously, I hope they go on being produced. I have a feeling that despite all their particularness, certainly at least *Streamers* and *Sticks and Bones* have a kind of distance about them, they have another aspect to them. If they hold up as theater, as written works, I think they'll be done as long as there are theaters willing to deal with their confrontational nature. But they may not. None of those plays has ever had a major production in England, for example. I don't know why that is—maybe they're not good enough, or maybe it's the answer to your question. But I think that if it's anything, it's that they're too confrontational. My plays don't get done in summer stock, they can't be, because people don't want to go to their little summer theater and see these plays. Universities will do them, and serious regional theaters will redo them or revive them. But I don't know—the end result is that I really don't know.

Bibliography

Bryan, C.D.B. *Friendly Fire*. New York: Putnam, 1976.

Calley, William Laws, with John Sack. *Lieutenant Calley: His Own Story*. New York: Viking Press, 1971.

Heinemann, Larry. *Close Quarters*. New York: Farrar, Straus & Giroux, 1974.

_____. *Paco's Story*. New York: Farrar, Straus & Giroux, 1986.

Herr, Michael. *Dispatches*. New York: Knopf, 1977.

Mailer, Norman. *The Armies of the Night: History as a Novel, The Novel as History*. New York: New American Library, 1968.

_____. *Why Are We in Vietnam?* New York: Putnam, 1967.

Mason, Bobbie Ann. *In Country*. South Yarmouth, MA: Curley, 1985.

O'Brien, Tim. *If I Die in a Combat Zone*. New York: Delacorte, 1973.

_____. *Going After Cacciato*. New York: Delacorte, 1978.

_____. *The Things They Carried*. New York: Houghton Mifflin/Seymour Lawrence, 1990.

Rabe, David. *"The Basic Training of Pavlo Hummel" and "Sticks and Bones."* New York: Viking Press, 1973.

_____. *Streamers*. New York: Knopf, 1975.

Sack, John. *M*. New York: New American Library, 1966.

_____. *The Man-Eating Machine*. New York: Farrar, Straus & Giroux, 1967.

Stone, Robert. *Dog Soldiers*. Boston: Houghton Mifflin, 1974.

Terry, Wallace. *Bloods: An Oral History of the Vietnam War by Black Veterans*. New York: Random House, 1984.

Weigl, Bruce. *The Monkey Wars*. Athens: University of Georgia Press, 1985.

_____. *A Romance*. Pittsburgh: University of Pittsburgh Press, 1979.

_____. *Song of Napalm*. New York: Atlantic Monthly Press, 1988.

Index

About the Author

Eric James Schroeder is a Lecturer in English and Director of Composition at the University of California, Davis. His primary field of scholarship is the literature of the Vietnam war. He has also published articles and given numerous conference papers on topics related to composition and, in particular, computer-assisted instruction. Dr. Schroeder is a co-founder and editor of *Writing on the Edge*, a journal concerned with the art of writing and the teaching of it. He is currently working on a second book about the Vietnam war.